Forgotten Futures,
Colonized Pasts

Forgotten Futures, Colonized Pasts

Transnational Collaboration in Nineteenth-Century Greater Mexico

CARA ANNE KINNALLY

Bucknell UNIVERSITY
UNIVERSITY PRESS

Lewisburg, Pennsylvania

Library of Congress Cataloging-in-Publication Data

Names: Kinnally, Cara A., author.
Title: Forgotten futures, colonized pasts : transnational collaboration in
nineteenth-century greater Mexico / by Cara Anne Kinnally.
Description: Lewisburg, PA : Bucknell University Press, [2019]
| Includes bibliographical references and index.
Identifiers: LCCN 2018031886 | ISBN 9781684481231 (cloth) | ISBN 9781684481224 (pbk.)
Subjects: LCSH: Mexican literature—19th century—History and criticism.
| Mexican American literature (Spanish)—History and criticism. | American
literature—Mexican American authors—History and criticism. | Literature and
transnationalism—Mexican-American Border Region. | Mexican-American Border
Region—In literature. | Mexican-American Border Region—History. | Mexico—
History—19th century. | Texas—History—To 1846. | Texas—History—1846–1950.
Classification: LCC PQ7152 .K56 2019 | DDC 860.9/97209034—dc23
LC record available at https://lccn.loc.gov/2018031886

A British Cataloging-in-Publication record for this book is available from the British Library.

∞ The paper used in this publication meets the requirements of the American National
Standard for Information Sciences—Permanence of Paper for Printed Library Materials,
ANSI Z39.48-1992.

www.bucknell.edu/UniversityPress

Distributed worldwide by Rutgers University Press

Manufactured in the United States of America

Contents

A Note on Translations, Terminology, and the Limits of Language

The nineteenth century was a time of immense change in the Americas. National borders were drawn and redrawn; old and new categories of race, ethnicity, and caste clashed with and changed one another; new legal categories and social modes of belonging emerged and old ones evolved; and individuals contemplated and debated their identity at the individual, national, and international levels. Language could not always keep up. It is therefore difficult to use stable ethnic, racial, national, geographic, and regional descriptors for individuals and communities in the Americas during the nineteenth century because these could, and did, change rather quickly and depended to a great extent on context. This is in part what *Forgotten Futures, Colonized Pasts* is about: how national, racial, ethnic, communal, and individual terms of self-identification changed over time and in different contexts within the Americas. There are inherent limitations to language when it comes to naming entities that are in nearly constant flux, but I will attempt to be clear and precise about my use of these descriptors. Whenever possible, I strive to use the terms that the individuals and communities I am studying used for self-identification. Usually, these are connected to regional rather than national affiliations, but they also simultaneously carry cultural and sometimes racial or ethnic dimensions. Thus as each chapter of my book focuses on different regions and communities, I use regional terms employed by the authors for self-identification in their writing, such as Tejano, Yucateco, Californio, and Nuevomexicano; I use these terms as the authors use them, even when it is problematic or exclusionary. I include more detailed discussions of specific terminology in the notes to each chapter.

For similar reasons, I use the term *America* (and *American*) to refer to all the Americas, not just the United States of America. *Americano* was a term employed frequently in the nineteenth century by people from throughout the Americas, not just from the United States. I use the term *U.S. American* to refer to people from the United States so as to discursively detach *American* from belonging solely to the United States. Although use of *U.S. American* might at first appear somewhat awkward, my hope is that with more frequent use it will become less so.

I have chosen to maintain spelling, accent marks, antiquated grammatical features, lexical choices, and so on as they appear in the original texts. I do this in part to reflect the tone and feeling of the texts and because I want to convey the language and voices of the writers themselves as much as possible. This language can at times appear archaic or, at other times, convoluted, extravagant, and opaque. I have chosen not to modernize the language because I want readers to engage with this sometimes alienating aspect of the language in part as an attempt to recognize that the language of these texts, in great measure, is *not* the language of the masses but rather that of a community of *letrados*—the lettered elites, as Ángel Rama explains in *La ciudad letrada*, who are also the ruling classes. I include all quotations in the original language in which they were written and have provided English translations following the original Spanish; these are purposefully literal translations, again as part of my attempt to draw readers' attention to the (sometimes coded and oblique) language of the original. All translations are my own unless otherwise noted.

I have chosen to use the masculine ending for gender-variable terms such as *Hispano*, *Chicano*, and so on for several reasons. First, I find the constant use of the split variation (e.g., *Chicana/o*, *Latino/a*) grammatically and syntactically awkward. Second, although I considered using the feminine and masculine versions interchangeably (as some do with gender-specific singular pronouns in English), I find the feminine endings potentially confusing, as the feminine variation may inadvertently and erroneously convey the idea that I am speaking about a woman or a group of women (e.g., *Chicana* or *Chicanas*). Lastly, the writers I study in this book almost invariably use the masculine variation when referring to their own communities, thereby reflecting the patriarchal gender norms of their times and places. I ask readers to see my use of the masculine form not as an unquestioning reinforcement of gender inequality but as an attempt to acknowledge and represent, through the use of the normative masculine, the thorough marginalization of women—a marginalization that was so ingrained in society, even in language itself, that it was rarely even recognized as such in the nineteenth century. I follow the same logic that I use in maintaining the racial and cultural terms of self-identification employed by my writers, even when highly problematic, so as to not erase the violence inherent in naming. For example, while it is true that most Mexicans were biologically racially mixed by the nineteenth century and therefore could be described as mestizo (in our present-day use of the term), elites rarely self-identified as mestizo. Lastly, although I recognize the socially and culturally constructed nature of race and ethnicity, for sake of reading fluidity, I do not place racial or ethnic terms within quotation marks unless I desire to specifically emphasize the constructed or self-reflective nature of the term being used. For the same reasons, I also avoid excessive use of quotation marks with words like civilization, modern/modernization, barbaric/barbarism, progress, and so on, although I once again ask readers to consider these terms as discursive constructs that nonetheless have immense meaning and power for the writers I analyze and their audiences.

Language is tricky, and the words we use to describe people are especially fraught with cultural baggage. It seems that in choosing any word, one immediately privileges some and excludes others, often unintentionally. My hope is that the terms I use in this book are understood less as static terms and more as markers for larger ideas that cannot always be accurately described through the limited language at my disposal. I ask readers to understand my use of these terms, similar to my decision to use masculine noun and adjective forms, as a recognition—not an endorsement—of how these terms and categories were used for both empowerment and disempowerment in the nineteenth century. These terms offer a critical reflection on the ways in which hierarchies of inclusion and exclusion permeate and reproduce themselves within society at every level, including through language itself.

**Forgotten Futures,
Colonized Pasts**

Introduction

◦○▸

A Novel and a History
"Yellowed and Tattered
with Age"

> Here he would create a new empire, and
> his place the finest of them all. Here, he
> could rear his family and keep the old
> ways and traditions safely away from the
> perfidious influences of Mexico City and
> the infiltration of foreign doctrines; not
> only for himself but for the generations
> to come.
> —*Caballero: A Historical Novel*

In the 1930s, a Mexican American woman from South Texas and an Anglo American woman from Missouri coauthored and attempted to publish an English-language novel, *Caballero: A Historical Novel*, a romance of historical fiction set in nineteenth-century South Texas.[1] Although little is known about the Anglo American, Margaret Eimer (who wrote under the pen name Eve Raleigh), we know more about the Mexican American woman, Jovita González, who was one of the first Mexican American academic folklorists of Texas Mexican[2] and Mexican American culture and history, and the first Mexican American woman to earn a master's degree in anthropology at the University of Texas, in 1930.[3] *Caballero* tells the story of an elite Tejano family with deep, proud Spanish roots living in the disputed territory of South Texas during the U.S.-Mexican War in 1846–1848. It is a romance about how the Tejano children in that family form romantic unions with recently arrived Anglos and build—quite literally—a future multicultural Texas through their offspring.[4]

1

Forgotten for more than forty years, *Caballero* was not recovered and published until the 1990s.[5] It fascinates me because it has proven to be such an enigma. The fact that it was never published during González's lifetime suggests that publishers did not believe it would be popular with a wide audience.[6] Due to its ambiguous portrayals of both Tejanos and Anglos; its setting at the margins of Texas, the United States, and Mexican national territories; and its seemingly incongruous combination of both progressive and simultaneously elitist and racist discourses, critics have long debated how to categorize and understand this novel. From the time González and Eimer first sent this novel out to publishers in the late 1930s until the present day, this novel has evaded stable categorization and has not found a firm home in any literary canon or tradition.[7] Yet this novel, like any text, was not written in a vacuum. To or for whom did the authors imagine this novel would speak? With what literary and cultural traditions did the authors see their novel engaging? What literary, social, or political contexts might help this novel make sense? Rather than discard this novel as an anomaly or a failure, I understand the manuscript, with its "more than five hundred typed pages yellowed and tattered with age,"[8] as an almost ghostlike apparition, quite literally gathering dust in an attic, that hints at the existence of another tradition and history of Greater Mexico. This novel, I propose, is a remnant of a now largely forgotten tradition of hemispheric community-building and transnational collaboration between elite Anglos and Hispanos—and a tradition that was much stronger and more clearly articulated in the nineteenth century. This is the tradition that I work to more fully illuminate in *Forgotten Futures* through analyses of narratives, novels, essays, letters, and histories that articulate multiple visions of transnational community-building between Anglos and Hispanos in the nineteenth century. However, this concept of community was frequently imagined on shifting categories of identity that empowered elites and simultaneously reinforced deeply problematic hierarchies of power and belonging that distanced elites in Greater Mexico from marginalized "others" within their own communities. As I will discuss, *Caballero*'s content harkens back to this alternative tradition, and its repeated rejection by publishers and its eventual relegation to the attic/archives mirror the ways in which this tradition of transnational and intercultural community-building has been gradually rejected and excised from U.S. American, Mexican, and Chicano historical narratives of community formation.

In *Caballero*, González and Eimer construct a narrative of collaboration between elite Mexicanos and Anglos in the nineteenth century and also highlight the problematic foundations of such a relationship. *Caballero* is in many ways a transnational novel. It takes place at the borders of multiple nations and reimagines a foundational moment in Texas, Mexican, and U.S. history: the U.S.-Mexican War of 1846–1848. It is a foundational fiction that allegorically imagines Anglos and Tejanos as complementary components of a multicultural society.[9] It does so, however, by joining *elite* Anglos and Tejanos, who are portrayed as fair-skinned, cultured, and of pure Spanish ancestry.[10] In general, the novel is disparaging of poor whites; mestizo *peones*, the unskilled laborers who make the hacienda profitable, are afforded little representation, except as dutiful servants who benefit from a new capitalist system; and nonassimilated, non-Christianized indigenous characters are almost completely absent. On the one hand, the novel appears quite progressive in its aim to represent female characters as agents in this history and in its attempt to write Tejanos (and more broadly, Mexicans and Mexican Americans) into U.S. and Texan history.[11] It is important to point out that this was a fairly radical idea given the gender norms at the time González and Eimer were writing the novel and the tense state of race relations between Anglos and Tejanos in Texas in the 1930s, which marked the beginning of the mass deportation of Mexicans and Mexican Americans, the destruction of traditional Mexican American barrios in the Southwest, and the rise of the eugenicist movement aimed at defining Mexicans and Mexican Americans as a new racial category.[12] But on the other hand, the novel articulates this progressive stance with regard to women and Tejanos in part by relying on elitist and racist rhetoric.[13]

The transnational community of elites imagined in *Caballero* thus simultaneously highlights the socioeconomic, racial, and regional divisions within Greater Mexico. As the quotation at the beginning of this introduction illustrates, when the patriarch of the central Tejano family in *Caballero* expresses his desire to isolate his family from the "perfidious influences" of central Mexico (portrayed as antithetical to the more conservative culture of Texas), he also draws attention to the cultural and political divisions that existed between the different regions of Mexico. These still exist today, but they were certainly more pronounced during the nineteenth century, when border zones like Texas were even more isolated from central Mexico. As this same quotation also indicates, many elites from throughout Greater Mexico, who often saw themselves, as does the patriarch in this quotation, as embodying and preserving Spanish and/or European tradition and culture, sought not to do away with class and ethnic hierarchies but rather to rule over a "new empire" of mestizos, subjugated Indians, and the poor. The dominant nationalist discourse that persists even today in Mexico emphasizes the mestizo origins of Mexico and does little to recognize fragmentation and conflict—racial, regional, and socioeconomic—as essential parts of Mexican history. *Caballero*, on the other hand, perhaps unintentionally reveals the social, racial, and regional divisions—the "patrias chicas"—that exist (and existed) within Greater Mexico. As a foundational fiction, *Caballero* allegorically incorporates Mexican Americans into the United States, but it does so through the establishment and reinforcement of problematic hierarchies of belonging that privilege rich, elite, fair-skinned Tejanos while excluding the poor, mestizos, indigenous, Afro-Tejanos, and other groups perceived as racially or socially undesirable.

Lastly, *Caballero* appears to reinforce the pervasive dichotomy of civilization versus barbarism, with the United States representing a civilizing and modernizing force. The novel, for example, portrays the arrival of a new U.S. capitalist economic system as an improved, more egalitarian and modern economic and social system that will do away with a backward, semifeudal economic system, a remnant of Spanish colonization. However, *Caballero* does not discard all aspects of Mexican (or Spanish) culture as antiquated; it hints at the ways in which the United States and Mexico might combine complementary cultural forces in order to achieve a new, better community in Texas. In one of the earlier chapters of the novel, for instance, the elite Tejano men meet to discuss the recent arrival of Anglos to Texas. Although the Anglos may have material wealth, Padre Pierre, the local parish priest and a voice of moral authority throughout the novel, notes that the Anglos are deficient when it comes to cultural matters: "Most of them lack what we [Tejanos] have: dignity, self-respect, pride, nobility, traditions, an old and sound religion."[14] He also encourages the elite Tejanos to show the Anglo officials "that we have much to give them in culture, that we are not the ignorant people they take us to be, that to remain as we are will neither harm nor be a disgrace to their union of states."[15] In *Caballero*, elite Tejanos, in other words, have much to offer in terms of their refined upbringing, appreciation for high culture (music, art, literature, etc.), and (Catholic) spirituality. As the novel shows allegorically through the successful marriages of Tejana women with Anglo men, the combination of these two cultures could create a new, modern culture that values capitalist commerce and also safeguards those aspects of Tejano culture deemed worthy of preservation while discarding those that have supposedly kept Texas (and Mexico) from becoming modern.[16] In terms of content, then, *Caballero* certainly reinforces a pervasive discourse that views and portrays the United States as a new and more benevolent empire—an empire of modernization and civilization. Yet at the same time, the novel suggests that the United States would benefit from being tempered by Tejano, and more broadly Hispanic and Catholic, culture as well—especially highbrow culture, "the best" that Mexico has to offer, according to Padre Pierre in the novel.

In its representation of the U.S.-Mexican War and its immediate aftermath, a foundational historical moment, *Caballero* shows readers a different version of Texan history in which Anglos and Tejanos work together, but it also reveals many conflicts and divisions within Greater Mexico and reproduces many deeply problematic racial, social, and political discourses of belonging that supported the building, real or imagined, of such elite transnational communities. The publication history of *Caballero*, by contrast, mirrors a gradual removal of transnational collaboration from national histories and a disavowal of many of the sociocultural hierarchies and politics of difference that made this specific mode of elite relationship-building possible in the first place.

Caballero was rejected by various groups of people for very different reasons and at distinct moments throughout the twentieth century. In the 1930s and 1940s, González and Eimer attempted to publish *Caballero* with several popular presses in the United States without success.[17] Although these two women could imagine an intercultural collaborative history in Texas, the rejection of their novel by popular English-language presses in the United States suggests that editors did not believe that the Anglo-dominated public would be as willing to imagine a romantic and sexual union, even historically removed to the past, between Anglos and Hispanos. By the 1930s, segregation between Mexican Americans and Anglos was firmly in place, and Mexicans and Mexican Americans were being legally defined as nonwhite, making these sorts of unions much less palatable to whites in the United States. *Caballero*'s rejection in the 1930s and 1940s therefore reflects the pervasive racism of that time and mainstream Anglo Americans' refusal to acknowledge or permit multicultural and multilingual histories of the United States.

According to an interview conducted in the 1970s with González and her husband, E. E. Mireles, Mireles expressed relief that the novel had not been published in the 1940s because the "racial-political climate in the 1940s would have made the novel's publication controversial for them as public school teachers in Corpus Christi, [Texas]."[18] However, even during the 1960s and 1970s, a period that saw the opening up of the U.S. literary market to more works written by minorities and women, González did not renew her efforts to publish *Caballero*, even with a Chicano literary press. Although we cannot know her reasoning for not seeking publication again, Mireles seems to have had the impression that his wife's novel would have been just as unpopular with Chicano nationalists in the 1970s as it might have been for bigoted Anglos in the 1940s. In José E. Limón's retelling of that same interview, Mireles reportedly remarked that "even if it [the novel] existed, he would not have wanted the manuscript published *then* in the 1970s, as he feared for its reception in the Chicano literary nationalist ambience of the period."[19] By the 1970s, the idea of intercultural collaboration—as we see in *Caballero*—not only ceased to be an option but was actively rejected by many in the Mexican American community and especially in the Chicano nationalist movement, which largely eschewed any assimilationist tendencies and promoted an idea of Chicano culture that was different from and resistant to dominant Anglo American culture and politics.[20] One of the results was that texts that did not fit the narrative of resistance and antagonism, like *Caballero*, were often deemed inauthentic representations of Chicano culture and history. It was also in the 1960s and 1970s that Chicano nationalist literature solidified an image of Chicano culture and identity as working class, heteronormative, mestizo, and able-bodied.[21] *Caballero*, unlike Chicano nationalist literature, focuses on elites, disparages the working poor, and minimizes indigenous influences in its representations of Tejano history and culture. Even today, María Cotera (daughter of Marta Cotera, who originally interviewed González and her husband) notes that *Caballero* is often read as a "failed Chicano/a text, a novel in which an essentially anti-imperial thrust is undercut by the author's flawed ideologies of race and class."[22] This argument, she further explains, "is founded on the many examples of collaboration within the narrative, especially the romantic entanglements of its Anglo and Mexican characters."[23] In sum, *Caballero*'s rejection by Anglo-dominated popular presses in the 1930s and 1940s demonstrates that transnational community-building and cultural accommodation were options for neither bigoted Anglos in the 1940s nor Chicano nationalists in the 1970s. And as Cotera indicates, its inclusion within the Chicano literary canon remains problematic even today.[24]

What I would like to suggest is that *Caballero* was either rejected or viewed as unpublishable by two different groups of people—Chicanos and Anglos— because it speaks to a tradition of transnational and intercultural community-building that has, over time, been eclipsed from both Anglo-centric histories in the United States and progressive narratives of community formation in Greater Mexico, although for very different reasons. Yet it is important to note that this is not because it is an anachronistic representation of Tejano, Mexican, and U.S. history.[25] In fact, while the novel is certainly a romantic and romanticized history, research shows that there was indeed a period of time in the decades following the U.S.-Mexican War when elite Anglos and Tejanos intermarried, worked together in commercial enterprises, and sought out intercultural political alliances.[26] It is therefore in many ways unsurprising that the plot of *Caballero* returns to the nineteenth century in order to insert itself within this different historical tradition, one in which elite Tejanos might be white *enough* to be considered compatible with Anglo Americans. Racial, cultural, and national identities were still being defined and debated throughout the Americas in the nineteenth century, and the people of Greater Mexico were not always already defined or did not always imagine themselves as unequivocally nonwhite or off-white in relation to Anglo Americans. As Raúl Coronado reveals in his insightful monograph *A World Not to Come: A History of Latino Writing and Print Culture*, the late eighteenth and early nineteenth centuries were a period when the worldview of Mexicanos, and Hispanos more generally, came crashing down, and they were forced to consider divergent modes of viewing and of understanding the world.[27] This was a foundational moment in American history in which nations and communities were being constructed, literally and figuratively. *Caballero* goes back to the nineteenth century in an attempt to show that Mexicans had not always been defined or identified as nonwhite. Instead, it asserts that elite Tejanos and Anglos once might have had much in common, including some form of whiteness and a desire for civilization, modernization, and progress—a better (in their eyes) and distinctly American future. I understand *Caballero* as a remnant of this alternative tradition of transnational collaboration and community-building between elite Anglos and Mexicanos—a tradition and discourse that was much stronger in the nineteenth century, which is perhaps why the novel returns to this period to rearticulate a similar collaborative and intercultural vision of a broadly American history.[28]

This is the tradition with which I see *Caballero* dialoguing, and it is the history I outline in *Forgotten Futures*: a time when Mexicans and Mexican Americans imagined and debated a multiplicity of possible futures for their relationship with the United States, as well as with Spain and Europe, and an era that shows a vast transformation in the ways in which the elites of Greater Mexico imagined, saw, and portrayed themselves, especially in terms of race and ethnicity. It is a story about the gradual formation of Greater Mexico but also the divisions that had to be forgotten in order to make that cohesion possible; it is about the missed opportunities and the leftover splinters of histories and discourses that are perhaps no longer possible for us to recognize or even imagine as once possible today and an exploration of why that is.

It is fitting that *Caballero* was lost for so many years in the Mireles's attic (or perhaps an unused desk drawer) because the attic, Rodrigo Lazo postulates, functions metaphorically as "a site that emphasizes the multiplicity of objects within an archive." An attic "emphasizes the passing of time and forgotten objects," and attics, Lazo reminds us, "are filled in a haphazard way and they contain (or hide) items that might otherwise be thrown away."[29] The metaphorical attic is where we find the letters, documents, and objects that appear out of place and do not meld with contemporary notions of Chicano or Latino (and, I would add, Mexican) identity, such as, in Lazo's example, a U.S. Confederate flag in the "Latino attic."[30] Building on Lazo's potent metaphor of the attic, I suggest that critics find it difficult to fit *Caballero* into existing Latino, Chicano, or Mexican literary and cultural narratives because *Caballero* belongs to a different archive—one relegated to the "attic" and one that reveals some troublesome aspects of a Latino, Chicano, and Mexicano past.

Like the novel *Caballero*, which goes back in time to show a different, more amicable relationship between elite Anglos and Hispanos and which itself, as an archival object, was relegated to the "attic" for so long, *Forgotten Futures* similarly turns to nineteenth-century archives that might be found in the metaphorical attic—forgotten political essays, travel narratives, novels, literary magazines, and newspapers of nineteenth-century Mexicans and Mexican Americans—in order to uncover the lost discourses of transnational collaboration and community-building they imagined during this turbulent time. Many of these texts have not made it into the canons of either U.S. or Mexican literature or have done so only relatively recently. Yet, as I will show, the texts and authors discussed in *Forgotten Futures* are far from anomalies; they reveal the types of debates, divisions, and conflicts that were representative of the time and have since been relegated to dusty archives.

The story I outline in *Forgotten Futures*, through analyses of writings from key moments from throughout Greater Mexico during the nineteenth century, is one that traces an alternative genealogy of now-forgotten imaginings of how Mexicans and Mexican Americans might define themselves and their relationship with Mexico, Spain, and the United States. As I will discuss, this history has been largely eclipsed from nationalist narratives because it does not always culminate in nation formation or in the nations of Mexico and the United States as they exist and are envisioned today. It is about ideas of community that are so divergent from the dominant conception that they ultimately question the stability of the nation and the coherence of the nation(al) and other community identities as we understand them today. Indeed, part of the reason it is so difficult to use descriptors in this book is because today we rely so much on nationality as an essential component of our communal and individual identities. Thus my chapters focus on moments of rupture rather than cohesion, on moments of impending change or tipping points, on instances of potential rather than fruition. I look at writers who peer out from uncertain moments and ponder possibilities, sometimes even dead ends, but not results.

The voices, discourses, authors, and texts that I examine in this book speak to a tradition and a history that are sometimes hard for us in the twenty-first century to decipher because it is difficult to avoid teleological interpretations of history, since we already know what happened (or think we do) and which discourses became dominant. Historical and cultural analyses have shown how Hispanos became racialized and marginalized within the United States and, more broadly, Western culture.[31] A whole generation of cultural and literary critics have explored and exposed the imperial foundations of U.S. history and culture and the diverse ways in which the United States established itself as a new imperial power during the nineteenth and twentieth centuries—often through the racialization and conquest of different communities in the Americas who were portrayed as barbaric others.[32] As any student or even casual observer of American history and culture can readily recognize, Mexican Americans and other racial(ized) minorities in the United States have long been battling negative stereotypes and systematic marginalization and oppression. As students and critics of literature, culture, and history, we often search for the germ of a revolutionary spirit, the seed of an anticolonial impetus, or a narrative thread of resistance to Anglo American and U.S. empire in Mexican American and Mexican literature. And like a self-fulfilling prophecy, it is easy to find if one already knows what to look for. When we look at the archive, however, we need to be ready, as Lazo says, to "unearth corpses": we need to be prepared for unexpected items in the archive that "will not necessarily run parallel to the progressive political positions of a Latino present."[33]

Following this idea, the premise of *Forgotten Futures* is that the nineteenth century is a lot messier and more conflicted than the teleological narratives of nation and identity formation presuppose; the outcome is much more uncertain from the viewpoint of the nineteenth century than our vantage point in the twenty-first century; and if we look closely, we can witness this fragmentation and uncertainty in the literature and writings of that time period. Ultimately, this untold story highlights the instability of the nation and the national—in both Mexico and the United States. It reveals the divisions within the nation—racial, ethnic, cultural, political, socioeconomic. The myth of the cohesive nation—whether political or cultural—is one that was constructed over time. As I will show, that supposed cohesion relies on a silencing of the community's fractures and imperfections, past and present.[34] I argue that it is this suppression of internal histories of colonialism, racism, classism, and sexism that in fact allowed the nation and nationalism(s) to emerge. *Forgotten Futures* digs into the divisions and structures of inequality that allowed some Mexicanos to picture a hemispheric future joined together with other American elites. Their visions show how the nation has always been "imperfect"—fractured, incoherent, divided. The ideal of the cohesive, liberal nation-state can only be achieved through the repression of voices of discord and the erasing of inequalities that are a constitutive part of that nation and its people.[35]

In the remainder of this introduction, I explain the theoretical underpinnings of *Forgotten Futures*, including a discussion of nations, nationalism, and transnationalism.[36] I define the competing discourses of civilization/whiteness and barbarism/blackness through and against which I see Mexicanos exploring potential avenues for transnational and intercultural collaboration. I elaborate on how I find it most fruitful to situate Greater Mexico within the theoretical fields of postcolonial literary and cultural studies—at the intersection of multiple national(ist) histories. I explain why literature—both fiction and nonfiction—offers a valuable vantage point from which to critically examine the history and culture of Greater Mexico. And lastly, I describe the organization of *Forgotten Futures* and provide a brief overview of the chapters.

Nations, Nationalism, and Greater Mexico

I find it theoretically impossible and irresponsible to limit the study of literature written by Mexicans and Mexican Americans, especially in the nineteenth century, to one national category (Mexico or the United States) or one language (Spanish or English). Instead, I find it more fruitful to examine these writers as part of a larger transnational and multilingual field of inquiry: Greater Mexico.[37] I borrow this term from the Chicano public intellectual and pioneer in border studies and Chicano studies Américo Paredes.[38] Like Paredes, I use this term to refer to "all the areas inhabited by people of a Mexican culture—not only within the present limits of the Republic of Mexico but in the United States as well—in a cultural rather than a political sense."[39]

My use of the term *Greater Mexico* adheres to Paredes's original definition: it is capacious and goes beyond a national focus, emphasizing the border as a "contact zone" between different groups and communities that can exist in other spaces in addition to the spaces along and around geopolitically defined borders. Mary Louise Pratt defines a contact zone as "the space of colonial encounters, the space in which peoples geographically and historically separated come into contact with each other and establish ongoing relations, usually involving conditions of coercion, radical inequality, and intractable conflict."[40] Pratt explains that this term foregrounds "the interactive, improvisational dimensions of colonial encounters so easily ignored or suppressed by diffusionist accounts of conquest and domination. A 'contact' perspective emphasizes how subjects are constituted in and by their relations to each other. It treats the relations among colonizers and colonized, or travelers and 'travelees,' not in terms of separateness or apartheid, but in terms of copresence, interaction, interlocking understandings and practices, often within radically asymmetrical relations of power."[41] The idea of a contact zone emphasizes complex networks of exchange and of negotiation rather than boundary-making, while seeking to understand the unequal distribution of power—and accompanying violence—that is a vital component of these interactions.

I conceive of borderlands as an expansive designation that includes all areas of the present-day United States that formed part of Mexican national territory in the nineteenth century. In addition, I use the term to refer to the large swath of land both between and bordering Mexico and the United States; both sides of the (present-day) U.S.-Mexican border are included in this definition.[42] Whenever possible, I label states/territories with more regional specificity, as the culture, history, and communities of the borderlands are heterogeneous and should not be viewed as a cohesive whole. It is important to note that the term *Greater Mexico*, as I use it in this book, is not synonymous with borderlands; rather, *Greater Mexico* refers to people in any area of Mexico or the United States who are culturally and/or historically connected to Mexico—as Gloria Anzaldúa explains it, "*mexicanos del otro lado* and *mexicanos de este lado*"[43] [Mexicans from the other side and Mexicans from this side][44]—while *borderlands* refers to the areas immediately on both sides of (present-day) national borders, the periphery of the (Mexican) nation, and those areas of the present-day United States that once formed a part of Mexico. *Greater Mexico*, as I use it, invokes a cultural definition of *mexicanidad*.

Thus the borderlands are part of Greater Mexico, but not all of Greater Mexico is included in the Mexican borderlands.

Following the call by both Paredes and Anzaldúa for a recognition of the links between people of Mexican descent from both sides of the border (and for brevity's sake), I frequently use the term *Mexicanos* to refer to the inhabitants of Greater Mexico; I employ *Mexicanos* as a cultural descriptor and not as a synonym for Mexican. I have chosen to use the term *Mexican American* when speaking about a new, more broadly defined identity and community of people with cultural or ancestral ties to Mexico living in and forming part of the U.S. national body after 1848.[45] *Chicano*, as I understand and use it, refers specifically to a chosen political identity tied to Chicano nationalism and Raza movements that emerged in the United States in the 1960s and 1970s.[46] It is therefore a term I use sparingly in this book. To refer to a very broad community of Spanish-speakers from throughout the Americas, when I wish to move beyond national or regional communities, I often employ the terms *Hispano, Hispanoamericano*, and *Spanish American*.

Although it is not often included in studies of the U.S.-Mexico borderlands, Yucatán, I argue, is another type of contact zone, and I consider it part of the Mexican borderlands. While Yucatán does not share a geopolitical border with the United States, it has existed—and still does, in many ways—on the margins of the Mexican nation, often having more in common with the Caribbean and other ports in the Gulf of Mexico, such as New Orleans, than with central Mexico and the nation's capital, Mexico City, which Mexicans frequently referred to (and still do today) with the telling synecdoche "México."[47] Although understudied in comparison to other parts of the U.S.-Mexican border, as I will discuss in more detail in chapter 2, the Gulf of Mexico, as a whole, is a site of complex transnational cultural and economic exchange— what Kirsten Silva Gruesz terms a "Latino-Anglo border system"—and should be recognized as another primary field for border studies.[48] Like Pratt's idea of the contact zone or Anzaldúa's concept of borderlands as "*una herida abierta* [an open wound] where the Third world grates against the first and bleeds . . . a dividing line, . . . a vague and undetermined place created by the emotional residue of an unnatural boundary," Yucatán in the nineteenth century was a region where diverse cultures and communities interacted, clashed, and negotiated with one another, where national and sociocultural boundaries became fuzzy and people passed and lived between them.[49] As my analysis of Yucatán (my area of focus in the Gulf) will show, an engagement with Yucatán as a border zone questions reified notions of the border as well as the nation.

While *Forgotten Futures* is *necessarily* a transnational exploration of writing by Mexicanos, the national and the regional—or "patria chica"—remain key theoretical components of my transnational approach. As my analysis reveals, statesmen, nation-builders, writers, and other cultural workers operating within national political and cultural fields were also embedded within and influenced by broader international political, cultural, and literary fields.[50] However, while the cultural workers whom I analyze sought or were sometimes forced to look beyond the regional and national (as geopolitical borders changed, for example), they also defined themselves within and against emerging and ever-changing national boundaries, both geopolitical and cultural. Perhaps precisely because of the instability of the nation-state in the nineteenth century, there was an increased need to define and categorize the national so that the nation(al) might be recognized outside of the borders of the nation, at an *international* level. Thus even as the writers I study look across national borders, they also do so in order to reflect back at their own (sometimes nebulous) concept of the national, the regional, and the local. For this reason, I find the concept of Greater Mexico, which simultaneously emphasizes both the importance of the nation and that which exceeds the nation, so useful for this study.

Many critics have emphasized the progressive potential of transnational approaches to literature and cultures. *Forgotten Futures*, however, explores the flip side of this coin—the imperialist, exclusionary, and sometimes racist imaginings of the transnational—in order to better understand the conversations in which both "sides" of the coin were participating.[51] While the transnational can certainly challenge the cohesiveness and omnipotence of the nation-state, it is not inherently liberating; similarly, the liberal nation-state is not inherently restrictive or, put more simply, bad.[52] Furthermore, revealing the transnational history of a community does not necessarily entail an undermining of the nation-state or a questioning of the hierarchies and structures of inequality that are constitutive of the nation-state.[53] In fact, the obfuscation of the nation(al) can, perhaps unwittingly, deny the existence of these political and social structures of inequality and exclusion that continue to shape communities in the present day.[54]

In *Forgotten Futures*, I read texts not only as vehicles for national consolidation but also as forums for debate and as venues in which intellectuals and cultural workers pondered, argued about, and commented on the conflicts and discourses that were changing their world and their ambivalence about their place within those discourses. These texts and authors offer insight into the divisions—sometimes fiercely fought over and enforced—that were an integral part of life in nineteenth-century Greater Mexico. They speak to the violence, discursive as well as corporeal, that has frequently been suppressed from the *internal* history of Greater Mexico. Underlying *Forgotten Futures* is an assumption that writing both reflects and forms the communities and readers for which it is produced. As countless critics have clearly shown, in Latin America, there was (and is) an intimate, generative connection between writing and sociopolitical projects.[55]

Experts in the field of early Mexican print literature have convincingly argued that the role of literature in nation-making and community-building was perhaps even more important in nineteenth-century Mexico, which was fragmented along social and racial lines and economically as well as politically unstable.[56] In fact, the question should not be why Mexico had such trouble consolidating as a country but rather how the country came together at all given its precarious economic and political situations and the hierarchical and deeply divided nature of its social structures.[57] The answer for many critics, at least in part, is literature. As Mexican historian José Ortiz Monasterio eloquently explains, literature provided the initial *virtual* space—which would eventually become a physical, political, and economic space—for the creation, or invention, of a new nation-state: "Cuando no había un poder hegemónico estable, cuando el mercado nacional prácticamente no existía, la literatura abrió un espacio *virtual* con la proposición de que en la medida de que se creara una literatura nacional, a ésta le seguiría un Estado nacional estable"[58] [When there was no stable hegemonic power, when the national market practically did not exist, literature opened up a *virtual* space with the idea that to the extent that a national literature was created, a stable national State would follow]. Tomás Pérez Vejo similarly explains that the most difficult aspect or most decisive moment of nation-building is not necessarily the establishment of legal systems or geographic boundaries; it is instead "el convencer a los habitantes del territorio independizado de que son parte de una entidad homogénea, distinta y claramente diferenciada del resto de los habitantes del planeta; que el ser italiano, o persas o eslovacos, es parte esencial de su identidad como personas"[59] [the convincing of the inhabitants of an independent territory that they are part of an entity that is homogeneous, distinct, and clearly differentiated from the rest of the planet's inhabitants; that being Italian, or Persian or Slovakian, is an essential part of their identity as people]. The nation, he continues, "necesita ser querida, no sólo ser obedecida"[60] [needs to be loved, not just obeyed]. Literature—which in the nineteenth century was understood to encompass a much broader array of genres than it does today, as I will discuss—plays a decisive role in the construction of new communities, such as the nation, in nineteenth-century Greater Mexico.

However, while *Forgotten Futures* is intensely interested in the nation, it also ponders literature's unique ability to imagine and voice alternatives to the nation as we know it today and its ability to reach beyond the national to an international community. Recent research on the publication and international circulation of Spanish-language texts, including the writing of exiles, points to how literature could be used not only for nation-building but also for the development of an international consciousness.[61] Rather than assuming that nation formation is the inevitable social and political goal of these nineteenth-century writers and cultural workers, I offer a nonteleological approach to the relationship between literature and nation formation while still recognizing literature's vital function in nineteenth-century Greater

Mexico as a virtual space for imagining, debating, and pondering the creation and distinctive qualities of a community. In other words, I propose that literature can also offer perspectives that decenter the nation, question the seemingly inevitable process of nation formation, and reveal, through analyses of the often unrecognized silences in these texts written by elites, the voices of those people and groups who were never included as a part of the nation(al). As I will discuss in further detail in my chapters, travel narratives (the focus of the first two chapters of *Forgotten Futures*) and literary texts that were excluded from *national* literary canons (the focus of the latter two chapters of *Forgotten Futures*) are particularly useful vantage points from which to explore the creation of concepts of community that extend beyond the nation, that question the limits of the nation, or that are hyperaware of possibilities outside of national borders as we know and recognize them today.

The Multiple Empires of Elite Mexicanos

The vexed history I trace in *Forgotten Futures* relies on diverse discourses of power and belonging that evolve throughout the nineteenth century. I contrast two different sets of discourses that I designate broadly as "discourses of civilization and whiteness" and "discourses of barbarism and blackness." These discourses change and take on different dimensions throughout the nineteenth century. In the first half of the book, I look at how Mexican travelers comment on and sometimes question the connections between republicanism, modernization, racial inequality, and U.S. neocolonialist endeavors in an attempt to make their identities recognizable to an international community of "civilized" nations and peoples. In the second half, I examine how Mexican American writers rely on similar discourses—civilization, modernization, Spanishness, and whiteness—as modes of belonging and empowerment for elite Mexican Americans within a social and cultural context in the United States that is increasingly hostile to all Mexicanos.

Forgotten Futures seeks to understand how the inhabitants of Greater Mexico understood these changing discourses and how they imagined their own places within both old and new hierarchies of power as they transitioned from Spanish colonialism, through postcolonial formations, and eventually to U.S. neocolonialism. The stories and histories included in this book reveal the debates, fighting, and divisions *within* the communities of Greater Mexico told from the perspective of Mexicanos. I start with the premise that the identities of the inhabitants of Greater Mexico were not, and are not, formed solely by resistance to Anglo American and European discourses. *Forgotten Futures* shows how people throughout Greater Mexico used, understood, and manipulated diverse discourses themselves as they developed their own identities as individuals and as part of larger communities.

Within the broad discourses of civilization/whiteness and barbarism/ blackness, Spain and Spanishness emerge as central figures through which these discourses are articulated in Greater Mexico. *Spanishness*, as I use it throughout this book, is linked specifically to Spain and the imagined, mythical idea of a pure Spanish culture, history, and ethnic identity. Spanishness in the nineteenth century is a surprisingly volatile concept. It could be perceived as a link to Europeanness, whiteness, and cultural sophistication; but this image was also constantly in tension with negative representations of Spain and Spanishness, such as the Black Legend, which painted Spain, Spaniards, and the Spanish empire as barbarous, morally blackened, and culturally degenerate. As I will discuss in each chapter, the slipperiness of these figures made Spain and Spanishness a constant site of negotiation and preoccupation through which inhabitants of Greater Mexico both affirmed and contested their whiteness (or blackness) and level of civilization (or barbarism).[62] Although not a term used by speakers in the nineteenth century, I use the concept of off-whiteness to discuss the gradations of whiteness and blackness that were perceptible in the nineteenth century.[63]

Figures of empire, imperialism, and colonization form the second thorny category around which Mexicanos contemplated and formulated their positions within the dichotomies of civilization/whiteness and barbarism/blackness. Mexicanos saw connections between themselves and two different and competing empires: one of the future (the United States) and one of the past (Spain). On the one hand, they recognized a new U.S. empire of capitalist commerce emerging from a comparable history of colonialism: a fellow American country linked to supposedly more modern and egalitarian forms of governance, such as republicanism and democracy, but also new types of present and future colonialism, such as economic colonialism. On the other hand, they perceived a dying Spanish empire bound to old (European) ways of understanding the world, such as monarchy and Catholicism, but also an empire with a potentially valuable past—a history of military prowess and cultural innovation (the Spanish Golden Age of arts and literature, for example) widely recognized as evidence of greatness by an international community.[64] As I will show in each chapter, Mexicanos were constantly questioning their place within and their links to these competing empires and different forms of colonialism—past, present, and future. As with the figures of Spain and Spanishness, figures of imperialism and colonialism emerge as contested sites of meaning and representation that Mexicanos could manipulate to fit their needs and a variety of contexts. At the same time, the tenuousness of these figures of Spain, Spanishness, and empire meant that they were dangerously fragile—they could be used by Mexicanos in certain situations as sources of empowerment, but they could also just as easily be used against Mexicanos as a form of exclusion or disenfranchisement.

The precarious position of Mexicano elites within blackness/whiteness and civilization/barbarism highlights the instability of these dichotomies and the inadequacy of terms such as *postcolonial, subaltern,* or *marginalized* for homogenously describing Greater Mexico (or more broadly, Spanish America).[65] It can be argued not only that there are multiple colonial powers at play in Spanish America but that the end of formal Spanish colonialism implied neither the end of different types of internal colonization nor the relinquishment of imperial designs for many communities in Spanish America.[66] With these issues in mind, Walter Mignolo has called for a more precise distinction between the terms *colonialism* and *coloniality*. For Mignolo, "'colonialism' refers to specific historical periods and places of imperial domination . . . [while] 'coloniality' refers to the logical structure of colonial domination underlying the Spanish, Dutch, British, and US control of the Atlantic economy and politics."[67] As I also use it throughout this book, *coloniality* is a type of logic that sustains systems of domination. So when I use the term *colonialist*, I am not referring to a formal colonial system (colonialism); rather, I am referring to a hierarchical way of ordering society, a remnant of the Spanish colonial past that continues to structure society in the postindependence, nineteenth-century present of the authors' works I examine in this book. Even though Mexico was politically independent for most of the nineteenth century, it was still a *colonialist* state in many ways. Racial and cultural hierarchies established during the Spanish colonial period still existed, even if they were not always labeled or recognized as such, and certain sectors of the population enjoyed privileges such as citizenship while other sectors of the population were refused these same privileges. Historically, many of these groups, such as Indians, had been treated politically and/or socially as equals under neither the Spanish monarchy nor the independent Mexican government. Thus for many sectors of the Mexican population, a colonialist hierarchy was sustained after formal political independence.

The elite voices that I focus on in *Forgotten Futures* train our sights on the wide range of experiences of different groups within Greater Mexico. Critics in Chicano and Latino studies, Latin American studies, and American studies have also moved toward a more critical recognition of this diversity of experiences as well as the internal divisions and repressions that are an integral, but little recognized, part of the history, literature, and culture of Greater Mexico, especially in the nineteenth century. My book builds on and dialogues with the work of literary and cultural critics such as Jesse Alemán, José F. Aranda, Nicole M. Guidotti-Hernández, Manuel M. Martín Rodríguez, and others who seek to move away from master narratives that view social resistance to and conflict with Anglo Americans as the defining characteristic of the literary and cultural production of Greater Mexico. Alemán and Martín Rodríguez have called for greater attention to the rhizomatic, dialogic, hybrid, and interlingual aspects of Chicano literary production, moving away from mono-logical and teleological paradigms.[68] And Aranda and Guidotti-Hernández have brought to light the layers of colonial history and complex power strug-gles *within* Greater Mexico that need to be acknowledged as essential compo-nents of the Chicano or Mexican American experience. Aranda advocates for a "New Chicano/a Studies" that would seek to reveal "the history of this [Mexi-can American] community on its own complicated internal terms, not simply terms that suggest an oppositional relationship to Anglo America."[69] This "New Chicano/a Studies" engages with the overlapping histories of colonialism experienced by Mexican Americans, carefully examining how "Chicanos/as are the descendants of colonizers, as well as the colonized."[70] Guidotti-Hernández perhaps most concisely articulates the central problem with the resistance paradigm in Chicano, Latino, and American studies: embedded within the celebratory discourses of mestizaje, hybridity, and nationalism, which form essential components of the resistance paradigm, there are also repressed stories of intracultural violence enacted literally and figuratively on racialized and gendered others through the silencing or repression of those stories.[71] These histories of intracultural violence and oppression are some-thing few scholars write or talk about "because they pose a direct challenge to nationalist ideologies that celebrate the cultural heritage of Mexico and, in particular, of its indigenous roots."[72] Guidotti-Hernández concludes that there "is a disjuncture between the celebratory narratives of mestizaje (social, racial, and cultural hybridity as a formation of the Spanish colonial collision with Indians in the Americas) and hybridity that compose Mexican, Chicana/o, and other nationalisms and the literally unspeakable violence that character-ized the borderlands in the nineteenth century and the early twentieth."[73]

Responding to these new calls for work that is sensitive to the hybrid, dia-logic characteristics of Chicano (and more broadly, American) literature and that recognizes the intracultural violence and layers of colonial(ist) histo-ries, *Forgotten Futures* seeks to move beyond the idea of resistance to Anglo America or antagonism between Anglos and Mexicans/Mexican Americans as the essential characteristic of Mexican and Mexican American identity forma-tion. I instead look at how writers, through their texts, imagined the potential for a different dynamic between elite Anglos and Mexicans/Mexican Ameri-cans in which fruitful intercultural and transnational collaborative coalitions were possible and sometimes desired. As I will discuss in more detail in each chapter, at different moments throughout the nineteenth century, Mexica-nos imagined political unions with the United States, economic partnerships, joint colonial enterprises in the borderlands, and cultural and racial mixing between Anglos and Hispanos. As I will show, these relationships between elite Mexicanos and Anglos were often envisioned or created at the expense of racial and social others within Greater Mexico—an inflicting of both literal and discursive violence on those "othered" groups. This violence has subsequently been written out of linear and progressive histories of national cohesion and community formation in Greater Mexico. These transnational and intercultural coalitions and collaborative relationships between Mexicanos and Anglo Americans constitute an obscured transnational and inter-American history that, since the nineteenth century, has not been given adequate attention in Latin American, U.S. Latino, or American studies because the resistant/antagonistic vision of Anglo-Hispano relations has dominated so thoroughly since at least the mid-twentieth century and because they pose a threat to dominant discourses of national and cultural consolidation.

Before I end this section, I wish to emphasize that I do not see my research, or that of the critics I have discussed here, as "doing away" with the idea of subaltern or (post)colonial subjects. Indeed, oppression of Mexican Americans and other Latinos happened and continues today, and imperial discourses and colonial systems have very real and tangible consequences, especially for marginalized communities, such as Latinos in the United States. However, it is problematic to lump all groups in Greater Mexico into one category of postcolonial, marginal, or subaltern. We must take context into account and more carefully scrutinize the complex relationships between oppressor and oppressed, between colonizer and colonized. This is not to say that colonialism is a balanced relationship between equal partners; rather, this more nuanced understanding of the complexity of the (post)colonial experience opens up new ways of envisioning different types of dialogue and exchange. It exposes ways in which marginalized groups, such as Mexican Americans in the Anglo-dominated United States, have also been able to alternatively subvert or insert themselves into these ideologies of domination.

Rather than assuming either a submissive acquiescence or an antagonistic rejection of imperial and neocolonial formations, the approach that I take acknowledges the complexity and diversity of Greater Mexico and questions a one-way flow of information and power from (Anglo) center to (Greater Mexico) periphery. My approach seeks not to discard or to dispel the narratives of resistance and antagonism, which are valuable and important, but rather to complement and enrich them. Forgotten Futures recognizes the communities of Greater Mexico for their unique discursive location in the nineteenth century: between two empires and two forms of colonialism yet never completely devoid of their own colonialist intentions and internal hierarchies.

Chapter Outlines and Organization

Each chapter of Forgotten Futures focuses on a different moment of internal discord in Greater Mexico and thus also a moment of possibility and uncertainty. The texts I study in each chapter offer glimpses into these moments of introspection, when their authors examined their own identities and the different discourses they might use or manipulate to place themselves and others like them in positions of power.

My study moves roughly chronologically through the nineteenth century and is divided into two parts. The year 1848 is a pivotal moment around which this book navigates: the first half of the book focuses on the period before and during the U.S.-Mexican War (through 1848), and the second half focuses on Greater Mexico following the war (post-1848). To say that the U.S.-Mexican War was an important moment in the history of Greater Mexico would be a gross understatement. Yet while many studies have rightly looked at 1848 as a key turning point, they have often simultaneously looked at it as a moment of definitive and unambiguous change—as an already determined and understood crucial moment of rupture. The year 1848 certainly marks a profound shift in the types of imaginings that were possible for Mexicanos, but this was not a transformation that occurred overnight the moment that the Tratado de Guadalupe Hidalgo [Treaty of Guadalupe Hidalgo] was signed on February 2, 1848, nor was it understood and felt in the same way throughout the diverse and diffuse communities of Greater Mexico. In short, 1848 does not mark a moment of complete and definitive rupture from previous ways of imagining community in Greater Mexico, especially for elites. I understand 1848 as a moment of great importance, but because it advanced possibility as well as uncertainty, not definitiveness.

In *Forgotten Futures* I focus on several literary works that are considered "first" or early works: the first known novel published by a Mexican American woman in English, the first novels written by a New Mexican author in Spanish, and the first travel narrative about U.S. democracy. Although with time we may unearth earlier works, these texts will remain significant because, as early works, they represent a moment that triggered some sort of shift in thinking. As some of the first who are writing about these topics, debates, and concerns, they often do not necessarily have an "answer" yet; they meditate on possibilities and potential, not necessarily outcomes. For this reason, they are also significant because they give us a glimpse into an uncertain moment of change, thereby revealing the competing discourses and ideas of the moment—some of which are now difficult to detect. My use of "first" works or early works is not intended to uncover a linear moment of origin or some incipient, deepest, and most "original" or authentic articulation of identity. Instead, I employ these early texts because, as Gruesz explains, they can "disrupt traditional structures of periodization and refresh our ideas about intertextuality, originality, and the evolution of literary form."[74] These sorts of early recovered texts, Gruesz argues, "are important not only for the places where they display analogues to later cultural expressions—where they become recognizable to us—but for the ways in which they memorialize lost concerns, extinct modes of relation, the dead ends of historical paths not taken."[75] Indeed, my goal is to think about not just how these works "fit" into established canons but also where they diverge from now well-established parameters of national literary canons and narratives of cultural cohesion.

In order to evaluate popular (in the sense of widespread) discourses, I turn to readily available and easily disseminated types of writing. With this in mind, the first half of this book focuses on nontraditional literature: travel narratives, letters, political essays, newspapers, and published diaries. While these are often seen as private or nonliterary forms of writing today, in the nineteenth century the line between private and public writing was not so clear-cut. Many individuals who wrote personal narratives, such as diaries or personal letters, did so with full knowledge—and sometimes even the intention—that these could and would be shared with others back at home through circulation and semipublic readings or with a broader public through publication in newspapers and other venues. Likewise, the understanding of literary genres was different in Greater Mexico in the earlier part of the nineteenth century than it is today.[76] As Jean Franco explains, the clear distinctions we have today between imaginative and scientific works, or between poetry and narrative, do not correspond to early nineteenth-century categories.[77] Texts that we might not find in the literature sections of bookstores today, such as the travel narrative (or guide), allegory, religious sermon, economic treatise, or political essay, were not only popular but also considered serious literary works with broad international audiences; individuals read them and shared them with others for their political and social usefulness.[78]

Newspapers, a somewhat ephemeral but ubiquitous presence in nineteenth-century America, were key forms of communication and also debate; indeed, they were some of the earliest forms of easily accessible and widely circulated print media.[79] In Greater Mexico in the nineteenth century, newspapers did not merely report news; newspapers served as vehicles for debating and critiquing not just politicians and the public but also other editors and newspapers. Newspapers in Greater Mexico usually had strong political and ideological platforms, which they did not try to hide. In fact, they openly sought to sway readers with argumentative articles, and original novels and poetry, as well as articles about politics, culture, and history, were all part of what they found worth publishing as part of their political and ideological platforms.[80]

Even though these types of nonfiction literature were of great cultural and political significance, especially in the early decades of the nineteenth century, they are not frequently included in national literary canons, especially in the U.S. literary canon. Today, they exist largely in archives. As publishing became professionalized, "ephemeral" literature such as newspapers and magazines, as well as literature that did not fit with emerging definitions of belle-lettristic "literature" (educational texts, how-to manuals, songbooks, religious tracts, political speeches, etc.), were "dropped out of the history books" and excluded from the canon as nonliterature.[81] As Nancy Vogeley, Nicolás Kanellos, and others have convincingly argued, this serves as a way of erasing a multilingual literary presence—and more specifically, Latino voices—from the U.S. literary canon, even though if we look at the field of nonfiction, as we should, Latinos have a long and rich history of publishing in the United States, starting in the first decades of the nineteenth century.[82] At the same time, this lack of acknowledgment of the existence of early Latino and Spanish-language non-fiction also erroneously—and using circular logic—confirms that U.S. literature has long been English-language centered.[83] As critics involved in recovery work and research on early presses and print communities in the United States have clearly demonstrated, this is not accurate.[84] The fact is that in the eighteenth and early nineteenth centuries, nonfiction made up much of what American readers were consuming; literary histories that do not take this into account are only partial.[85] In this way, I also see my inclusion of nonfiction narratives, newspapers, and other "ephemeral" nonfiction texts—especially those written originally in Spanish—as evidence of the multilingual and transnational roots of U.S. literature and as an important contribution to the recovery of the Latino literary presence within the U.S. national literary canon as well as a recovery of texts that would eventually be excluded from national(ized) literary canons.

Within Mexican (and more broadly, Spanish American) literary and historical canons, *Forgotten Futures* highlights Mexico's intimate relationship with the United States and a broader American and European community of elites. Through acknowledgment of the important voices and discourses that did not ultimately come to form a part of the way that Mexican national identity is conceptualized today, my book helps reveal and question how history and nation-building have been (re)written in Mexico as a cohesive narrative of political progress, harmonious mestizaje, and the triumph of the liberal nation-state.[86]

Chapters 1 and 2 revolve around two pivotal periods of uncertainty and fragmentation for Greater Mexico: the 1830s, its early years as an independent nation; and 1846–1848, during the U.S.-Mexican War and the start of the Caste War in Yucatán. Chapter 1, "Imperial Republics: Lorenzo de Zavala's Travels between Civilization and Barbarism," focuses on the Yucatecan man of letters, influential politician, and later first vice-president of independent Texas, Lorenzo de Zavala, who was writing and working during the turbulent early national period of Mexico, when federalists and centralists were waging war over the future and form of their country. I explore Zavala's travel narrative, *Viage a los Estados-Unidos del Norte de América* [*Journey to the United States of*

North America], published in Paris in 1834, as a commentary and lesson to his fellow Mexicanos on what the racial and political makeup of a liberal democratic American nation should—or could—look like. In *Viage*, Zavala ponders potential avenues for the future economic, political, and cultural development of Mexico. He does so through two competing and seemingly oppositional images of the United States and Mexico, as both barbaric remnants of a colonial past and harbingers of a modern and civilized future. Through analysis of Zavala's representations of slavery, slave-like imitation, and racial(ized) others in both the United States and Mexico, I demonstrate how he creates a sense of shared American barbarism and degeneracy that is the result of centuries of colonialism in both countries. In his more panegyrical depictions of U.S. industry, innovation, and equality, however, he also points to the possibility of a future union between the United States and Mexico through the spread of liberal ideologies. At the same time, he hints at the "dark side" of republicanism in the United States: its inability to incorporate racial others, its dependence on the exclusion of racial others, and its (future) neocolonial endeavors. In this chapter I show how Zavala's proposed partnerships between the United States and Mexico are part of a long history of imagined transnational collaboration between Greater Mexico and the United States. This was a collaborative discourse, however, that simultaneously embraced elitist racial and class hierarchies and considered new modes of internal colonization within Mexico. This chapter sets the stage for the rest of the book by highlighting key competing discourses of blackness/barbarism and whiteness/civilization and how elite Mexicans in the first decades of the nineteenth century understood and sought to ascertain their place within those dichotomies.

Chapter 2, "A Proposed Intercultural and (Neo)colonial Coalition: Justo Sierra O'Reilly's Yucatecan Borderlands," starts in 1847, at the outset of the Caste War in Yucatán and in the midst of the United States' imperial conquest of Mexican territory during the U.S.-Mexican War. I look to the margins of the Mexican nation—Yucatán, which had seceded from Mexico at this time—in order to understand how even during a moment of intense violence between the United States and Mexico, we can still see elites contemplating and debating a variety of potential routes for cooperation between themselves and U.S. Anglos. As a way of highlighting the presence of these discourses, I examine Justo Sierra O'Reilly's travel diary, *Diario de nuestro viaje a los Estados Unidos (La pretendida anexión de Yucatán)* [Diary of our travels to the United States (The attempted annexation of Yucatán)], written between 1847 and 1848 while the author was in the United States as a representative of the Yucatecan government, along with other personal correspondence and newspaper articles about Yucatán in Mexican and U.S. presses. Sierra O'Reilly uses complementary discourses of whiteness, progress, and hemispheric solidarity as ways of strategically linking elite Yucatecos with a new imperial power, the

United States, while simultaneously distancing Yucatecos from the barbarism and racial degeneracy associated with the Spanish imperial past. Through his manipulation of these discourses, he works to position European-descended elites in Yucatán in a strategic alliance with government officials and the Anglo American public in the United States in order to secure a stable space of agency for Yucatecos in the broader Americas and to protect Yucatecos from both U.S. and Mexican military aggression. At the same time, I explore how Sierra O'Reilly engages with and promotes U.S.-centered neocolonial formations, such as informal economic imperialism, Indian removal/extermination, and a narrative that imagines the United States as a progressive and beneficent empire, as potential ways of saving the "civilized" white population in Yucatán from perceived racial extermination at the hands of the "barbaric" Maya Indians. As I reveal, Sierra O'Reilly's sense of hemispheric solidarity is based on a common drive to whiten communities (in this case, in Yucatán), thus also speaking to a shared hemispheric history of neocolonialism in the postindependence era. Underlying this chapter is an understanding of Yucatán as another type of borderland, a region on the periphery of the (Mexican) nation that ultimately helps us question reified notions of not only national borders but also borderlands.

In chapters 3 and 4, the focus shifts to the U.S. American side of the border and fictional narratives by writers from the U.S. side of the borderlands in the decades following the U.S.-Mexican War. I look more closely at the process of incorporation of Mexican Americans into the United States to see how discourses of barbarism/blackness and civilization/whiteness continue to manifest themselves in diverse ways in the communities of Greater Mexico following the pivotal U.S.-Mexican War. This second half of the book focuses on a highly versatile literary form that gains popularity and cultural capital in the second half of the nineteenth century: long forms of narrative fiction such as the novel and novella. While newspapers and nonfiction narrative literary genres continue to have a strong presence in Spanish American culture and politics, the novel emerges in the second half of the nineteenth century as an influential genre through which writers and cultural workers debate and comment on the form of their nations and communities.[87] As Doris Sommer, Lee Joan Skinner, Jean Franco, and numerous others have shown, narrative fiction—and particularly the romance and historical novel—became increasingly important and popular forums for imagining and debating the substance and character of newly emerging identities and communities in the latter half of the nineteenth century.[88] This period, following the U.S.-Mexican War, was also a time when Mexicanos were reevaluating and reimagining their relationship with the United States and Anglo America and their changing place and options within that relationship. My readings of literary works by different authors from throughout Greater Mexico reveal that this second half of the century is a time of both possibility and uncertainty, especially with regard to racial, social, and political configurations. As with the texts I cover in the first half of *Forgotten Futures*, the narrative fictions I discuss in these chapters are texts that did not, at least initially, make it into any national(ized) literary canons. It is precisely in these sorts of texts that were not accepted, however, that we can see the lost imaginings of different sorts of community-building—that is, community-building outside of the nation(al) as we know it today.

Chapter 3, "A Transnational Romance: María Amparo Ruiz de Burton's *Who Would Have Thought It?*," concentrates on a moment in U.S. history when debates raged about how to integrate, or impede the integration of, Mexican Americans into the United States. I uncover how Ruiz de Burton's *Who Would Have Thought It?* (1872), the first known English-language novel written by a Mexican American woman in the United States, participates in and helps construct a transnational and intercultural Mexican American literary tradition that emphasizes collaboration rather than resistance as a desirable characteristic of Mexican-U.S. and Anglo-Hispano cultural and political negotiations. I explore how Ruiz de Burton manipulates discourses of whiteness and European cosmopolitanism as ways of linking elites from across the Americas. In addition, I move toward a more nuanced understanding of the multiple and overlapping colonialist formations that influenced how elite Mexicans and Mexican Americans such as Ruiz de Burton saw themselves and imagined their relationship to Anglo Americans in the nineteenth century. In her novel, Ruiz de Burton looks at two pivotal moments—the French Intervention in Mexico (1861–1867) and the U.S. Civil War (1861–1865)—in order to show how elite Anglos and Mexicanos share similar European roots and a similar capacity to overcome barbarism; but she also reveals, perhaps unintentionally, the imperialist and racist foundations of such a shared, cosmopolitan, future-oriented, modernizing project. Pushing back against interpretations of this novel as a decolonial or anti-imperial text, I argue that it can only be interpreted as such within a U.S. context. Within the broader context of Greater Mexico, Ruiz de Burton upholds racial and social hierarchies that placed elite Mexicanos at the top at the expense of African Americans in the United States and indigenous communities within Greater Mexico. To leave this aspect unrecognized, I contend, is to erase histories of racism and elitism within Greater Mexico, thereby enacting further violence against those already marginalized by these discourses in the nineteenth century.

Chapter 4, "Between Two Empires: The Black Legend and Off-Whiteness in Eusebio Chacón's New Mexican Literary Tradition," focuses on a key moment in New Mexican community development—the last decades of the nineteenth century, when New Mexico was fighting to be recognized as a state. I look at the literary and political writings of Eusebio Chacón, a prominent community leader, lawyer, writer, and advocate for Hispano rights in New Mexico and southern Colorado, as a window into the experiences of Nuevomexicanos during this turbulent period. I concentrate on his two novelettes, *El hijo de la tempestad* [*The Son of the Storm*] and *Tras la tormenta la calma* [*The Calm after the Storm*] (1892), credited as the first Spanish-language New Mexican novels. Chacón's work highlights the different strategies used by Nuevomexicanos to position themselves in proximity to both Spain and Anglo America while eliding cultural, racial, and political connections with Mexico. On the one hand, Chacón draws on Spanish cultural forms and utilizes the concept of blood purity, which linked elite Nuevomexicanos to Spanish conquistadors, as a means of establishing Nuevomexicano heritage as white and Nuevomexicanos as therefore fit for self-governance. On the other, he maintains a political distance from Spain and demonstrates Nuevomexicanos' compatibility with U.S. political principles in an effort to secure his community's right to self-governance as a new U.S. state. At the same time, his works seem to jump from one imperial context (Spain) to the next (United States), completely ignoring New Mexico's Mexican history in an attempt to eschew any connection with the racial miscegenation popularly assumed by Anglo Americans to be an inherent and degenerate/degenerating component of Mexican identity. Through analysis of these two novelettes, I show how Chacón, like so many of his fellow Nuevomexicanos, was forced to negotiate the fine line between the Old World and the New. His novelettes look toward the Old World—Spain—as proof of European heritage and whiteness while shunning the trappings of the old, backward, and barbarous Spain and moving toward the new (in this case a "New" Mexican) literary tradition distinct from both Mexico and the United States. His work highlights a moment when Nuevomexicanos fought to create political coalitions with Anglo Americans even as they simultaneously worked to preserve their own culture, language, and history and establish a space of agency for themselves within U.S. society. Chacón's work, like that of the other authors studied in my book, consequently forms part of an alternative literary and cultural tradition that sought out affinities between elites of Greater Mexico and the United States but did so on ever-shifting and seminegotiable grounds of privilege and belonging.

The authors and works I study in *Forgotten Futures* often speak from a place of privilege. I have at times been ambivalent about bringing to light and focusing on the voices of elites. So much work remains to be done to recover the voices and words of marginalized communities and individuals, and elites are, in general, already overrepresented in history books and literary studies. I nonetheless continue to find value in this project because these voices reveal the internal divisions within the communities of Greater Mexico—the class schisms and racial hierarchies that continued to structure Greater Mexico, to varying degrees, before and after the U.S.-Mexican War. These internal rifts, however, were strategically forgotten as Mexicans moved toward national consolidation and as Mexican Americans joined ranks in the face of an even more repressive power: the United States and a culturally, politically, and economically imposed Anglo American dominance. Nonetheless, these internal repressed voices—or rather, the echo of the repressed, who do not find a voice in these texts—need to be acknowledged as a fundamental part of the history of Greater Mexico. Moreover, although the *reading* public became increasingly democratized throughout the nineteenth century, it was largely elites who were *writing* in the nineteenth century and who had the means to publish as well as access to publishers.[89] This fact should not be glossed over. Part of the larger goal of this book is thus the recovery and analysis of the stories of violence and subjugation *as well as* the corresponding discourses of privilege that were integral parts of the communities of nineteenth-century Greater Mexico. To erase this history of conflict and to erase this repression from a foundational moment in American history and culture is to further marginalize those already ignored by elites in the first place.

In addition, there seems to be a tendency to look at recovered texts written by Hispanos in the United States and either praise them for their mere existence, with little attention paid to the content, or focus on the more progressive (anti-imperial, antiracist, etc.) aspects. Both of these approaches, in my opinion, oversimplify an incredibly rich and complicated corpus and avoid uncomfortable conversations about privilege and violence within the Latino community. To avoid these conversations, however, is also to erase the presence of racism, elitism, and different forms of colonialism from American and Mexican histories. *Forgotten Futures* instead seeks to engage with this difficult history through an understanding of these texts as sites of struggle and discord and as evidence of the violence that was an intrinsic component of nineteenth-century community formation in Greater Mexico.

In our present day, U.S. Latino literature, and more broadly U.S. Latino identity, is frequently imagined as existing in the present and future but denied a past.[90] If Latinos are always seen as new arrivals to the United States and/ or immigrants, as a new community always *about to* emerge (future-oriented), Gruesz astutely notes, this means that Latinos "are denied *the common occupation of past time* with other U.S. Americans."[91] *Forgotten Futures* attempts to reveal the interconnectedness of U.S. and Mexican nation-based literary canons as well as the points of contact between our (now) national(ized) histories. At the same time, I caution against automatically assuming continuity between present-day and nineteenth-century notions of *latinidad* and against uncritically foisting a progressive political narrative onto the Hispanic archive. While this book is not a broadly Latino literary history, I make gestures in each chapter toward a larger American context in an attempt to place these authors in dialogue with other Hispanos from throughout the hemisphere and in an effort to recognize the coevalness of a Latino and Anglo past, as well as (a) Latino future(s). Due to its proximity and its intimate connections with the United States, Mexico is certainly unique in some ways, but the discourses and ideas I pull out in these texts circulated throughout the Americas.

Forgotten Futures focuses on nineteenth-century Greater Mexico, but its implications for how we identify, talk about, and study such foundational moments extend into our present. Today, in the United States, talking about race, much less racism, is becoming increasingly taboo. The coded language of racial color-blindness is becoming more and more prevalent,[92] even as racism, xenophobia, and white supremacy are on the rise.[93] Socioeconomic disparity is increasing as wealth is concentrated into fewer and fewer hands.[94] Now more than ever, we need to recognize and talk openly about violence, racism, classism, and other hierarchies of power and understand how they have formed American history and culture. This, perhaps more than anything else, is our shared, dark, unhappy, American history.

fic & nonfic
literature of elites in Greater Mexico
in the c...

1

Imperial Republics

———————————————————————◇—

Lorenzo de Zavala's Travels
between Civilization and
Barbarism

In one of the early chapters of Lorenzo de Zavala's 1834 narrative about his
travels as an exile in the United States, *Viage a los Estados-Unidos del Norte
de América*,[1] he recounts his time passing through Missouri, remarking on an
"hecho curioso," or "curious affair," that he says "da idea asimismo de la situacion civil de aquellos remotos paises" (*Viage*, 51) [gives an idea of the civil situation of these remote lands (*Journey*, 30)]. He describes how during an attempt
to drive off a squatter, a landowner decides to take matters into his own hands
through violence. Zavala reports that the landowner ultimately decided not
to fire on the squatter only because he was worried that his daughter, who had
retrieved his gun for him, might be found guilty as an accomplice if the squatter were killed. Zavala explains to his readers that this sort of occurrence is
"muy comun en los estados y territorios occidentales de los Estados-Unidos, y
en Tejas, California y Nuevo-Méjico de nuestra república, el que los primeros
venidos tomen posesion de un terreno sin ningun título, le cultiven y vivan en
él hasta que un propietario legal venga á ocuparle" (*Viage*, 52) [very common
in the western states and territories of the United States, and in Texas, California and New Mexico of our republic, that those who get there first take possession of lands without any title, cultivate them and live on them until a legal
owner may come to occupy them (*Journey*, 31)]. He also notes that "los inhab-
itantes de esta parte de los Estados-Unidos son generalmente poco civilizados,
y hay muchos que se aprocsiman á nuestros Indios, aunque siempre son más
orgullosos" (*Viage*, 50) [the inhabitants of this part of the United States are

generally not very civilized, and there are many who are much like our Indians, although they are always more proud (*Journey*, 30)]. During this "hecho curioso," Zavala thus uses a comparative mode to show the "not very civilized" people, frontier zones, and impediments to progress that exist in both the United States and Mexico.

Zavala employs this comparative frame throughout his narrative of exile. He writes about U.S. customs, political governance, and daily life, and then he compares these practices, institutions, and lifestyles with places, people, and customs in Mexico—familiar faces and places for his Mexican readership. His encounters as an exile with other cultures and ways of life in the host country help generate and develop this comparative approach. In *The Politics of Exile in Latin America*, Mario Sznajder and Luis Roniger explain that exile typically entails a confrontation with "new models of organization that transform them [exiles], willingly or not."[2] This exposure to new ideas and forms of social and political organizations in turn "challenges the displaced persons to reconsider the ideals they came with and their notions of both the host country and the homeland that they left behind."[3] Exiles indeed played an important role in reimagining and (re)defining national identities and boundaries in nineteenth-century Spanish America. They became more aware of their identity as belonging to a nation and helped more clearly define the boundaries and borders of a nation when they were, as Sznajder and Roniger put it, "translocated" outside of their homeland.[4] At the same time, the experience of translocation and displacement also made individuals more aware of their nation's image in and relationship to a broader transnational public sphere. Sznajder and Roniger explain, "The very exclusion of exiles from the domestic public arena shaped, however, a transnational public sphere and multistate politics in the Americas and beyond, in which some of the exiles learned how to play their national politics from afar and the states were drawn into play politics on an international and, later, global scale."[5] Zavala's constant use of comparison between the United States and Mexico, then, is about more than just teaching his fellow Mexicans about democracy and republicanism through concrete and local references that they could more easily grasp. It is also about defining a new concept of the Mexican nation and creating, or at least imagining, a meaningful link between U.S. Americans and Mexicans in a broader international and transnational arena. As I will show, this link is envisioned as a racial, political, and cultural connection between elites, and it is established through two seemingly contradictory images of the countries and their relationship. On the one hand, Zavala focuses on a mutual lack of civilization (in certain areas/aspects of the national imaginary) and a common history of moral as well as political degeneracy; he shows how both countries are embroiled in similar though not completely analogous fights against corrupted and "blackened" components of their cultures and histories that continue to haunt each country in different ways. On the other hand, Zavala also at times uses comparison to present the United States as a model for its fellow American republic, Mexico. In these instances, Zavala presents the United States as a new—at times benevolent—imperial model and force in the hemisphere. Zavala praises free labor, industry, and modern innovation in the United States as motors of a new type of capitalist republicanism that he ultimately sees spreading to Mexico and thereby linking Mexico and the United States in a new type of republican union in the future.

In this chapter, I explore how Zavala's conflicting representations of Mexico and the United States can be understood as links between the two nascent republics, which he portrays as similarly fighting forces of barbarism, in an attempt to move toward progress and true liberalism. I examine how Zavala links Mexicans and Anglo Americans in his exilic travel narrative through a shared history of slavery, colonialism, and degeneracy, as well as an emergent capitalist republicanism that is dependent on newly emerging racial hierarchies and exclusions. Lastly, I explore his portrayal of both countries as potential harbingers of modernity and progress if, his narrative suggests, they are able to move beyond the degenerate and "blackened" aspects of both their past and present and toward civilization, progress, and republicanism. Ultimately, I argue that Zavala, one of the first authors to write explicitly about the intimate geographical, philosophical, and political connections between the United States and Mexico, articulates an alternative imagining of an inter-American relationship that unites elites from both countries. His perspective from exile frames his experiences, allowing him to critique his homeland from afar, confront new models of governance, and envision a new Mexico that is intimately connected to other young American republics within a larger transnational community. This alternative imagining, though perhaps lost to us today, is key to understanding the Mexican and Mexican American experience in the nineteenth century. As I will show, it reveals the deep racial, ethnic, and class-based fissures that should be recognized as foundational to identity formation in Greater Mexico.

Comparative Barbarisms

In the decades following independence in Mexico, the dominant creed of the nation was unequivocally liberalism.[6] But what exactly liberalism might mean on the ground in Mexico in these first decades of independence was hotly contested. The most ardent liberals—*puros*, or doctrinaire liberals—believed in individual freedom and equality unrestrained by government or corporate interests, such as the Catholic Church, the army, guilds, and Indian communities.[7] Freedom and equality, according to the *puros*, would be achieved through the "protection of civil liberties, representative institutions, the separation of powers, federalism, and municipal autonomy," and the establishment of a sec-ular, republican state.[8] This concept of liberalism "embraced a vision of social progress and economic development."[9] I use the terms *liberal* and *liberalism* in these first two chapters to refer to this political movement to establish a secu-lar, federal democratic republic based on the ideals of freedom, equality, and progress through the cultivation of the enlightened individual.

Originally from Yucatán, Lorenzo de Zavala (1788–1836) was an influential Mexican statesman, writer, and editor and a strident liberal, well schooled in the political philosophy of European Enlightenment thinkers such as Voltaire and Rousseau. Like other historians and writers from this time period, Zavala was a politician first and a man of letters second.[10] He was a principal architect of the Mexican Constitution of 1824, and during his lifetime he also served as governor of the state of Mexico, as Secretary of the Treasury in Vicente Guer-rero's government, and as the first minister plenipotentiary of the Mexican legation in Paris under Santa Anna. He was recognized by his contemporaries, both political allies and enemies, as one of the most influential liberal reform-ers in Mexico.[11] Within Mexican historiography, Zavala remains today a key figure in early independence history.[12] Yet his role in U.S. history, literature, and politics is less well documented, despite his contributions to culture and to politics on both sides of the border—specifically in the Texas Revolution and the Republic of Texas.

In late 1829, Zavala fled Mexico and traveled to the United States as a political exile. Labeled a traitor by his fellow Mexicans because of his federal-ist stances and radical liberal policies, Zavala toured throughout the United States as an exile until late 1832, when power shifted back to federalist allies in Mexico. He then returned to his homeland to resume his position as gov-ernor of the state of Mexico.[13] He was named Yucatán's representative to Congress in 1833 and immediately recommenced implementing liberal, anti-clerical reforms in state and national government.[14] Later, in 1833, President Santa Anna appointed him as the first Mexican minister to the French court. Zavala was honored by his nomination and accepted the position, but in real-ity, angry supporters of the Catholic Church had urged Santa Anna to do so as a way of removing Zavala, if only temporarily, from Mexico City and Mexican politics.[15] His stint in France was thus a type of what Sznajder and Roniger call "translocation," a mechanism of political exclusion frequently employed in the early independence era in Latin America as a way of removing dissenting par-ties without bloodshed, therefore avoiding outright war, which could weaken or topple already unstable governments and leaders.[16]

Zavala's political tenure in France was short. In 1834, upon learning about Santa Anna's installation of a new cabinet, the election of a new centralist con-gress, and the restoration of special privileges to both the Catholic Church and the military back in Mexico, Zavala resigned from his political appointment, having served only six months as the minister in France.[17] While in Paris in 1834, Zavala published *Viage a los Estados-Unidos del Norte de América*, a travel narrative reflecting on his earlier experiences as an exile in the United States and one of the earliest meditations on U.S. democracy (before Alexis de Tocqueville's *Democracy in America*, first published in 1835).[18] Although Zavala published *Viage* before leaving France as an exile for the second time, he was surely contemplating the possibility of future exile. As he wrote and prepared his narrative for publication, he became increasingly aware of the fact that he had been sent to France as a way of limiting his involvement in Mexican politics.[19] In early 1835, he sailed for New York, eventually relocating to Texas, where he planned an attempt to oust Santa Anna with federalist support. The plan failed. He became active in Texas politics, where he urged separation—not necessarily independence—from Mexico, later helped draft the first Texas constitution, and served as Texas's first vice-president.[20]

Zavala's position from exile allows him to be critical of his home nation in its process of nation-building. In his prologue to *Viage*, Zavala explains that he was driven to write it because "nada puede dar lecciones mas útiles de política á mis conciudadanos, que el conocimiento de las costumbres, usos, hábitos y gobierno de los Estados-Unidos" (*Viage*, 1) [nothing can give more useful lessons in politics to my fellow citizens than the knowledge of the manners, customs, habits and government of the United States (*Journey*, i)]. Thus while ostensibly his narrative is written about the United States, Zavala directs it to his fellow Mexicans and intends it to be used as a tool for learning about republican ideals and their potential realization in Mexico. The future of liberalism and republicanism in Mexico was indeed a principal concern for Mexican statesmen and intellectuals during this time. While Mexico was formally organized as a federalist republic with the Constitution of 1824, Mexicans were split on how to actually enact those republican ideals within their country. Moreover, in the early decades of the nineteenth century, Mexican leaders and thinkers hotly debated—and waged battle over—whether the Mexican masses were ready for or capable of participating in a nation that adhered to republican ideals. Although at first glance it may seem odd that Zavala claims to be writing about his homeland and to his fellow Mexicans in a book published outside of his country that focuses on his time spent traveling outside of Mexico, this gesture directed back at his native land is actually typical for exiles and other dislocated individuals who "lose the entitlements attached to citizenship but, at the same time, . . . become even more attached than before to what is perceived as the 'national soul.'"[21] In fact, this sense of national belonging is often discovered, recognized, or deepened through the process of dislocation, leading many exiles and displaced individuals "to reconstruct their bonds of solidarity in terms of the collective home identity."[22]

Reflecting in *Viage* on his past experiences as an exile, and perhaps steeling himself for the imminent possibility of another bout in exile, Zavala recognizes his unique and somewhat distanced vantage point, which permits him to critique his homeland while attempting to affect changes in and shape his country from afar. In the early independence period in Spanish America, exiles were important political figures and strong voices of dissent, writing from their position outside the control of a ruling national party or individuals in power. It is during this time that the "expatriation of central political figures . . . starts a tradition in which the absent leader becomes the pole of attraction and political consultation for actors in the home society."[23] Similarly, Zavala's role in Mexican politics did not decrease when he was in exile the first time or in France as he wrote *Viage*. In fact, as historian Raymond Estep makes clear, it was during his first stint in exile that Zavala became a major public voice in the reorganization of politics in Mexico following Bustamente and the centralists' fall from national control.[24] Furthermore, Zavala had already established his reputation as a political player and thinker at the national level in Mexico with his popular *Ensayo histórico de las revoluciones de México* [Historical essay on the revolutions of Mexico] (also published in France, during his first exile) before writing *Viage*, and his writings in France were most likely eagerly awaited by the reading public in Mexico.[25] Zavala, as an absent leader, continued to be a political threat and a voice of critique in the political happenings in his home country.[26]

Thus it is no coincidence that Mexico's cultural, political, and moral shortcomings emerge as primary preoccupations in *Viage*; he continues to critique his country from afar, knowing his voice still holds weight in the political arena back in Mexico. In the very first chapter of his narrative, he does not pull any punches when he describes his fellow compatriots:

El Mejicano es ligero, perezoso, intolerante, generoso y casi pródigo, vano, guerrero, supersticioso, ignorante y enemigo de todo yugo. El Norte-Americano trabaja, el Mejicano se divierte; el primero gasta lo menos que puede, el segundo hasta lo que no tiene: aquel lleva á efecto las empresas mas arduas hasta su conclusion, este las abandona á los primeros pasos: el uno vive en su casa, la adorna, la amuebla, la preserva de las inclemencias; el otro pasa su tiempo en la calle, huye la habitacion, y en un suelo en donde no hay estaciones poco cuida del lugar de su descanso. En los Estados del Norte todos son propietarios y tienden á aumentar su fortuna; en Méjico los pocos que hay la descuidan y algunos la dilapidan. (*Viage*, iv)

[The Mexican is easy going, lazy, intolerant, generous almost to prodigality, vain, belligerent, superstitious, ignorant, and an enemy of all restraint. The North American works, the Mexican has a good time; the first spends less than he has, the second even that which he does not have; the former carries out the most arduous enterprises to their conclusion, the latter abandons them in their early states; the one lives in his house, decorates it, furnishes it, preserves it against inclement weather; the other spends his time in the street, flees from his home, and in a land where there are no seasons he worries little about a place to rest. In the United States all men are property owners and tend to increase their fortune: in Mexico the few who have anything are careless with it and fritter it away.] (*Journey*, 2–3)

Zavala in fact critiques Mexican politics and culture so often in *Viage*, especially in comparison to the United States, that he preemptively answers his readers' outrage in his very first chapter: "Parece que oigo á algunos de mis paisanos gritar: ¡Qué horror! ved cómo nos desacredita este indigno Mejicano, y nos presenta á la vista de los pueblos civilizados" (*Viage*, v) [I seem to hear some of my fellow countrymen yelling: "How awful! See how the unworthy Mexican belittles and exposes us to the view of civilized peoples!" (*Journey*, 3)]. He responds, "Tranquilizaos, señores, que ya otros han dicho eso y mucho mas de nosotros y de nuestros padres los Españoles. ¿Quereis que no se diga? Enmendaos" (*Viage*, v) [Just calm down, gentlemen, for others have already said that and much more about us and about our forefathers, the Spaniards. Do you not want it said? Then mend your ways (*Journey*, 3)]. But how will Mexicans fix themselves? By learning from their mistakes, which he brings to light for them in this very book, of course. He explains, "Tú, amigo lector, procura leer este libro con atencion, y espero que cuando lo hayas concluido habrás cambiadado muchas de tus ideas" (*Viage*, vii) [You, my dear reader, try to read this book with attention, and I hope that when you have finished it you will have changed many of your ideas (*Journey*, 3)]. Writing to and about his fellow Mexicans, Zavala thus appears to be aware of the weight his criticism will continue to have in his homeland and in a more international arena despite (or perhaps because of) his location outside of the nation.[27] His firsthand experience as both insider and outsider to Mexico and the United States alike makes him highly qualified to critique as well as to teach his fellow Mexicans.

As literary critic John-Michael Rivera has pointed out, Zavala praises the United States in many passages throughout *Viage*, almost to the point of seeming like a utopian representation of U.S. culture and governance.[28] But the careful reader will also note many ambivalent or sometimes explicitly critical portrayals of the United States. Zavala's first impressions as his ship approaches his first stop in the United States, New Orleans, for example, are not very positive:

Las playas son tan bajas que no se perciben . . . mas que unos montones de tierra al nivel de las aguas, sobre los que hay unas miserables chozas en donde apenas puede concebirse como habitan seres racionales. Se ven desembocar grandes trozos de madera, árboles enteros que la fuerza de los huracanes arranca á dos ó tres mil millas y vienen arrastrados por las corrientes impetuosas de los rios tributarios del Misisipí. El aspecto de esta entrada y aun el curso del rio hasta el fuerte Placamino es desagradable, pues solo se ven juncos y arbustos miserables, cuya vista aparece tanto mas fastidiosa cuanto que solo presenta montones de lodo y una innumerable cantidad de lagartos que semejan trozos de madera seca. (*Viage*, 6)

[The beaches are so low that they are seen . . . as nothing more than mounds of earth at the level of the water, upon which there are a few miserable huts where it is scarcely conceivable that rational beings live. Floating on the current can be seen great pieces of wood, entire trees, that the forces of hurricanes pulled loose two or three thousand miles away and which have been dragged along by the roaring currents of the tributaries of the Mississippi. The view of this entrance and even the course of the river (Mississippi) as far as Fort Placquemines is unpleasant, for the only thing to be seen are reeds and wretched shrubs, the sight of which appears all the more distasteful because there are only mountains of mud and an endless number of lizards that look like pieces of dried wood.] (*Journey*, 6–7)

The environment not only is ugly but also feeds on Zavala and his fellow travelers, causing them bodily harm and contributing to an unhealthy atmosphere. He mentions that they are constantly bothered by "el zumbido de infinidad de mosquitos que nos chupaban la sangre" (*Viage*, 7) [the buzzing of an infinite number of mosquitoes that sucked our blood (*Journey*, 7)]. When Zavala finally reaches the city itself, he dryly remarks that "el aspecto de la ciudad no ofrece nada que pueda agradar la vista del viagero, no hay cúpulas, ni torres, ni columnas, ni edificios de bella apariencia y arquitectura esquisita. Su situacion, mas baja que la superficie del rio y rodeada de lagunas y pantanos, la hace sombría y en estremo malsana" (*Viage*, 8) [the overall view of the city offers nothing that can please the eyes of the traveler; there are no cupolas, nor towers, nor columns, nor buildings of handsome appearance and exquisite architecture. Its location, lower than the surface of the river and surrounded by lagoons and swamps, makes it gloomy and unhealthful (*Journey*, 7)].

In these first impressions of New Orleans, which are also his first impressions of the United States, it is significant that Zavala begins by highlighting not the city itself but instead the ways in which nature—the uncivilized—remains an uncontrolled and uncontrollable presence in New Orleans and its surroundings: the brute strength of hurricanes litter the "unruly" river ("corrientes impetuosas") with obstacles, mosquitos that suck travelers' blood, and swampy lands that make the city an unhealthy place (*Viage*, 6). In addition, when he does finally reach the city, his descriptions emphasize the lack of architectural components that he associates with a developed center of civilization; it is not a truly modern city in every aspect. Although Zavala does go on to say positive things about New Orleans and its inhabitants, these very first impressions of New Orleans and the United States alert his readers to the idea that there are still liminal spaces in the United States that civilization and modernization have not yet quite reached—or, at the very least, have not yet dominated.

In the narrative as a whole, Zavala's positive representations of the United States, especially of the Northern states, stand out to the reader as more admiring because of a contrast with some of his more critical comments about the U.S. South and frontier zones, such as the areas around New Orleans.[29] I suggest that for Zavala, who might be characterized as somewhat obsessed with what he saw as Mexico's inferiority and its political and cultural shortcomings, the idea that a fellow new republic like the United States might also still be overcoming its own pockets of barbarity or backwardness, as seen in his descriptions of both the Arkansas Territory and New Orleans, might have been a comforting thought. These more disparaging comments and portrayals of the United States and Mexico link these countries through a common fight against degeneracy and, subsequently, a call to move toward a true liberal democracy of moral, political, and cultural progress. I begin by focusing on one particular image of barbaric degeneracy that appears in multiple guises throughout Zavala's narrative and that would have provoked particularly strong reactions for nineteenth-century liberal readers and writers—that of slavery.

The Limits of Liberalism in the United States and Mexico

Zavala's narrative intimates that both the United States and Mexico are linked by histories of and constant battles against slavery. Abolitionists throughout the Western world viewed and portrayed slavery first and foremost as a moral and humanitarian problem, and Zavala likewise highlights this aspect in his critique of U.S. slavery.[30] When reflecting on his time in New Orleans, he voices one of his most forceful critiques of U.S. democracy, the continuation of slavery, which he describes as "degradante" [degrading] and "humillante" [humiliating], enforced by "leyes que contienen principios sumamente antiliberales" (*Viage*, 34) [laws that contained extremely antiliberal provisions (*Journey*, 21)] and "medidas de represion tan ofensivas á los derechos del hombre" (*Viage*, 36) [such offensive measures of repression against the rights of man (*Journey*, 22)]. Moreover, he argues that slavery leads to moral decadence and political as well as cultural stagnation. He writes that laws permitting slavery have "una influencia estraordinaria sobre el progreso moral y la civilizacion de los

Estados que permiten esclavos" (*Viage*, 36) [an extraordinary influence on the moral progress and the civilization of the states that permit slaves (*Journey*, 23)]. As evidence, he compares the current state of publishing in free and slave states in the United States. In free states, he shows, the number of newspapers has increased dramatically over the last twenty years, while in slave states, the number has remained somewhat static or has even decreased, as in the case of Louisiana (*Viage*, 37). Zavala portrays literacy, publishing, and education as proof of progress. His critique of slavery in the United States thus clearly highlights one more impediment to the realization of a truly liberal U.S. republic. Yet as I will discuss, for all Zavala's commitment to and promotion of liberalism and republicanism, he, like many of his fellow liberals throughout the Americas, is not necessarily committed to racial equality—especially not as we understand it today. In fact, his travel narrative highlights how liberalism and republicanism are only made possible through racial inequality.

As I have said, abolitionists throughout the Western world critiqued slavery first and foremost on moral grounds. But they also portrayed it as an economic issue. Historian Robin Blackburn notes that "abolitionists claimed that the labour of free men was always more productive than that of slaves."[31] In fact, the abolition of slavery was seen and represented by abolitionists as "the cause defining progress in the Atlantic World."[32] Moreover, the concept of progress itself also contained an economic aspect, with the main thrust of the argument against slavery being that it "was incompatible with a rising industrial capitalism and that this explained why abolitionism appealed not only to the idealistic, and those capable of great empathy, but also to hard-headed—and hard-hearted—governments."[33] Zavala's discussion of publishing in the U.S. South, while certainly voicing a moral critique, also underscores the financial aspects of publishing and the economic setbacks in slave states; he concludes that Southern slave states are following "un curso contrario al progreso de la civilizacion y comercio" (*Viage*, 37) [a course that is contrary to the progress of civilization and trade (*Journey*, 23)] through their lack of development of the printing industry. For Zavala, as for other critics of slavery, slavery is an obstacle for not just political or moral but also economic progress. And in fact, economic progress is inseparable from moral or political progress; they are complementary factors that must all be present in order to achieve true civilization as envisioned by the early nineteenth-century intellectual and statesman.

Zavala also indicates that slavery will continue to disrupt liberal projects in the United States even after blacks are formally freed. For example, Zavala portrays colonization efforts in Liberia as possible options that will help move toward abolition and the realization of liberal ideals for both whites and blacks. He explains that freed slaves might be civilized in Liberia, "una nacion de negros civilizados en las costas de Africa" (*Viage*, 262) [a nation of civilized blacks on the coast of Africa (*Journey*, 142)], because they have been given the tools to be economically successful and the opportunities to move toward republicanism. But in the United States, where there is no mixing of races, they would be doomed to be "una clase distinta, degradada é infeliz" (*Viage*, 262) [a distinct, degraded, and unfortunate class (*Journey*, 142)]. Zavala reports his understanding of the general feelings in the United States about the situation of free blacks:

> De consiguiente cuando se hayan roto sus cadenas, ... es claro que este pais se encontrará cubierto con una poblacion tan inútil como miserable; una poblacion que con su aumento disminuirá nuestras fuerzas, y su número solo traerá crímenes y pobreza. Esclava ó libre siempre será para nosotros una calamidad. (*Viage*, 262–263)

> [When their chains have been broken, ... it is clear that this country will find itself covered with a population as useless as it is miserable, a population which with its increases will lessen our strength, and its numbers will only bring crime and poverty. Slave or free it will always be for us a calamity.] (*Journey*, 142)

Zavala in these examples is quoting Mr. North, the president of Union College, whom Zavala sees as representative of public opinion in the United States.[34] He offers no contradictory remarks to North's assessments, indicating a tacit agreement. In these examples, Zavala considers how the effects of slavery might linger in the United States because blacks, even once freed, are not being incorporated into the civilizing and modernizing process. In his description of the free black community in New York, for instance, he explains that "á pesar de esta emancipacion de la clase africana y su posteridad, ecsiste una especie de proscripcion social, que la excluye de todos los derechos políticos, y aun del comercio comun con los demas, viviendo en cierta manera como escomulgados" (*Viage*, 162) [in spite of this emancipation of the African class and its descendants, it is excluded from all political rights, and even from the common trade with the others, living to a certain degree as though excommunicated (*Journey*, 90)]. Acknowledging the disjuncture between the professed liberalism of the United States and its inability to enact that liberalism when it comes to its racial minorities, Zavala wryly concludes that "esta situacion es poco natural en un pais donde se profesan los principios de la mas amplia libertad" (*Viage*, 162) [this situation is not very natural in a country where they profess the principles of the widest liberty (*Journey*, 90)].

Perhaps more significantly, however, it is not clear whether it is possible or desirable to incorporate blacks into the United States. Again describing the situation of the free black community in New York, he observes the exclusion of blacks from U.S. society and the lasting effects this has on the black community:

> Las gentes de color tienen sus habitaciones, sus posadas, sus templos separados: son los judíos de la América del Norte. Esta repulsion de la sociedad los envilece y les quita los estímulos al trabajo: se entregan á la ociosidad, y no procuran mejorar una situacion sin esperanzas, encerrada en tan estrechos límites en que apenas pueden tener lugar los cálculos del interes. De aquí los vicios y la pereza, que con muy pocas escepciones retienen á casi toda esta clase en los últimos rangos de la sociedad. (*Viage*, 163)

> [The colored people have their separate homes, hotels, and churches; they are the Jews of North America. This rejection by society degrades them and takes from them the incentive to work; they resign themselves to idleness and do not try to improve a hopeless situation, circumscribed within limits so narrow that there is scarcely room to calculate self-interest. Hence the vices and laziness which with very few exceptions holds (*sic*) this whole class down to the lowest ranks of society.] (*Journey*, 90)

Even once freed, social and economic ostracization creates a vilified black community that cannot easily be incorporated into a civilizing and modern(izing) nation. Following this discussion, Zavala rhetorically questions his readers: "Pero ¿cómo se remedia esa situacion embarazosa de las gentes de color libres en el centro de la sociedad Americana? ¿Llegará un dia en que se incorporen al Estado y formen una parte integrante de la comunidad?" (*Viage*, 164) [But how does one remedy that embarrassing situation of free colored people in the center of American society? Will the day come when they will be incorporated into the state and form an integral part of the community? (*Journey*, 91)]. He responds to his own question, "Debemos esperarlo" (*Viage*, 164) [We must hope so (*Journey*, 91)]. Yet how or when this will occur remains uncertain. Zavala's observations and questioning about the future of blacks in the United States reflect a common preoccupation of his time: politicians, statesmen, and even abolitionists throughout the Americas worried about how to incorporate (or the impossibility of incorporating) racial others into the nation, and particularly a republican nation, after emancipation. As Blackburn explains, one of "the difficulties in winning elite support for emancipation was explaining what would then become of the freedmen and women. Many abolitionists feared that slavery had degraded the slaves and that it would take a long time to teach them how to handle liberty."[35]

As Zavala's critique of the situation of free blacks in the United States demonstrates, U.S. democracy and the very roots of its civilization, its moral as well as economic cornerstones, are similarly undermined by the racial "other" (the slave as well as the ex-slave) whom it refuses to incorporate into its supposedly liberal project. Reflecting on the colonization efforts in Liberia and the current situation of free blacks in the United States, Zavala concedes, "No es cierto que mezcladas las castas jamas desaparecerian sus estigmas naturales" (*Viage*, 263) [It is not certain that once the castes were mixed the natural stigma would never disappear (*Journey*, 143)]. In other words, it is possible that the mixing of race could eventually lead to the dispelling of racial stigmas or prejudice. However, even at the sentence level, his convoluted double negative under-scores his uncertainty with regard to the future of newly freed blacks. He also ponders other options for the United States besides waiting for racial mixture to erase, smooth over, or whiten the black "other":

> Pero ¿cuántos siglos se necesitarian para que esto se verificase? Y entre tanto los inconvenientes de la permanencia de la casta negra en los Estados-Unidos son de mucha consideracion, para que un pueblo previsor y que calcula admirablemente sus intereses deje de tomar providencias que le libren de los males ó que al menos los disminuyan. (*Viage*, 263)

> [But how many centuries would be needed for this (racial mixing) to take place? And in the meantime the difficulties of the permanent residence of the black people in the United States are a matter of too much concern for a far-sighted people that look well to their interests to fail to make provisions to free themselves from the ills or at least to lessen them.] (*Journey*, 143)

For Zavala, the answer to the question of what to do with the uncivilized racial other in the United States does not seem to necessarily be the incorporation of blacks into society. Liberia, for example, is presented in fairly positive terms and as an option for moving toward a more civilized nation in the United States (*Viage*, 261–262). While the black colonization movement has been understood by many historians as a proslavery deportation project, David Kazanjian reveals that in the earlier stages of its development and implementation, from the 1770s until the 1830s, "the project was primarily planned and supported by a complex and uneasy coalition of free and enslaved blacks as well as white abolitionists (most of whom were Northerners) and slaveholders who were vaguely 'troubled' by the existence of slavery."[36] Furthermore, those factions that supported this type of colonization during this period saw it as "consistent with, indeed as the completion of, the American Revolution's emancipatory promise of universal equality."[37] Thus Zavala's apparent acceptance of the colonization/deportation project in Liberia would not necessarily have been understood as being at odds with republican ideals of freedom and equality.

In Zavala's depictions of the United States, the free blacks who remain excluded from national projects certainly reveal a fundamental shortcoming of U.S. liberalism. But this racial other is simultaneously portrayed as an (or perhaps *the*) insurmountable impediment to the realization of U.S. liberalism. The paradox unfolds: blacks, the embodiment of the racial other, cannot be incorporated into the national project of progress because U.S. liberalism is incomplete and flawed, but liberalism and progress will never be realized if uncivilized blacks remain in the United States. Colonization projects such as the one Zavala mentions offered a possible resolution to this dilemma through the promise of formal equality and emancipation and, of equal importance, through the purification of the white domestic space with the removal of black bodies.[38] Through his discussion of this new colonial endeavor, what Zavala also uncovers is how colonization—what many might consider as contrary to the ideals of universal equality and freedom—can come to be portrayed as a type of freedom. It means literal freedom for blacks in Liberia, but it also allows the United States to maintain its claim on universal equality while removing troublesome black bodies from its national boundaries. What Zavala also reveals, then, is how U.S. republicanism is inextricably tied up with—indeed, dependent on—the exclusion of racial others.[39] In much broader terms, Zavala additionally highlights how slavery and its legacy will continue to haunt the United States and impede its move toward progress (economic, moral, and political).

In his discussion of both free and enslaved blacks, Zavala confronts one of the main (perceived) obstacles to the implementation of liberal ideals in both Mexico and the United States: racial difference. Throughout the Americas and western Europe, equality was a concept that liberals found difficult to incorporate into their democratic institutions when it came to racial others, especially Indians and blacks. As historian Beatriz Urías Horcasitas explains, for liberals in Mexico in the first half of the nineteenth century, equality and how that would play out in the Mexican context was a constant source of conflict and debate.[40] Although freedom and the right to life were widely accepted in Mexico, "la posibilidad de que el orden democrático igualara a criollos, mestizos e indios causó profundo rechazo"[41] [the possibility that the democratic order would make criollos, mestizos, and Indians equal provoked profound rejection (translation mine)].[42] In short, for many liberals—even more radical *puros*—differences of class, caste, or race represented an essentially insurmountable barrier to the development of liberal ideals and institutions.[43]

In *Viage*, the racial(ized) other surfaces as a central preoccupation in Zavala's descriptions of Mexico as well as the United States. Although slavery had already been abolished in Mexico by the time he published *Viage*, Zavala continues to use the vocabulary and images of slavery, though on a more metaphorical level, when he talks about blind imitation and inherited colonial cultural formations as other forms of slavery and degeneracy in his narrative. In the section mentioned earlier about his travels through Arkansas and

Missouri, he compares the uncivilized U.S. frontier to his homeland, remarking, "En nuestros pueblos los mas recónditos, se palpan los efectos de la esclavitud en que hemos vivido bajo la antigua dominacion" (*Viage*, 50) [In our most remote small towns, one can feel the effects of the slavery under which we lived under the old regime (*Journey*, 30)]. He explains that it is not true civilization that exists in these parts of Mexico but rather "los efectos del terror impreso en los ánimos de los habitantes" (*Viage*, 50) [the effects of terror impressed upon the spirits of the inhabitants (translation mine)], which make Mexicans merely appear civilized. He suggests that Mexico is not really civilized—at least not in all regions. Democratic institutions have been imposed in Mexico, but the true character of the Mexican people remains uncivilized. Zavala explicitly links this lack of true civilization with Mexico's Spanish colonial history: Mexico's backwardness is the result of hundreds of years of oppression (which he labels a type of slavery) imposed and sustained by its mother country, Spain.[44] When Zavala describes this history in Mexico and the resultant lack of civilization in the present, he articulates another central dilemma that liberals throughout Spanish America confronted: the contradiction between liberal ideals of equality and the impossibility of implementing those ideals in a society structured by inequality. In the early decades of the nineteenth century, Mexican liberals perceived that they had formally instituted a democratic system that did not match their social reality, a vastly diverse society marked by severe economic and social inequalities that they saw as a reflection and product of centuries of colonial domination.[45] Indeed, for historian Stephen J. Mexal, this is the crux of Zavala's narrative: Mexal reads *Viage* as more than just a critique of slavery; it is also a commentary on "the impossibility of reconciling democratic praxis with liberal theory, an impossibility that cuts to the heart of modern liberal democratic rule."[46]

Throughout *Viage*, a history of Spanish colonial domination continues to impede Mexico's democratic venture much in the same way that slavery continues to trouble the United States' liberal project. In the conclusion, Zavala describes the Mexican nation as "jóven, sin esperiencia, llena de vida y deseosa de sacudir los restos de sus antiguas cadenas" (*Viage*, 365) [young and inexperienced, full of life and desirous of shaking off the remains of its ancient chains (*Journey*, 194)]. Mexico's "antiguas cadenas" [ancient chains], still in the process of being dismantled, reference this other type of slavery, a cultural degeneracy inherited from and imposed by Spain, which continues to impact Mexico's development as a liberal republic even in his present.

Zavala's portrayal of Spain as a degenerate or blackened empire reproduces a well-known trope in the Americas and Europe by the nineteenth century that painted Spain and its colonies as part of an antimodern empire. While this view of the blackened Spaniard and the degenerate Spanish empire was certainly prevalent in the United States and northern Europe, criollo elites in

Spanish America also internalized this discourse, often pondering their supposed inherited degeneracy and resultant lack of modernity.[47] In addition, intellectuals, politicians, and nation builders throughout the Western world used the terms *civilization* and *progress* to articulate this idea of modernity. So when Zavala talks about civilization and progress, he is also talking about modernity and confronting a quandary faced by nineteenth-century Spanish American leaders, writers, and cultural workers: modernity was some-' thing they desired but was also a discourse from which they were constantly excluded, in part because of their links with the antimodern Spanish empire.[48]

As María DeGuzmán, Alejandro Mejías-López, Walter Mignolo, and numerous others have shown, the exclusion of Spaniards and Spanish Americans from modernity was cast in increasingly racialized terms. The antimodern Spanish legacy is likewise linked to racial(ized) others for Zavala and other Mexican liberals. During colonial rule, indigenous communities in Mexico had been legally considered minors and restricted from many rights of full citizenship. This long history of oppression during Spanish colonial rule had created, in the minds of many Mexican liberals, a community that was ill prepared for participation in democratic governance. When documenting the state of printing and education in the United States, for instance, Zavala contrasts it with the situation in Mexico. He notes the low literacy rates and lack of educational opportunities for the masses in Mexico, concluding,

> Añádase á esto que en Yucatan hay á lo menos un tercio de los habitantes que no hablan el castellano, y en el Estado de Méjico un quinto. Los que cuentan por nada el grado de civilizacion de las masas para dar *instituciones á los pueblos, ó son sumamente ignorantes, ó son estremadamente perversos*. (*Viage*, 302–303; emphasis in original)

> [Add to this that in Yucatan there are at least a third of the people who do not speak Spanish, and in the state of Mexico one fifth. Those who consider the degree of civilization of the masses as no reason (not) to give institutions to the people are either dismally ignorant or they are extremely perverse.] (*Journey*, 163)

Zavala indicates that Mexico's colonial history has created subjects—in this case, the indigenous masses who do not speak Spanish—unfit for participation in many truly democratic institutions.

Many Mexican liberals like Zavala who originally fought for indigenous rights and inclusion within the national body politic eventually came to perceive this move for inclusion and integration of the masses, particularly the indigenous masses, as a threat of social *dis*integration.[49] Zavala's reflections on Mexico's slave-like past tap into a discourse that portrayed Spain and its colonies as morally unsound and, as biological definitions of race gained

precedence throughout the nineteenth century, increasingly racially degenerate. Mexico, in this view, is an imitation of an already degenerate empire that
has created morally, culturally, and racially degenerate communities. Echoing
his discussion of Liberia and free blacks in the United States, Zavala indicates
that Mexico also must confront its own racial others—indigenous Mexicans,
"los habitantes que no hablan el castellano" (*Viage*, 303) [the people who do
not speak Spanish (*Journey*, 163)], who are the remnants of hundreds of years
of slave-like oppression and a moral and political blackness akin to the United
States' continued support of human slavery. Through this comparative mode,
Zavala thus points to commonalities in the histories of the United States and
Mexico. These histories of slavery and colonization have created racial(ized)
others who are not seen as very compatible with or ready for the demands of
responsible citizenship within a democratic nation. Marissa K. López also
points out these similarities and the creation of racial others within both Mexico and the United States but reads the "liberal state's necessary construction
of a racial other that it is unable to incorporate" as evidence of the failure of a
transamerican ideal grounded in liberal democracy.[50] Yet what I am suggesting
is that Zavala shows this failure in both counties in order to actually connect
Mexico and the United States, revealing how slavery and political, moral, and
racial degeneracy exist in both countries. They are similar young nations fighting antiliberal legacies and pondering what to do with the racial(ized) others
in their midst. Moreover, he shows how liberalism itself, in both countries, is
both reliant on and imperfect because of the exclusion of (increasingly) racialized groups within the national community.

Models for the Future: Labor, Capitalism, and Public Morality

Although Zavala spends quite a bit of time discussing the barbarism and
degeneracy that still exist in both Mexico and the United States, he has many
positive things to report about the United States as well. Throughout the narrative, he reminds his readers that the United States is "el modelo á todos los
pueblos civilizados" (*Viage*, 222) [the model of all civilized peoples (*Journey*,
121)]. In one of his earlier chapters, Zavala describes the images he would use
to represent the United States:

> Si yo tratase de hacer una obra de lujo y con estampas, desde luego haria grabar
> hermosas láminas en que se representasen buques de vapor; obreros nivelando el
> terreno y colocando planchas de madera y hierro para formar caminos; praderas
> bañadas de arroyos; ciudades divididas por rios navegables; poblaciones naci-
> endo de la tierra y dedicándose á mejorarla luego, luego; salones cubiertos de
> niños de ambos secsos aprendiendo á leer y escribir; labradores y artesanos con
> el arado ó el instrumento en la mano y el periódico en la otra; seis mil templos

de diversos cultos en que el hombre eleva al Creador sus votos, conforme se lo dicta el corazon; en suma la tranquilidad y la abundancia haciendo felices á quince millones de habitantes. Tal es la idea que tengo de los Estados-Unidos del Norte y las impresiones que recibí desde Nueva-Orleans á Cincinati. (*Viage*, 89)

[If I were trying to produce a work that was a luxury item with engravings, I would have prepared immediately beautiful plates on which would be pictured steamboats, workmen leveling the land and laying planks of wood and iron to form roads, meadows bathed by streams, cities divided by navigable rivers, cities being born of the earth and dedicating themselves to improving it immediately, rooms filled with children of both sexes learning to read and to write, workers and craftsmen with plow or instrument in one hand and the newspaper in the other, six thousand temples of diverse cults in which man raises his vows to the Creator in accordance with the dictates of his heart, in short tranquility and abundance bringing happiness to fifteen million people. Such is the idea that I have of the United States of the North and the impressions that I received from New Orleans to Cincinnati.] (*Journey*, 50–51)

Through these images he succinctly indicates the aspects of the United States that he hopes Mexicans will imitate in their development of republican values: industry, scientific and mechanical innovation, education, freedom of religion, freedom of press, and equality. These are the aspects he sees as embodying the future of republicanism in the Americas.

As the passage above indicates with its references to workers domesticating the land, constructing roads, navigating rivers, and so on, labor and industry emerge as central interests for Zavala. His favorable portrayals of free laborers stand out, particularly given his previous negative discussions of slavery. While Zavala's renderings of the U.S. South frequently ruminate on slaves, slavery, and the resultant degeneracy—both real and metaphorical—his focus when commenting more positively on U.S. culture and progress often turns toward depictions of free capitalist labor (especially, but not solely, in the northeastern states).

Zavala continues to employ comparison when describing the U.S. North, free labor, and an emergent capitalism, but his use of comparison changes: he instead compares the countries in order to highlight the differences between them and presents the United States as a model—though imperfect—from which Mexico can learn about progress and modernization. However, as I will discuss, even as he puts forth the United States as a new model of American republicanism and progress, he also ponders the ways in which U.S. republicanism and capitalism are tied to a new form of colonialism, with free and slave labor jointly working as its motor. Thus while Zavala's descriptions of different types of slavery link Mexico and the United States through shared barbarity,

his representations of free labor, industry, and scientific and mechanical innovation link Mexico and the United States through a new vision of republicanism that is simultaneously—and perhaps somewhat paradoxically—a new
form of colonization. I thus now turn to Zavala's impressions of free labor,
commerce, and industry. His depictions of New England, often viewed and
portrayed as the embodiment of U.S. founding principles of hard work
and industry, offer ample commentary on these aspects and how he views
them.

Reflecting on the character of the people in the United States, Zavala
describes them as "egoista, incomunicativa y desconfiada . . . [con] cierta asper-
eza en su trato, que hace desagradable su sociedad" (*Viage*, 73) [self-centered,
uncommunicative and distrustful . . . [with a] certain harshness in their deal-
ings that makes their society unpleasant (*Journey*, 42)]. However, he also
notes that this is caused by the culture of hard work and industry, explaining to
his readers that "se puede asegurar que no hay pueblo mas moral que el de los
Estados-Unidos del Norte. La aplicacion constante al trabajo hace á los hombres virtuosos ó independientes; pero al mismo tiempo orgullosos y descon-
fiados" (*Viage*, 74) [one may be sure that there are no more moral people than
those of the United States of the North. Constant application to work makes
men virtuous or independent, but at the same time proud and distrustful
(*Journey*, 42)]. Although he is not always admiring in his representation of
U.S. culture, as his comments about the disagreeable and unsociable nature
of U.S. Americans indicate, he explains that this is the result of a different history and culture—based on individual hard work and independence.
He contrasts this description of the people in the United States with his fellow countrymen in Mexico, exclaiming, "¡Qué diferencia entre esta y la
poblacion mejicana! Nosotros somos comunicativos por esencia; parece que
somos impelidos á entrar en relaciones con todos los que se nos acercan, de
cualquiera clase y condicion que sean. . . . Yo no sé si en nuestra amabilidad
estremada hay un poco de servilismo, ó de hábito de obediencia pasiva" (*Viage*,
74–75) [What a difference between these people and those of Mexico! We are
essentially outgoing; it seems that we are impelled to become involved with
all those about us, of whatever class and condition they may be. . . . I do not
know whether or not in our extreme amiability there is a touch of servility or
of the habit of passive obedience (*Journey*, 42)]. Through comparison, Zavala
praises the industry of U.S. Americans while still noting some of the less desirable results it has on the personality and character of its people, and he deni-
grates what he sees as a major shortcoming of Mexican culture—its passivity
and servility—even as he also points out some of the positive aspects of Mexican culture. As these passages indicate, however, industry and hard work hold
high moral value for Zavala, and he was certainly not alone in this stance. This
view of labor as a moral duty is a cornerstone of U.S. culture and a value he

also seems to be reinforcing in *Viage*.[51] The moral worth of industry and hard work seems to outweigh any less attractive effects, such as the coldness and selfishness he sees as a resultant part of the Anglo American character.

Technical and scientific innovations in the United States are also linked to industry in Zavala's narrative and receive some of his highest praise. On his list of the most influential and important men in history, for example, he includes the inventor of the steam engine, rhetorically questioning his readers, "¿Habria cosa mas justa que erigir en cada poblacion de aquellas una estatua de bronce al inmortal Fulton que aplicó el vapor á la navegacion? ¡Tanta es la grandeza de un hombre de genio, que hace una revolucion benéfica al género humano! Gioya, Juan de Guttemberg, Colon y Fulton vivirán eternamente" (*Viage*, 49) [Could there be anything more fitting than to erect in each town a bronze statue to the immortal Fulton who applied steam to navigation? Such is the greatness of a man of genius who brings about a revolution beneficial to humankind! Gioya, John Guttemberg (*sic*), Columbus and Fulton will live eternally (*Journey*, 29)]. Robert Fulton, a U.S. American widely credited with the development of the first commercially successful steamboat, is on the same list as no less than the likes of Christopher Columbus and Johannes Gutenberg, the inventor of mechanical moveable-type printing—two men who, for good or bad, radically changed the world and the way we understand it. Through his inclusion of Fulton on this list of groundbreaking men, Zavala once again comments on the power of industry and innovation as revolutionary forces.

In Zavala's descriptions of the United States, free labor and capitalism emerge as the motors that drive U.S. progress. Zavala's recollections of his entry into New England offer a sharp contrast to his first impressions of New Orleans. Upon entry into New England, he notices an immediate improvement in his surroundings, stating that "desde el momento en que se entra en Nueva-Inglaterra se advierte una mejora en los caminos, posadas, agricultura, belleza de casas y jardines, en fin en todo lo que rodea el viagero y ha podido adquirir perfeccion con la ayuda de la industria" (*Viage*, 278) [from the moment that one enters New England one notes an improvement in the roads, inns, agriculture, beauty of houses and gardens, in short everything that surrounds the traveler and that can be perfected with the aid of hard work (*Journey*, 150)]. In contrast to his very first impressions of New Orleans, in which he focuses on nature's potency and notes the surprising lack of modern development in the city's architecture, here he centers on the visible signs of man-made progress (streets, hotels, houses). Even his references to nature—agriculture and beautiful gardens—demonstrate how in New England man has conquered and knows how to control nature. In his praise of New England—particularly its industry, which is what supports its success—Zavala articulates a political ideology that was emerging in the United States in the early nineteenth century that identified the U.S. North as the home of free labor and also served as "an affirmation of the superiority of the social system of the North—a dynamic, expanding capitalist market."[52]

Lowell, Massachusetts, and its textile factories offer one of Zavala's most striking reinforcements of the concept of free labor and capitalism as part of a morally and economically superior social system. Describing the textile factories there, he expounds on the progress made possible through mechanical innovation: "En las sociedades modernas, los progresos de la mecánica han producido las manufacturas que prometen ser para el género humano, una fuente inagotable de prosperidad y bienestar" (*Viage*, 286) [In modern societies mechanical progress has produced factories that promise to be for the human race an inexhaustible source of prosperity and well-being (*Journey*, 154–155)]. He also reports favorably on the salaries and the quality of life of the workers there, which he says are better than the situations of workers in Europe (*Viage*, 289). Lastly, what is unique about Lowell in Zavala's eyes is its morality as well as its industry. Despite the fact that it is mostly unchaperoned young women who work in the textile factories in Lowell, Zavala makes clear that the women are—with only a few exceptions—well-behaved, happy, industrious, and of equal importance, well-protected by the companies and their extensive systems of rules and regulations, which govern all aspects of the young women's lives, both within and outside of the factory (*Viage*, 291–292). The factories in Lowell, then, are both economically profitable and morally good for workers and society alike. Zavala offers this as a possible model of free labor and capitalist democracy for his fellow Mexicans.

In a telling moment in this same chapter, Zavala compares the factories in Lowell to an entity with which his Mexican readership would be quite familiar: a Catholic monastery. He explains that "como Lowell es una poblacion de obreros que todos estan sujetos á estos reglamentos de la compañía, se concibe bien que es como un vasto monasterio, en donde poco tiene que hacer la autoridad civil" (*Viage*, 292) [since Lowell is a workers' town where everybody is subject to company rules, it is evident that it is like a vast monastery where civil authority is little concerned (*Journey*, 157)]. He further illustrates the character of the factories in Lowell and the atmosphere created by them:

> Los reglamentos de las compañías se observan religiosamente en Lowell. En las fábricas, que son edificios de una grande estension, hay campanarios para llamar las gentes al trabajo, de manera que parecen conventos de una de nuestras ciudades. Pero en Lowell no hay demandantes con santos, no hay limosneros, no hay andrajosos y gentes miserables: en vez de ocuparse estas monjas del siglo diez y nueve en hacer relicarios, escapularios y sudarios, se emplean en hilar algodon y hacer tejidos de todas calidades. (*Viage*, 293–294)

[The company rules are religiously observed in Lowell. In the factories which are buildings of great extent there are bells to call the people to work so that they resemble the convents of one of our cities. But in Lowell there are no supplicants with saints, there are no beggars, there are no ragged and poverty stricken people. These nineteenth-century nuns, instead of keeping busy making relicaries, scapularies and shrouds, are employed in spinning cotton and weaving textiles of all qualities.] (*Journey*, 158)

For the twenty-first-century reader, this appears, at first glance, as perhaps nothing more than an odd comparison. But for Zavala and his contemporary Mexican readership, who were in the midst of heated debates about the role of the Catholic Church and the power it should have in Mexican culture and politics, as well as its economy, this comparison holds special significance. Since the writing of the Mexican Constitution of 1824, liberals (federalists) and conservatives (centralists) had literally and figuratively been waging battles over its implementation; one of the biggest debates was over the rights and powers of the Catholic Church and its clergy. The constitution had named Roman Catholicism as the sole official religion, protected by the nation, and it also preserved special *fueros*, or privileges, for the Catholic Church that exempted clergymen from standing trial in civil courts.[53] Zavala, like many other liberals, was critical of the church's power and was a proponent of freedom of religion, secularized education, and a reform of the church that would include the secularization of missions and the confiscation of church funds and properties.[54] The debates—and battles—over the Catholic Church's power and privileges were about morality as well as politics and economics for many conservatives, many of whom "still held that religious toleration was somehow incompatible with public morality."[55] Thus Zavala's description of Lowell as a new type of monastery, complete with nuns ("monjas del siglo diez y nueve") piously working in convent-like factories and with bell towers ("campanarios") dutifully tolling the work hours, has special meaning for his Mexican readers. He is presenting the image of a modern society that is also virtuous, but without the presence of the Catholic Church. It is a productive society, aided by modern machinery. The young women work to produce useful commodities—textiles and spun cotton—out of raw materials. And the factory itself seems to also simultaneously be producing the modern woman. The traditional nuns he describes do in fact produce something as well, but the items they produce look to the past. The reliquaries and shrouds that he imagines them producing are items associated with death and remembrance. These items serve no modern purpose and are not future oriented but rather steeped in the past, just as the nuns themselves will produce no future offspring. Lowell is a model for a new type of public morality, a modern-day, modernized, and modernizing convent that helps produce and is produced by its own secular—but none-theless morally upright—community.

Zavala's comments in fact suggest that the community in Lowell is more moral *because* the church does not control it. Throughout *Viage*, Zavala time and again comments on the formative—and negative—influence that the Catholic Church has had and continues to have on Mexico. At one point, he argues that the Catholic tradition has negatively influenced and shaped Mexican culture, especially in terms of its work ethic:

> Los descendientes de los conquistadores heredaban de sus padres los Españoles el gusto por la música y las diversiones, que se conciliaban con el culto católico, cuya cabeza en Roma daba el impulso á todo género de espectáculos. En vez pues de dedicarse al trabajo de la tierra ó á otras ocupaciones penosas, se entregaban á las bulliciosas fiestas á que por otra parte convidan sus climas cálidos, ó templa-dos. (*Viage*, 128)

> [The descendants of the conquerors inherited from their parents the Spaniards the taste for music and entertainment, which were in accord with the Catholic religion, whose head in Rome gave encouragement to all sorts of spectacles. Instead of dedicating themselves to working the land or to other arduous occu-pations, they gave themselves over to noisy festivals to which on the other hand their warm or temperate climates invited them.] (*Journey*, 71)

In Zavala's eyes, the Catholic Church's devotion to pomp and spectacle, com-bined with the Spanish penchant for festivities, has created Mexicans who, further influenced by tropical climates, naturally prefer boisterous celebrations over hard work. Zavala's work thus once again feeds into the Black Legend of (Catholic) Spanish decadence.

When describing the young female factory workers in Lowell, Zavala simi-larly notes that these same women would not fare as well in Catholic countries such as France or Mexico because "la educación protestante traza al rededor de cada individuo un círculo mas difícil de penetrar que el que forma la educa-cion católica" (*Viage*, 290) [Protestant education draws around each individual a circle much more difficult to penetrate than that drawn by Catholic educa-tion (*Journey*, 156)]. He further explains, "Por una parte hay, es verdad, mas frialdad, menos comunicacion en las relaciones sociales, una ausencia mas ó menos absoluta de efusion y de confianza; pero por la otra se encuentra mas respeto, mas consideraciones por la personalidad de otros" (*Viage*, 290) [For one thing there is, indeed, more coldness, less communication in social rela-tions, more or less an absolute absence of free expression and confidence. But on the other hand, one finds more respect, more consideration for the person-ality of others (*Journey*, 156)]. Zavala attributes cultural differences to different religious backgrounds, which create distinct types of citizens. Catholicism, from his viewpoint, creates a citizen that prefers festivities and spectacle over hard work and values community over the individual, which can all be detrimental to economic as well as political progress.

As a liberal reformer, Zavala's negative views on the Catholic Church were not unusual. Zavala, like other doctrinaire liberals, believed that many of the problems Mexico was having in the popular adaptation of formally implemented republican reforms stemmed from the influence of the Catholic Church. In Zavala's earlier published work, he attributes many of Mexico's difficulties adapting to republicanism "al cambio súbito que se produjo en una sociedad en donde durante tres siglos de dominio colonial la ortodoxia católica había sido la base del sistema político"[56] [to the sudden change that was generated in a society in which, during three centuries of colonial domination, Catholic orthodoxy had served as the base of the political order].[57] In this work, Zavala appears particularly invested in showing how Spain had established and normalized a regime based on ignorance, terror, and passive obedience to authority during Mexico's most formative years as a colony.[58] For Zavala, Catholicism—as practiced and implemented in Mexico—has prepared the Mexican populace not for republicanism but rather the opposite: despotism, monarchy, and servility.

Religion as a formative influence thus appears as yet one more central concern and interest for Zavala—and apparently he thought it would be of interest to his readers as well. For example, he also spends quite a bit of time reflecting on the famous "camp meeting," a type of revivalism popular in the western frontier and U.S. South that usually involved a large gathering of hundreds or thousands of people. Such gatherings featured preaching—day and night, usually for a week or more—by passionate Presbyterian, Baptist, and Methodist ministers.[59] The camp meetings became famous for their powerful, catchy music and "electrifying" results, which included "participants falling down as if struck dead, while others laughed out loud, barked like dogs, or experienced 'the jerks.'"[60] Although a version of the camp meeting had existed in Europe, it took on new life and cultural dimensions in the United States, where it gained immense popularity in the first decades of the nineteenth century.[61] The camp meeting was such a novelty that it became a must-see attraction and experience for many travelers passing through the frontier and U.S. South. Not all travelers found the camp meeting attractive, however, and it was frequently mocked by foreigners in travelogues and other publications.[62]

While he recognizes some of the absurd elements of the camp meeting, Zavala nonetheless seems to agree that it also has positive influences on the community (*Viage*, 58–59). He contrasts the camp meeting's influence on its people to the influence that Catholic religious holidays and celebrations have on the people in Mexico: "La misa dicha en latin en voz baja, aprisa y como por formula; la predicacion, generalmente hablando, es un tejido de palabras sin coherencia, sin conciencia y sin uncion. El resto del dia, despues de estas ceremonias, el pueblo bajo bebe y come; la gente de categoría juega y baila" (*Viage*, 60) [The mass is said in Latin in a low voice, hurriedly and according to formula; the preaching generally speaking is a weaving of words without coherence, without conscience and without divine comfort. The rest of the day, after the ceremonies, the lower classes eat and drink; those of the upper class play and dance (*Journey*, 35)]. He finishes this comparison of religious celebrations in the two countries by remarking on (what he sees as) the corruption and ignorance that continue to permeate Mexican society:

> ¿Y qué diremos de las [fiestas religiosas] de los Indios en Chalma, en Guadalupe y en los otros santuarios? ¡Ah! la pluma cae de la mano para no esponer á la vista del mundo civilizado, una turba de idólatras que vienen á entregar en manos de frailes holgazanes, el fruto de sus trabajos anuales para enriquecerlos, mientras ellos, sus hijos y sus mugeres no tienen un vestido, ni una cama. ¡Y á esto han osado llamar religion los Españoles nuestros padres! (*Viage*, 50)

> [And what shall we say of the Indians in Chalma, in Guadalupe and in other shrines. Ah! The pen falls from the hand in order not to expose to the civilized world a horde of idolaters who come to deliver into the hands of lazy friars the fruits of their year's work to enrich them, while they, their women and children have no clothing, not even a bed. And the Spaniards, our fathers, have dared call this religion!] (*Journey*, 35)

The description of the Indian masses as a horde of idolaters—"una turba de idólatras"—echoes his earlier discussion of civilization in Mexico, which he argued had been formally instituted through republican institutions but had done little to change the underlying character of Mexico, especially its indigenous communities, leaving the country with only the mere appearance of civilization and republicanism enforced paradoxically through terror. Similarly, his description here indicates that the type of religion that is practiced by and offered to the Indian masses in Mexico is not true religion but rather a more simplistic brand of idolatry that further reflects Mexico's barbarism and corruption. As in his discussion of civilization and republicanism, Zavala indicates that the Catholic religion as practiced in Mexico—at least in some parts, and particularly by Indians—gives the appearance of civilized religion but is actually something much more barbaric.

Zavala's comparison between the practices of religion among the masses in Mexico and the United States is significant because this sort of religious revivalism in the United States was seen and portrayed as a new and democratic form of Christianity, as it appealed to all "types and levels of society. . . .

[and preached] the same message to all."[63] These sorts of revivals, therefore, "were 'liberal' in the nineteenth-century sense of the term because they based organization and social activity on the determined action of individuals."[64] Ministers even used the same democratic vocabularies of liberation and equality to express the tenets of their newfound revivalist faiths. In this new type of Christianity, power was given to the people, not the clergy: the common people were allowed and encouraged to define their faith in their own way rather than through orthodox doctrines and a dense hierarchy of clergymen.[65] Contrast this with Zavala's description of the Latin mass, "dicha en latin en voz baja, aprisa y como por formula" (*Viage*, 60) [said in Latin in a low voice, hurriedly and according to formula (*Journey*, 35)], and the Catholic sermon as "un tejido de palabras sin coherencia, sin conciencia y sin uncion" (*Viage*, 60) [a weaving of words without coherence, without conscience and without divine comfort (*Journey*, 35)]. With the example of the camp meeting, Zavala indicates how U.S. Americans have adapted a European religious form to a new American context: they have democratized Christianity. The Catholic mass, on the other hand, retains its rigid structure. It is carried out in a language (Latin) that few common people comprehend—especially Indians, many of whom do not even speak Spanish, as Zavala points out, much less Latin. And it follows a set formula that is performed by rote, with the average individual understanding very little of deeper value. The religious practices he describes in Mexico further enmesh those communities within old and nondemocratic systems. For Zavala, Catholicism (the institution and the religion as it was taught and practiced in Zavala's present-day Mexico) appears as one more remnant of the lasting Spanish legacy of barbarism and backwardness, while U.S. Protestantism, on the other hand, is portrayed as helping prepare its community for freedom and independence.

While Catholicism is an all-invasive force that has negatively influenced and shaped Mexican culture, Zavala indicates that Protestant culture—which reinforces the values of industry, hard work, and individualism—feeds capitalist free labor and the resultant progress. Thus, to return to Zavala's descriptions of Lowell, when Zavala calls the young women working in the textile factories nineteenth-century nuns ("monjas del siglo diez y nueve"), he also indirectly comments on how these women—like the nuns who are the instruments of the Catholic Church—work as agents of a new type of power, a new colonizing force that uses free labor and republicanism as an effective means to achieve its goals. The women of Lowell are industrious because they come from a culture highly influenced by Protestant values, but they are also simultaneously the machinery that helps produce and reproduce that culture through their work and, eventually, their offspring. Even as he presents Lowell as a model from which Mexicans can learn about a different future for their country, he also hints at the coming of a new colonizing force that employs less overtly violent methods—such as capitalist expansion and mechanical innovations—than warfare and direct subjugation.

Ambivalent Colonialism

Zavala alludes to new types of colonialism throughout *Viage*, and in one of the later chapters, he more concretely argues for the power of industry over war and physical violence, unequivocally stating, "No es la guerra, esta *ultima ratio regum*, la que puede elevar un pueblo ó una nacion á la prosperidad. Un campo de batalla escitará el horror, ó el entusiamso febril, ó la piedad y el asombro. La fuerza del hombre aplicada á producir, es mas magestuosa que la fuerza humana aplicada á matar" (*Viage*, 284) [It is not war, that last rationale of kings, that can lift a people or a nation up to prosperity. A battlefield will excite horror, or feverish enthusiasm, or piety and fear. The strength of man applied to production is more majestic than human strength applied to killing (*Journey*, 154)]. He goes on to further explain the power of industry and innovation:

> Las pirámides y los templos de dimensiones colosales de Tebas; el coliseo ó la iglesia de San Pedro de Roma, descubren mas grandeza que un campo de batalla cubierto de muertos y escombros, aun cuando hubiese trecientos mil cadáveres tendidos.... Nada hay en el órden material de qué nuestra especie tenga mas derecho de gloriarse que de las invenciones mecánicas por medio de las cuales el hombre doma el vigor desordenado de la naturaleza ó desenvuelve su energía oculta. (*Viage*, 284–285)

> [The pyramids and the temples of colossal dimensions of Thebes, the Coliseum, or St. Peter's Church in Rome, disclose more grandeur than a battlefield covered with dead men and ashes, even when there were three hundred thousand corpses lying about.... There is nothing in the material order of which our species has more right to boast than the mechanical inventions by means of which man curbs the unordered vigor of nature or develops its hidden energy.] (*Journey*, 154)

What is interesting about this quotation is that while he seeks to highlight innovation and industry—rather than bloodshed—as future revolutionizing forces, he simultaneously hints at a different type of imperialist power exacted through more covert, but sometimes no less violent, methods than open warfare. The pyramids, for instance, were constructed on the backs of nameless thousands, and the grand cathedrals of Europe were built with riches extracted from American colonies and often made possible only through the subjugation and suffering of the predominantly Indian masses. Thus while Zavala comments on the power of innovation and hard work as moral and

revolutionary forces, he also perhaps inadvertently reveals how these can similarly be used to prop up an imperial power. Zavala astutely recognizes yet again
one of the paradoxes of U.S. republicanism: it is seen and portrayed as based
on the Enlightenment ideals of individual freedom and equality, but it simultaneously seeks to impose those ideals on others—particularly racial(ized)
others—who are not seen as or given the rights of equals. Moreover, on some
level, Zavala also points to how the Enlightenment ideals so central to the
development of U.S. politics and culture are both constructed on and also construct racial otherness.

Throughout *Viage*, Zavala records different moments in which he glimpses
the United States and its brand of capitalist republicanism as a new colonizing force spreading throughout the Americas—including southern Canada
and northern Mexico.[66] In one of the earlier chapters, he ponders the possible future of the northern Mexican border states such as New Mexico and
California and calculates that "antes de muchos años aquellas vastas comarcas
serán pobladas por estrangeros que buscan mejores climas y tierras baldías para
formar sus establacimientos, y entonces se verá descender por el rio Bravo del
Norte, viageros que habrán entrado por el de San-Lorenzo, por Nueva-York ó
el Misisipi" (*Viage*, 67) [before many years those vast lands will be populated
by strangers in search of a better climate and vacant lands to set up new estab-
lishments, and then one will see descending the Rio Grande travelers who will
have come by the St. Lawrence, through New York or along the Mississippi
(*Journey*, 38)]. In an eerie prediction of future U.S. expansion, he sees these
northern Mexican states as having a different future than the southern Mexican states because of their proximity to the United States and because of the
influx of immigrants from the United States, Canada, and Europe. He envisions U.S. civilization exceeding its national borders and spreading to Mexico
in its combat against barbarity: "Mientras los Estados del Sur de la república
mejicana ocupen de guerras civiles y querellas domésticas, los del Norte,
dedicados al comercio, á la agricultura y á la navegación, darán ejemplos de
moralidad y de trabajos útiles á sus hermanos disidentes, que pelearán por la
dominación y la supremacía" (*Viage*, 67) [While the states to the south in the
Mexican republic are occupied with civil wars and domestic quarrels, those of
the north, dedicated to trade, agriculture and navigation, will give examples
of morality and useful work to their quarrelsome brothers who will be fighting
for power and supremacy (*Journey*, 38–39)]. As in his descriptions of Lowell
and New England, Zavala sees the spread of republican ideals through trade,
industry, technical innovations, and commerce; these, he highlights once
again, will provide moral as well as economic success and political stability for
the northern Mexican states. Although he does not specifically use the terminology of "colonization," Zavala is in effect pondering a new type of colonization that conquers through republican ideologies of freedom and equality.

As he mulls over the future of colonization in Mexico—still an ongoing process in the frontiers of both the United States and Mexico in the first half of the nineteenth century—he contemplates the different dimensions that this new type of colonization appears to be taking in his present and that he foresees it taking in the future. First, there is a territorial colonization, with real people doing the colonizing, but it is different from the colonial enterprises of Spain or England in the Americas. Reflecting on this new type of colonization, he writes, "Un Ingles será Mejicano en Méjico, y un Mejicano Ingles en Londres" (*Viage*, 141) [An Englishman will be a Mexican in Mexico City, and a Mexican an Englishman in London (*Journey*, 79)], meaning that usually an immigrant or traveler would adapt to the culture around him or her and become part of that host country's culture. However, he does not see this as the future in the border zones of northern Mexico and the (south)western United States: "Lugares enteramente desiertos, bosques y florestas, inhabitadas hace doce años, convertidos en villas y pueblos repentinamente por Alemanes, Irlandeses, y Norte-Americanos, deben por necesidad formar una nacion enteramente diversa, y seria absurdo pretender que renunciasen á su religion, á sus costumbres y á sus profundas convicciones" (*Viage*, 141) [Completely empty woods and lands, uninhabited a dozen years ago, converted into villages and towns suddenly by Germans, Irish, and North Americans, must of necessity form an entirely different nation, and it would be absurd to try to get them to renounce their religion, their customs and their deepest convictions (*Journey*, 79)]. Because Anglo Americans and Europeans will be colonizing these frontier zones, which are sparsely settled by Mexicans, there will be little necessity for these new colonists to adapt to Mexican culture and politics; northern European and Anglo cultures will dominate, he postulates. Moreover, for Zavala, this does not appear to be negative, because he sees them as bringing more civilized cultural and political forms. In this very novel colonial context, he forecasts that these new types of colonists "no podrán sujetarse al régimen militar y gobierno eclesiástico, que por desgracia ha continuado en el territorio mejicano, á pesar de las constituciones repúblico-democráticas. Alegarán las instituciones que deben gobernar el pais, y querrán que no sean un engaño, una ilusion, sino una realidad" (*Viage*, 141–142) [will not allow themselves to be subjected to military regimes and ecclesiastical rule, such as unfortunately has continued in Mexican territory, in spite of its republican-democratic constitutions. They will argue for the institutions that should govern the country, and they will not want it to be a ruse, an illusion, but a reality (translation mine)]. He concludes,

> Dentro de pocos años esta feliz conquista de civilizacion continuará su curso por
> los otros Estados acia el sudoeste, y los de Tamaulipas, Nuevo Leon, San-Luis,
> Chihuahua, Durango, Jalisco y Zacatecas serán los mas libres en la confederacion

mejicana; mientras que los de Méjico, Puebla, Veracruz, Oajaca, Michoacan y Chiapas tendrán que esperimentar, durante algun tiempo, la influencia militar y eclesiástica. (*Viage*, 142)

[Within a few years this fortunate conquest of civilization will continue its course through other states towards the south, and those of Tamaulipas, Nuevo Leon, San Luis, Chihuahua, Durango, Jalisco and Zacatecas will be the freest ones in the Mexican confederation. Meanwhile, those of Mexico, Pueblo (*sic*), Veracruz, Oaxaca, Michoacan and Chiapas will have to experience for some time the military and ecclesiastical influence.] (*Journey*, 79–80)

Zavala foresees a future in which republican ideologies will gradually spread throughout his homeland, joining Mexico and the United States in a shared fight against barbarism, which appears naturalized and inherited (*Viage*, 142). Indeed, it is in these borderlands, like Texas, that Zavala imagines a new and heterogeneous generation of Mexicans (*Viage*, 141).[67] Zavala's enthusiasm for this "heterogeneous" generation could be read as favoring racial diversity.[68] However, heterogeneity can also be read—and was frequently employed in Latin America in the nineteenth century—as a whitening mechanism. Heterogeneity, from this viewpoint, was desirable because more European and Anglo (white) settlers would dilute the barbaric (and indigenous or mestizo) masses.[69] The United States' "feliz conquista de civilizacion" must ultimately also be understood as a racial and racially motivated conquest—and one that Zavala appears to embrace.

The second dimension that is key to the new type of colonialism that Zavala is pondering in *Viage* is economic in scope. Zavala is contemplating different types of empire and how exactly they are different. As historian Jeremy Adelman explains, it was during the late eighteenth and early nineteenth centuries that statesmen, intellectuals, and cultural workers throughout the Iberian Atlantic were forced to consider the differences between "empires of conquest, whose greatness was tied to the moment of conception, and empires of commerce, whose greatness was self-sustaining."[70] When Zavala discusses the differences between violence and innovation as distinct revolutionary forces, he is similarly recognizing a new form of imperialism, one spread as much through republican ideals as through capitalist commerce— the motor for the political, economic, and moral progress he sees in the United States. Zavala's emphasis on factory production, industry, and scientific and technical innovation all point to a new form of development, tied to capitalism, that he foresees eventually overtaking Mexico. Numerous historians and literary critics have certainly pointed out the existence of the United States' new brand of imperialism in Latin America, especially as it took root in the late nineteenth and early twentieth centuries.[71] Historian

Gilbert G. González, for example, argues that "the overriding objective of U.S. foreign policy with regard to Mexico and Latin America was the establishment of economic control to satisfy the very same ambitions that the British entertained in the search for and acquisition of their colonial possessions."[72] While González and others tend to focus on the period following the Civil War as the era when the United States launched a deliberate effort to economically dominate and subordinate Mexico to U.S. corporate interests, *Viage* marks a moment when this new type of imperialism—or the seed of it—is just starting to take shape. It has not yet fully emerged when Zavala is writing *Viage*, but he perceives the possibility of its development and potential power over Mexico in the future.

In contrast to the blackened and barbaric Spanish empire that has formed Mexican culture, Zavala portrays the new U.S. empire as a "feliz conquista de civilizacion" (*Viage*, 142)—a civilizing and benevolent empire that conquers through the spread of republican ideals, commerce, and white colonists who will diversify the new lands. However, even though Zavala does explicitly name the United States as a model for public morality, individual freedom, equality, and prosperity, as I have shown, we can catch fleeting glimpses in Zavala's text of concern—or at least some ambivalence—about what this new imperial force will mean for Mexicans, who are in a particularly vulnerable spot both geographically in their proximity to the United States and politically as they were in the unstable process of developing and defining their new nation during this time. Even as he attempts to portray the United States and Mexico as similarly fighting for civilization and progress, he also recognizes some of the contradictions in the United States' own republican project. It promises equality, but an equality that is only possible through the exclusion and racialization of certain communities, both internal and external to the nation. It promises freedom and democracy, but it does so through an imposition of those values—a new form of colonialism—the antithesis of freedom and democracy. It promises civilization and progress, but they will be enforced through a new imperial formation that conquers through more covert means than open warfare and violence.

Conclusions: An Unfinished Project and Bloody Future

Although contemporary critics have pointed to *Viage* as a key example of both the early Hispanic presence in the United States and Hispanic contributions to U.S. literature and culture, very little has been written in more depth about the content or the deeper ambiguities and intricacies of this text. In addition, critics have largely failed to take into account how Zavala's experiences as an exile frame his narrative and how his vantage point from exile in fact increases his symbolic capital back at home. As I have shown, through representations of slavery, slave-like imitation, and racial(ized) others in both the United States and Mexico, Zavala creates a sense of shared, very American barbarism and degeneracy that is the result of centuries of colonialism. Through his more panegyrical depictions of U.S. industry, innovation, and equality, he also paints the United States as a model for Mexico and points to the possibility of future union through the spread of liberal ideologies. But at the same time, he also ponders the dark side of U.S. republicanism: its inability to incorporate racial others, its dependence on the exclusion of racial others, and its future imperial endeavors.

When Zavala pits barbarism against civilization, he draws on a prevalent notion of history in which history is viewed as progress—slavery, for example, is understood and represented as a remnant of the old, of the barbaric, and as something that will eventually be overcome by progress and civilization. He also revives the popular image of Spain as the black and degenerate empire, which has, in turn, created degenerate colonies. And he bolsters the vision of the United States as a benevolent empire that spreads civilization and progress through industry, republicanism, and equality. However, while other critics have taken *Viage* as a somewhat simplistic reinforcement of Mexican stereotypes, I propose that this text is much more subtle and ambivalent than it might at first appear. He employs these discourses of degeneracy to, at times, create connections between Mexico and a new imperial power—the United States. But although he does portray the United States' possible future colonization in fairly favorable terms at certain points, he also highlights the interconnected nature of U.S. republicanism and imperialism—two concepts generally considered as contradictory. He ultimately suggests that the United States, ostensibly a republican nation, relies on antiliberal policies for its progress. Zavala is doing more than simply reinforcing Mexican stereotypes or bolstering U.S. imperialist discourses; he is revealing how civilization depends on the preservation and creation of barbaric others, just as liberalism is built on antiliberal practices. He is not necessarily critiquing this relationship of dependence but rather seeking to ascertain Mexico's place within a process of civilization.

Because of his prominent public voice as an exile, Zavala's critiques carry importance as an interlocutor both in the Mexican national political arena and also in a broader international community. Explicitly writing to his fellow countrymen from outside the nation, Zavala is deeply involved in imagining a new nation and its place in relationship to other young American republics. He offers lessons, through comparison, about the similar histories and challenges that both countries face; he posits that they must learn from one another, support one another, and offer guidance. But they must also think critically about their relationship with one another. They must not blindly follow one model.

As Zavala concludes his narrative, he again ponders the United States' future influence on Mexico:

> De consiguiente la influencia de los Estados-Unidos sobre Méjico, será con el tiempo un poder de opinion, de enseñanza de magisterio, tanto mas fuerte cuanto que será puramente moral; fundado sobre sus doctrinas y lecciones. . . . Estos colonos y negociantes [de los Estados Unidos] llevan con su industria los hábitos de libertad, de economía, de trabajo; sus costumbres austeras y religiosas, su independencia individual y su republicanismo. ¿Qué cambio no deberán hacer en la ecsistencia moral y material de los antiguos habitantes estos huéspedes emprendedores? . . . La república mejicana vendrá pues dentro de algunos años á ser amoldada sobre un regimen combinado del sistema americano con las costumbres y tradiciones españolas. (*Viage*, 366)

> [Consequently the influence of the United States upon Mexico will with time be a power of opinion, of teaching by guidance, all the stronger because it is purely moral, founded upon its doctrines and lessons. . . . These colonists and businessmen along with their hard work carry with them habits of freedom, economy, industry, their austere and religious ways, their individual independence and their republicanism. What change must these enterprising guests not make in the moral and material existence of the former inhabitants? . . . The Mexican republic then within a few years will come to be molded to a combined regimen of the American system and Spanish customs and traditions.] (*Journey*, 194)

Once more, he emphasizes the positive influences the United States will have on Mexico—again framed in terms of industry, economic advance, and republican values, which he says are all also morally good for the country.

In this final chapter, Zavala also reiterates the need to adapt—not merely translate or copy—these values to the Mexican context. With the same complex ambiguity with which he characterizes the United States throughout the text, he ends his narrative with this warning for his readers:

> El modelo era sublime; pero inimitable. Los que se aplican á copiar un cuadro de Rafael ó Miguel Angel, aciertan á veces a imitar algunas sombras, algunos rasgos que les acercan mas ó menos al original. Jamas sin embargo se llegan á igualar aquellas sublimes concepciones. Los artistas originales no copian ni imitan á los otros; inventan, crean sobre los modelos de la naturaleza y estudian sus secretos y misterios divinos. (*Viage*, 363–364)

> [The model was sublime, but not to be imitated. Those who set themselves to copy a painting of Raphael or of Michael Angelo at times succeed in imitating some of the shadows, some of the characteristics that bring them somewhere

within range of the original. However, they never manage to equal those sublime concepts. Original artists do not copy or imitate others; they invent, they create upon the models of nature, and they study her secrets and divine mysteries.] (*Journey*, 193)

Once again highlighting the importance of originality, Zavala suggests that the United States is a model that Mexicans must not submissively copy. They must study this model—as he himself is doing in *Viage*—and improve upon it, adapting it to their unique context.

At the same time, however, Zavala also warns about the difficulty of adapting and implementing U.S. models of governance, explaining that there will be, for some time to come, a schism between two different parts of the Mexican nation: "aquella parte poblada, disciplinada, fundada por decirlo asi, en los moldes de su antigua metrópoli" (*Viage*, 366) [that part populated, disciplined, founded, to put it thusly, in the mold of its former mother country (*Journey*, 195)], central Mexico, and "la parte desnuda de habitantes, y de consiguiente susceptible de una nueva poblacion, diversa enteramente de la otra" (*Viage*, 367) [the part bare of inhabitants, and consequently susceptible to a new population, completely different from the other one (*Journey*, 195)], northern Mexico. He goes on to explain the conflicts between the two:

> En la primera ecsistirá por muchos años todavía la lucha de principios opuestos que se han plantado en sus instituciones y será inevitable la guerra civil, mientras que en la segunda los colonos americanos, alemanes, irlandeses é ingleses forman pueblos enteramente libres, que prosperarán pacíficamente bajo la influencia de sus instituciones democráticas, y mas que todo de sus hábitos al trabajo, de sus ideas y convicciones acerca de la dignidad del hombre y del respeto que se debe á las leyes. (*Viage*, 367)

> [In the first there will exist for many years yet the struggle of opposing principles that have been planted in their institutions, and civil war will be inevitable, while in the second the American, German, Irish, and English colonies are establishing completely free settlements that will prosper peacefully under the influence of their democratic institutions, and even more of their work habits, their ideas and convictions concerning the dignity of man and the respect that is due the law.] (*Journey*, 195)

That part of the Mexican population who follow the old forms of governance will continue as before, "entregados al brazo militar y eclesiástico en pena de sus preocupaciones, de su ignorancia y superstición" (*Viage*, 367) [in the grip of the military and ecclesiastical arm as a penalty for their prejudices, their ignorance, and their superstition (*Journey*, 195)]. The new generation, conversely, will embrace the "instituciones adoptadas" (*Viage*, 367) [adopted institutions (*Journey*, 195)] from the United States; they will learn and teach "lecciones de libertad y de tolerancia" (*Viage*, 367) [lessons in liberty and tolerance (*Journey*, 195)].

His final paragraphs offer a wary optimism about the possibility of adapting, not merely copying, what he calls "americanismo"—U.S. liberal ideals—to Mexico:

> El término sin embargo será el triunfo de la libertad en estos Estados; y sobre los escombros góticos y de privilegios insostenibles, se levantará una generacion gloriosa é ilustrada, que poniendo en movimiento todos los elementos de riqueza de que abundan, asociará al fin esa clase indígena degradada y envilecida hasta hoy, á la familia civilizada, enseñándola á pensar y á estimar su dignidad elevando sus pensamientos. (*Viage*, 368)

> [The net result, however, will be the triumph of liberty in these states, and upon the Gothic ashes and the remains of untenable privileges there will be raised up a glorious and enlightened generation that will put into motion all the sources of wealth that abound and will bring into association with the civilized family that indigenous group, until today debased and vilified, and will teach them to think and to hold in esteem their dignity by lifting their thoughts to a higher level.] (*Journey*, 195)

This new generation offers the hope of civilizing indigenous masses. This triumph of freedom, in which the *degradada* (debased) Indian will finally be incorporated into the civilizing national project, however, comes at a price: there will be years of civil war as these two forces wage intellectual and physical battle over the future of their country. Nonetheless, Zavala indicates that until the indigenous masses—the racial others in Mexico—are incorporated into the nation, civilization will not be truly achieved in Mexico. Freedom, for Zavala, means the elimination of racial difference, and one way to achieve this is to modernize and civilize Mexico's Indians.

In the closing paragraph of *Viage*, Zavala uses a metaphor of a raging river to describe the spread of republicanism in Mexico:

> ¿Qué barrera podrá oponerse á este torrente que ha nacido hace veinticuatro años en un pequeño pueblo del Bagio, oscuro en su origen, sin direccion ni cauce, devastando cuanto encontraba, hoy un rio magestuoso que recibe aguas puras y cristalinas de otros paises, y que fecundará todo el territorio mejicano? Inútiles esfuerzos opondrá una generacion envilecida, heredera de las tradiciones y creencias castellanas, y defensora sin grandes resultados de sus antisociales

doctrinas. El sistema americano obtendrá una victoria completa aunque sangrienta. (*Viage*, 368)

[What barrier can oppose this torrent that was born twenty-four years ago in a small town in the Bagio (Bajío), obscure in its origins, without direction or channel, destroying everything in its path, today a majestic river that receives pure crystalline waters from other countries that will make fertile the entire Mexican territory? Unsuccessful efforts will oppose a debased generation, heir to Castilian traditions and beliefs and defender without great results of their antisocial doctrines. The American system will obtain a complete though bloody victory.] (*Journey*, 195).

Here Zavala appears optimistic about the spread of liberal republicanism and open to a new Pan-American political identity, although somewhat wary of the violence that will inevitably be a part of this radical transformation in Mexico. Through his allusion to Bajío, the cradle of the Mexican Independence movement, Zavala rhetorically positions American republicanism as emerging organically from within Mexico; it is not a simplistic copy of U.S. institutions but rather something that has origins in Mexico itself. The unstoppable river of American republican ideals starts with Mexico's Independence movement and is nourished by "pure crystalline waters" from other countries—like the United States, no doubt. Furthermore, Zavala also defines Spanish influences as *non*-American and, likewise, *non*republican: they are the forces against which Mexico must constantly fight. Rhetorically, Zavala accomplishes two feats with this positioning of Spanish culture and influence. First, he distances Mexico from Spain: Mexico contains the possibility—nay, inevitability, as the unrelenting waters of the raging river indicate—of escaping these inherited doctrines and cultural norms. Second, he couples Mexico with the United States as part of a natural and steadfast American impulse to (re)capture and implement republican values.

What remains ambiguous in the final sentence of *Viage*, however, is his use of "el sistema americano," the "American system," which will have, he proclaims, a complete though bloody victory. Is he optimistically including Mexico as part of a new, broadly American system of governance? Or is he voicing concern over the specter of U.S. domination and colonization? To whom does "el sistema americano" belong? Can it be adapted to a new context or only imperialistically imposed? Rather than give a definitive answer, this final and ambivalent statement forces his readers to think critically about the very text they have just finished reading. *Viage* can be understood optimistically, on the one hand, as offering guidelines for becoming a new liberal republic, emerging from the antiliberal legacies of a Spanish colonial past—a feat that will require necessary and honorable bloodshed. Or, on the other, we can read *Viage* and the final sentence of the book as a warning about a new type of colonization in Mexico and the violence that will accompany it. Perhaps, in choosing such an ambivalent statement to end his work, Zavala encourages his readers to understand it in both senses.

In this same concluding chapter, Zavala describes the United States as "aquel pueblo, lleno de vida y movimiento, [que] continua su curso á un fin" (*Viage*, 357) [that nation, full of life and movement, (that) continues its course towards a goal (*Journey*, 190)], implying that the United States has not yet reached that goal of progress and civilization. Thus even as he praises the United States for all it has accomplished, he also acknowledges that its project of civilization and progress, like Mexico's, is incomplete. The United States' future, as Mexico's, has yet to be written. For Zavala, the moment for reflection and change is now. In *Viage*, his experiences in exile confronting new forms of political and social organization press him to consider alternative possible futures for Mexico and help him critique, imagine, and (re)define his homeland in the present. Through comparison, he shows how both the United States and Mexico are working toward a liberal republic. Both countries must be wary of barbarism and corruption in all its forms—past, present, and future. Even as he points out many of the important differences between these countries, he sees them as joined together in a similar though still incomplete move toward a truly liberal Republic—what he calls civilization and progress—and in a fight against barbarism in its many guises.

As Zavala prepared his travel narrative for publication, he was no doubt acutely aware that this was a critical moment, a possible tipping point, in the development of the Mexican nation. This was the moment in which Mexicans were deciding—through battles as well as intellectual conversations and written works such as *Viage*—what their future nation would look like: its borders, its cultural and political institutions, and its citizenry. While U.S. American leaders such as Thomas Jefferson looked with admiration but also apprehension toward Europe as a model, Zavala's position is more complex, caught in a triangle between old European powers and new powers in the American hemisphere. He finds himself with an inadequate model, in his opinion, in Mexico's mother country, Spain. The United States presents another potential model, but it also represents the possibility of a new empire and a new type of colonization in Mexico, and it has roots in a very different cultural tradition that would be difficult to adapt to the Mexican context in Zavala's assessment. *Viage* thus meditates on Mexico's future at this unique moment in time as witness to the collapse of an old empire and the emergence of a new one. Zavala, as a voice of Greater Mexico, speaks to larger concerns for Mexicans during this early independence period. Where do Mexicans belong in the newly emerging racial, political, and cultural hierarchies of the Americas? What will that American future look like? In *Viage*, he articulates this moment of transition between old colonial formation and newly emerging and rapidly changing hierarchies, hoping to secure a space for Mexicans alongside U.S. Americans while still fearing the future.

For Zavala, this future of possibility would eventually materialize in Texas, where he fought alongside Anglo Texans against Santa Anna's centralized Mexican government. As the first vice-president of the Republic of Texas, he served as a bridge between Hispanic and Anglo culture and politics, fighting to position Mexicans at the forefront of what he considered progress and civilization. He died in 1836, before the annexation of Texas, the U.S.-Mexican War, and the marginalization and oppression of Mexicans within a new and supposedly liberal government. He thus died too soon to see the United States' "bloody victory," which ended up being a different sort of bloody victory than he had optimistically, some might say naively, hoped for. Nonetheless, *Viage*—one of the earliest works of literature that deals explicitly with the relationship among Mexico, the United States, and the borderlands caught in between these forces—opens up a moment when other possibilities for future Mexican-U.S. collaboration and support were seen as possible, even desirable. His text speaks to the possibility of a different future between the United States and Mexico and a different future for the Mexican borderlands, one in which Mexicans and Anglo Americans might fight side by side for progress and liberalism, with all its contradictory and problematic aspects—including its sometimes very antiliberal foundations. In his articulation of this possible future, he thus also exposes the deeply entrenched ethnoracial, social, and cultural divides that made liberal narratives of progress possible in the Americas. If liberalism has helped form broadly American concepts of identity and uniqueness, my reading of Zavala urges us to think through the dark side of this shared history and consider how entrenched racism and classism are within both Greater Mexico and the United States—so deeply enmeshed, in fact, that we do not always recognize them as a shared component of a hemispheric American history and culture.

2

A Proposed Intercultural
and (Neo)colonial
Coalition

<o>

Justo Sierra O'Reilly's
Yucatecan Borderlands

If you travel to the city of Mérida, a popular tourist destination in the north-western part of the Yucatán peninsula in Mexico, you will surely take a stroll—or perhaps a *turibus* or horse-drawn carriage—down one of the city's central avenues, Paseo de Montejo. Frequently touted as the material embodiment of Mérida's long-awaited entrance into modernity, this scenic thorough-fare was built in the style of the grandiose boulevards of nineteenth-century Paris. The avenue is lined with ornate turn-of-the-century mansions and stately palm trees and dotted with historic markers, monuments, and busts of important dead men. Paseo de Montejo and its mansions provide a nostalgic look back at the history of Mérida and the long-past era of the booming henequen industry that once made the city and peninsula so prosperous.[1] It was the cultivation and production of henequen—the famous "oro verde," or green gold—that made the construction of a grand boulevard like Paseo de Montejo both possible and desired by wealthy *meridanos*, who were seeking to establish themselves and their city as members of an international cosmopolitan elite.[2]

Today, although a few prominent families still reside on Paseo de Montejo, many of the grandest mansions have been turned into museums, hotels, and banks, fittingly reflecting the institutionalization of historical memory and the domination of multinational corporations in our present day.[3] On the Paseo de Montejo, a massive Walmart watches over a monument dedicated to Justo

Sierra O'Reilly (1814–1861), considered a founding father of Yucatecan literature. Further down the Paseo, in the middle of one of the largest roundabouts
in this city of one million inhabitants, sits the commanding Monumento
a la Patria—a monument dedicated to the Mexican *patria* (fatherland or
homeland)—sitting almost side by side with a McDonald's. Perhaps nothing
could be a more fitting commentary on Mexico's economic dependence and
U.S. cultural imperialism than this juxtaposition: in Mérida, the largest city in
Yucatán and one of the oldest continually inhabited European settlements
in America, built on the even older pre-Hispanic Maya site of T'Ho, one can
contemplate this hypernational monument while eating a cheeseburger inside
an air-conditioned McDonald's that is nearly identical to any McDonald's
almost anywhere in the world.[4]

The Walmart and McDonald's show the contemporary invasions of U.S.
capital and culture into Mexican life, but this U.S. presence actually has a
much longer history. Many of the other monuments along the Paseo, and in
particular the monument dedicated to Justo Sierra O'Reilly, instantiate how
long and how deeply Mexican and U.S. histories have been intertwined. Sierra
O'Reilly, an important nineteenth-century politician, writer, and cultural
worker, traveled from the Yucatán to the United States in 1847 as a representative of his regional government. His writings, as I will show in this chapter,
illuminate what has been left out of national(ized) Mexican histories, such
as that which has been compressed into the Monumento a la Patria. Sierra
O'Reilly's travel diary and other writings about his time in the United States
offer a glimpse of potential transnational community formation. At the
same time, his writings also shed light on how elite Yucatecos were able to
find common ground across national and cultural borders because of deeply
entrenched racial, ethnic, cultural, and socioeconomic hierarchies and
divisions within Greater Mexico.[5]

Transnationalism, as I discussed in the introduction, is not always subversive or liberating; similarly, the nation is not always repressive or limiting.[6]
Throughout *Forgotten Futures*, I explore how ideas about transnational community formation change during the nineteenth century for elites in Greater
Mexico. This chapter is about how histories are told, shaped, and retold. And
perhaps more importantly, it is about what is (sometimes necessarily) forgotten in that retelling. Sierra O'Reilly's texts reveal a (now) forgotten history of
transnational collaboration in which elite Yucatecos envisioned an alternative
to the nation(al) as we know and recognize it today. In this chapter, I examine
how oppressive racial hierarchies and categorizations circulated transnation-
ally among elites. This involves asking to what extent both national and transnational ideas of white supremacy, elitism, and racism should be considered
formative components of community history in Greater Mexico—and what it
means to erase these influential discourses from that community history.

Sierra O'Reilly's writings—both personal and public—offer a way to recapture the sorts of futures that elites in mid-nineteenth-century Yucatán imagined for themselves. These ideas about community looked beyond the nation to other sorts of economic, political, and literary networks of belonging in which elite criollo Yucatecos could insert themselves. Through manipulation of discourses of whiteness, progress, and hemispheric solidarity in his travel writings and letters, Sierra O'Reilly links Anglos and Yucatecos. At the same time, he uses these discourses in an attempt to distance Yucatecos from both Spain and indigenous Maya communities in Yucatán. The terminology he and others used to refer to themselves as a group reflects this distancing: the term *Yucateco*, for instance, did not include indigenous Maya.[7] Sent to the United States in a moment of uncertainty but also possibility, Sierra O'Reilly ponders the possible neocolonial formations that would make this union with the United States possible and that would also protect elite (criollo, white) Yucatecos from central Mexican aggression, U.S. imperialism, and indigenous Maya revolution. Sierra O'Reilly's writings thus speak to a history of internal violence that haunts Mexico's past and present. This history needs to be told, and Sierra O'Reilly's work provides a way to more deeply understand it.

I begin this chapter with a brief description of the historical and cultural context in which Sierra O'Reilly was living and writing before moving on to a closer textual analysis of his travel diary and other writings about his time in the United States. Sierra O'Reilly's writings ask us to reexamine the seemingly inevitable goal of national consolidation in Mexico and to recognize the histories of fragmentation, racism, and division that were characteristic of nineteenth-century Greater Mexico and were simultaneously erased from narratives of community formation as Mexico moved toward national(ized) consolidation. These legacies continue today in Yucatán and Greater Mexico but are often voiced in more subtle and coded ways. I therefore end with a return to the Paseo de Montejo and an analysis of the avenue and its monuments, which, like the forgotten history represented through Sierra O'Reilly's diary and writings, I read as a metaphor for the Mexican nation and how it has been created and continuously reimagined and rewritten.

The Yucatecan Borderlands

A liberal with a doctorate in both theology and law, Sierra O'Reilly held a number of political offices and was integral to the foundation of a Yucatecan literary tradition.[8] He is still well-known today in Yucatán for being one of the first historical novelists in Mexico and the founder of Yucatán's earliest literary magazines.[9] Sierra O'Reilly established the first Yucatecan literary newspaper, *El Museo Yucateco* (1841–1842), followed by *El Registro Yucateco* (1845–1849) and *El Fénix* (1848–1851). He penned historical novels (his most well known being *Un año en el Hospital de San Lázaro* [A year in Saint Lazarus hospital] [1845–1848] and *La hija del judío* [The Jew's daughter] [1848–1849]), novellas, and short stories and rewrote Yucatecan legends for his reading public.[10] Many of his literary works were published serially in *El Museo Yucateco* and *El Registro Yucateco*. Sierra O'Reilly was also deeply committed to recording Yucatecan history, editing and rescuing Yucatecan historical texts from oblivion, and writing biographies of important Yucatecan historical figures. In 1842, he edited and published a foundational text of Yucatecan historiography, Diego López de Cogolludo's *Historia de Yucatán* (1688), which Sierra O'Reilly published under the descriptive title *Los tres siglos de la dominación española, o sea historia de esta provincia, desde la conquista hasta la independencia* [Three centuries of Spanish domination, or history of this province, from conquest to independence].[11]

Sierra O'Reilly is less known, however, for his role in a little-discussed episode in Mexican and Yucatecan history: he was sent by the Yucatecan government to the United States in the midst of the U.S.-Mexican War (1846–1848) to seek annexation for Yucatán, which had declared itself independent from Mexico and neutral in the war between the United States and Mexico. Sierra O'Reilly thus quite literally follows in the footsteps of one of the other most influential early nineteenth-century Yucatecos, Lorenzo de Zavala. As readers will recall from chapter 1, Zavala was born in Yucatán, but he is often remembered for his importance to Texas, where he helped draft Texas's first constitution and served as its first vice-president. He was much vilified in Mexico for his participation in Texas's secession, a devastating act that helped lead to Mexico's greatest loss of territory following the U.S.-Mexican War. Sierra O'Reilly was similarly later criticized for his role in this failed mission to annex Yucatán. Some critics have even gone so far as to say that Sierra O'Reilly was so vilified that he never would have been recognized as a father of Yucatecan and Mexican literature if it had not been that his son, Justo Sierra Méndez, a prominent writer and politician during Porfirio Díaz's rule (1876–1911), rescued his father's public image and promoted him as a founding figure of Mexican and Yucatecan literature.[12]

In 1846, Sierra O'Reilly found himself, like Zavala before him, in a moment of crisis and national as well as regional disintegration. It was in this year, in the midst of the war between Mexico and the United States, that Sierra O'Reilly published Zavala's travel narrative as *Viaje a los Estados Unidos del Norte de América* [*Journey to the United States of North America*], accompanied by Sierra O'Reilly's own introduction to the text, "Noticia sobre la vida pública y escritos del Excmo. Sr. D. Lorenzo de Zavala, antiguo secretario de estado y ministro plenipotenciario de la república en París" [Note on the public life and writings of his excellency, don Lorenzo de Zavala, past Secretary of State and Plenipotentiary of the Republic of Paris].[13] "Noticia" provides a biography of Zavala as well as an explanation of the importance of Zavala's work and a defense of Zavala as a national hero. It is significant that when Zavala's narrative about his exilic travels in the United States was finally printed in his native country for the first time in 1846, it was printed not in Mexico City but in Mérida (Yucatán) and edited and introduced by Sierra O'Reilly, a fellow Yucateco.[14] Sierra O'Reilly's decision to reprint Zavala's text hints at the economic, cultural, and political connections between border zones such as Texas and Yucatán and brings to light the hostilities that existed within Greater Mexico, between central Mexico and its borderlands.

Sierra O'Reilly seems to recognize the delicacy of writing about a figure who was still much vilified in Mexico, especially as the war with the United States—over Texas, in large part—would have been ever-present in his thoughts as well as those of his readers in 1846. He even eliminates a discussion of Zavala's time in Texas, apart from a few footnotes, from his introduction to the new edition of Zavala's *Viaje a los Estados Unidos del Norte de América*. In one such footnote, Sierra O'Reilly defends the omission of this material:

> He creído conveniente omitir por ahora una gran parte de este escrito atento el estado actual que guardan nuestras relaciones con los Estados Unidos que han osado invadir nuestro territorio, y que no habrían hecho tal si a nuestros graves males políticos se hubiese aplicado oportuno remedio. Como yo creo a don Lorenzo de Zavala LIBRE de toda acusación y cargo por su conducta en Texas, y como para justificar esto habría sido preciso entrar en ciertos pormenores, me parece más cuerdo remitir las pruebas de este aserto para otra ocasión. Entretanto, suplico a los lectores suspendan su juicio, y no se preocupen contra nuestro digno compatriota.[15]

> [I believe it convenient to omit, for now, a large part of this text with regard to the current situation in which our relationship stands with the United States, who have dared to invade our territory. If some opportune remedy had been applied to our serious political ills, this is something that they otherwise would not have done. As I believe Mr. Lorenzo de Zavala FREE of all accusation and charge for his conduct in Texas, and as in order to justify this it would have been necessary to elaborate upon certain details, it appears prudent to delay such evidence for another occasion. Meanwhile, I ask kindly that the readers suspend their judgment and not condemn our honorable countryman.]

His hesitancy to pass preemptive judgment on this part of Zavala's biography conveys the importance of regional identity and the uncertainty of the position of both Yucatán and Texas in relation to Mexico in this moment.

As numerous historians have noted, national histories of nineteenth-century Mexico must be rooted, ironically, in the regional—the *patria chica*.[16]

And this is perhaps even more important for a region like Yucatán, which had experienced a troubled relationship with Mexico since independence from Spain. Because of geography, it actually shared much more in common with its Caribbean neighbors (Louisiana, Florida, Cuba) and Central America (especially Belize, a British stronghold) than with central Mexico. Distinct historical, cultural, and economic experiences had shaped Yucatán as a cultural and political sphere, separate in many ways from the rest of New Spain and, later, independent Mexico. Yucatán had been geographically isolated from New Spain; dense jungles and swamps hindered communication with the mainland, prompting Yucatecos to seek connections by sea with other areas of the Gulf of Mexico and the Caribbean.[17] The predominant indigenous group in Yucatán (Maya) was different than the indigenous groups in New Spain, thus producing notable cultural and linguistic differences that exist even today. Yucatán had also been governed differently than central New Spain during the colonial period: it had enjoyed greater autonomy as its own captaincy general since the seventeenth century and, later, as its own intendancy following the eighteenth-century Bourbon reforms.[18] Lastly, Yucatán had been granted a much greater degree of economic autonomy, freely trading with other nations and other Spanish colonies since 1814, thereby simultaneously establishing strong economic and cultural connections with other Caribbean ports, especially Cuba.[19] Thus historically it had been not only culturally distinct and geographically disconnected but also politically and economically separated from central Mexico.

Sierra O'Reilly's decision to publish Zavala's travel narrative—in 1846, in the midst of the U.S.-Mexican War—including an introductory biography full of praise for this vilified Tejano, highlights a broader history of cultural and political exchange among Yucatán, Texas, and the United States. It also opens up the possibility of reading Yucatán—as part of the Gulf of Mexico—as another type of borderland, caught between multiple countries and cultures, sharing much in common with other borderlands, such as Texas. Lastly, it offers a chance to look at how history is written and rewritten, and to question how histories of both cohesion and division are forgotten or remembered by different communities for different strategic purposes.

Sierra O'Reilly speaks from his social and cultural space within his community in Yucatán—which in turn forms part of the expansive Greater Mexico. Many scholars would fairly unambiguously consider Yucatán part of "Greater Mexico," defined by Américo Paredes as "all the areas inhabited by people of a Mexican culture—not only within the present limits of the Republic of Mexico but in the United States as well—in a cultural rather than a political sense."[20] Yet those who study and write about the Mexican borderlands rarely include Yucatán in their discussions, despite its commonalities with other border regions. Yucatán is a region where, historically, multiple cultures and peoples have come together, clashed, and negotiated their positions of power in relation to one another. Spaniards, Mayas, mestizos, and Afro-descendants have all shared this space, and not always peacefully.[21] Yucatán has served as a physical buffer zone between Mexico and other regions, nations, and communities; it has been (and is) a space of nearly constant negotiation, where multiple nations, cultures, and languages converge.[22] Central Mexico, Central America (including British-controlled Belize), the Caribbean (both British and Hispanic), South America, and—looking across the Gulf of Mexico—the United States have all come in contact with and played roles in Yucatán's history and development.

Yucatecos and Tejanos noticed some of these similarities and common experiences as peripheral borderlands too. In fact, in the 1830s and 1840s, Texas and Yucatán perceived one another as allies and as examples of how to fight a common enemy: Mexico.[23] Both Yucatán and Texas were stridently against any form of centralized government that would give more power to central Mexico. They looked to one another for support against what they perceived as an oppressive centralist government (Mexico) that sought to deny these regions the level of political, social, and economic autonomy they desired. Seen in this light, Sierra O'Reilly's choice to publish a text by a fellow Yucateco and much-maligned leader of Texas is evidence of an obscured history of division and regionalism, rather than national consolidation, in Mexico. It speaks to an alternative configuration of political, cultural, and economic networks of belonging in which Yucatecos and Tejanos—and even Anglo Texans—have much in common and might imagine a future for themselves distinct from central Mexico. While there were obviously important cultural elements that connected Yucatecos to Mexicans (e.g., Spanish colonialism, Catholicism, a common language), union with Mexico was not an inevitable conclusion for all Yucatecos in the first half of the nineteenth century. Sierra O'Reilly thus offers us a map for another type of border zone and system of multilingual, multicultural exchange (what Kirsten Silva Gruesz calls a "Latino-Anglo border system") that to this day goes largely unrecognized as a borderland: the Gulf of Mexico.[24]

The fact that critics have neglected to delve deeper into the intricate connections between these two important Yucatecos, Sierra O'Reilly and Zavala, is indicative of the ways in which critics have overlooked the moments of transnational collaboration that were taking place between parts of Greater Mexico and the United States even in the midst of the U.S.-Mexican War, a moment that would seemingly prevent such instances of collaboration but that in fact facilitated them in many ways. Unlike Zavala's travel narrative, which has recently received a resurgence of critical interest from scholars in Mexican, U.S., and Chicano literature and history,[25] Sierra O'Reilly's travel diary has been largely ignored by critics in both the United States and

Mexico.[26] This is in part, I suggest, because it does not neatly supplement narratives of national consolidation that were later established in both the United States and Mexico. Furthermore, it does not fit into a paradigm of cultural and political opposition between Spanish Americans (and later, Mexican Americans) and Anglo Americans. While cultural and political antagonism between Spanish America and Anglo America has a long and well-documented tradition, Sierra O'Reilly's diary and writing fall into an alternative historical, cultural, and political lineage that was well established in his time, although it has since been neglected.

Converging Histories of Violence

After independence from Spain, politicians in central Mexico fought over centralist or federalist forms of government. But in Yucatán, they were split over what type of federalism best suited the populace; federalism itself was largely a given for the vast majority of Yucatecos. In 1841, dissatisfied with Mexico's return to a centralized form of government, Yucatán declared its independence from Mexico. The Mexican army attempted to regain Yucatán, first with diplomacy and then by force, but its military invasion was ultimately unsuccessful. The Mexican government returned to federalism in 1846, and the Yucatecan government began to negotiate reunification with Mexico. But when war was officially declared between the United States and Mexico, the current ruling political party in Yucatán, headed by Sierra O'Reilly's father-in-law, Governor Santiago Méndez, feared entering a war with the United States, which already occupied key ports in Yucatán. They revolted against Mexico and once again declared Yucatecan independence. Hoping to regain control of key occupied ports, they also declared a position of neutrality in the U.S.-Mexican War and refused to provide troops or other forms of support to the Mexican government.[27]

At the same time, a different type of revolution was simmering in Yucatán. In July 1847, elite Yucatecos found themselves unable or unwilling to deliver on promises of land rights and tax breaks that they had previously made to Maya communities who had agreed to fight with Yucatecos against central Mexico in exchange for these promises. The Maya rebelled and the fighting quickly split Yucatán, with Maya Indians pitted against criollos and mestizos in what is now known as the Caste War.[28] Massacres occurred on both sides, but criollos and mestizos were far outnumbered and began losing ground to the Maya.[29] By the spring of 1848, Maya rebels had taken over most of the peninsula, with the exception of the criollo strongholds of Campeche and Mérida.

In the midst of the social and political upheaval of the Caste War and the U.S.-Mexican War, the ruling political party in Yucatán sent Sierra O'Reilly as its representative to the United States in September 1847. He was instructed to request three items from the United States: (1) the immediate evacuation of troops from Isla del Carmen, an important port in Yucatán; (2) special treatment that would protect Yucatecos from any repressive measures taken against them by the Mexican government due to Yucatán's declaration of neutrality and refusal to provide troops and other support to the Mexican government during the U.S.-Mexican War; and (3) help in the form of weapons, ammunition, troops, and money to aid the Yucatecan government in its war against the rebel Indians.[30]

The cultural and political work that Sierra O'Reilly was doing in the United States is cataloged in his diary, published as *Diario de nuestro viaje a los Estados Unidos (La pretendida anexión de Yucatán)* [Diary of our journey to the United States (The attempted annexation of Yucatán)] in 1938 in Mexico.[31] His diary was intended for his wife to read and in this sense can be understood as a private document. However, given his affinity for publishing Yucatecan travel narratives, it seems likely that he was also thinking about future readers even as he penned his private diary.[32]

Between 1849 and 1851, Sierra O'Reilly did in fact publish a four-volume travel narrative, *Impresiones de un viaje a los Estados Unidos de América y al Canadá* [Impressions of a journey to the United States of America and to Canada], that tells about his travels and time in the United States.[33] Although *Impresiones* is more comprehensive in some ways (it is, for one, much longer than *Diario de nuestro viaje*—the recently republished 2012 edition comes in at a hefty 704 pages), Sierra O'Reilly cuts out most information about his "secret" mission to annex Yucatán and seek the United States' help. He instead presents an edited, reorganized, polished, somewhat sanitized version of his experiences in the United States. By 1849, when Sierra O'Reilly started publishing *Impresiones*, he already knew the outcome of his trip: the U.S.-Mexican War was over, Yucatán had rejoined Mexico, and Yucatecos' position within the Mexican nation was somewhat stable once again. *Impresiones* thus offers a more cohesive retrospective on this moment in time and his experiences in the United States from the perspective of the eventual outcomes of the crises in motion at that time. But *Forgotten Futures* aims to look at moments of possibility—in all their uncertainty—in order to explore these lost stories and connections. So his more fragmentary recollections, as we see them in *Diario de nuestro viaje* rather than in *Impresiones*, are more valuable for uncovering his earlier position and that of Yucatán in its relation to both Mexico and the United States.

Diario de nuestro viaje offers a raw glimpse into a moment when Sierra O'Reilly could not yet have known the outcome of the U.S.-Mexican War, his mission in the United States, or the Caste War in Yucatán.[34] The entries in *Diario*, as in a traditional diary, are listed chronologically by date, with no grand narrative linking one entry to the next—how could there be when he did not yet know if they were important to where his "story" would end? A diary such as this one is by its nature fragmentary and discontinuous—unlike the much more edited, reorganized, and narrativized *Impresiones*, which shares more in common with the travel narrative or autobiography.[35]

As the eminent critic on diary studies Philippe Lejeune explains, autobiography is turned toward the past, because "you know the end point of the story, because you have reached it, and everything you write will lead up to this point, explaining how you got there."[36] The diary, in contrast, is inherently future oriented and always "unfinishable": you cannot know the end point of the story because you have never reached it; there is always one more day to write, or at least live, beyond the last entry.[37] A diary, he writes, "is turned towards the future, so if something is missing, it is not the beginning, but the end that changes in the course of writing it."[38] Rachael Langford and Russell West's introduction to *Marginal Voices, Marginal Forms: Diaries in European Literature and History*, similarly comments on how the diary exists in a liminal space, in terms of both genre and content: "The diary, as an uncertain genre uneasily balanced between literary and historical writing, between the spontaneity of reportage and the reflectiveness of the crafted text, between selfhood and events, between subjectivity and objectivity, between the private and the public, constantly disturbs attempts to summarise its characteristics within formalised boundaries. The diary is a misfit form of writing, inhabiting the frontiers between many neighboring or opposed domains, often belonging simultaneously to several 'genres' or 'species' and thus being condemned to exclusion from both at once."[39] A diary is also uneasily balanced between present and future. *Diario de nuestro viaje* captures a sense of an impending possibility, an undetermined future—and one that would be forgotten, rewritten, and reimagined later in a text like *Impresiones* in order to create a cohesive narrative of the past that leads to a culminating moment, unlike in a diary. His diary, like all diaries, exists in the in-between, on the borders, in the realm of speculation. Like Zavala's travel narrative examined in chapter 1, Sierra O'Reilly's *Diario de nuestro viaje* thus allows us to glimpse a (now) forgotten future in the midst of an uncertain present.

Diario de nuestro viaje, as it was edited and published in 1938, is useful also because it includes appendices with correspondence between Yucatecan and U.S. government officials, as well as excerpts from newspaper articles and congressional proceedings with regard to Sierra O'Reilly's "Yucatan Bill" in U.S. Congress. These were not part of his original diary, but they provide further insight into his ideas and thoughts during this time period and the cultural and political context in which he was enmeshed.

Sierra O'Reilly's diary and letters should also be understood as straddling a line between private and public writing. He was acutely aware of the fact that he was representing his homeland and the role that writing played in the construction of a national image and identity. He also knew that his letters to other politicians, for example, would most likely be publicly circulated or even published. As I noted in the introduction, texts that we might today consider "private" were often publicly shared in the nineteenth century: travel diaries and letters were frequently read out loud to larger audiences or family members, they were passed around to different people, and they were sometimes even published in local periodicals. On the front page of the third volume of his diary, Sierra O'Reilly explains that he wrote this diary, for example, "de orden de mi esposa, y en testimonio del fino y profundo amor que le profeso" (*Diario*, 19) [by order of my wife and as testament to the deep and profound love that I profess for her]. His diary was never intended to be an entirely private exercise in self-reflection.

Sierra O'Reilly's diary documents a moment when both the United States and Mexico were still working for national consolidation. The borders of both countries were indeterminate, the political form of the national government was still largely up for grabs in both countries, and the idea of what constituted the ideal citizen as well as the larger national population was being closely considered and debated in both countries.[40] Sierra O'Reilly's diary, along with his more public writing, demonstrates that this was a moment when certain groups of people sought out alternate coalitions that moved beyond already uncertain and sometimes weak national boundaries—a moment when criollos from Yucatán could imagine themselves as part of the United States and proposed that they might have more in common with Anglo Americans than with Mexicans from central Mexico.

In his diary, as the situation for criollos in Yucatán becomes more desperate and they begin to lose more and more towns to the Maya rebels, Sierra O'Reilly reveals how his own liberal ideals are embedded within racist and essentialist notions of indigenous groups. For readers today, this reveals the limits of and contradictions inherent in liberalism. He increasingly relies on a dichotomy that pits civilization against barbarism, with criollos on the side of civilization and progress—the same side, he argues, as the Anglo Americans to whom he was appealing for help and political recognition of his homeland. In his writing, Sierra O'Reilly uses complementary discourses of whiteness, progress, and hemispheric solidarity as a way of strategically linking elite Yucatecos with a new imperial power, the United States, while also distancing Yucatecos from the barbarism and racial degeneracy associated with the Spanish imperial past.

These discourses are not unique to Sierra O'Reilly; they circulated widely throughout Greater Mexico and Spanish America. During most of the nineteenth century, elite criollos in Spanish America saw and portrayed themselves as distinct from the indigenous, mestizos, and Afro-Latinos. While there was more flexibility within these categories and there were more opportunities to move between racial, ethnic, and social categories for individuals in Spanish America, this does not diminish the power of these hierarchies as omnipresent forms of sociocultural organization. In the context of Greater Mexico, these discourses continue a much longer history of social and cultural differentiation harkening back to the complex caste hierarchies of the colonial period. However, in the nineteenth century, these social and cultural categories take on increasingly racial and racist dimensions and begin to function in unique ways in Greater Mexico. This shift occurs as Greater Mexico is drawn into more frequent and intimate contact with the United States and Anglo American discourses of whiteness, blackness, civilization, and barbarism.

Thus while Yucatecos waged a literal battle on the ground, Sierra O'Reilly and other elite Yucatecos like him were engaged in what David Kazanjian calls a "guerra escrita"—a war of words over the past, present, and future of Yucatán itself.[41] Kazanjian's focus is on how criollos such as Sierra O'Reilly (re)wrote the Caste War, investing it "with meaning as a war about . . . 'the difference in skin color,' raza, or casta."[42] As he reveals, this process simultaneously racialized indigenous Maya and incorporated them into (a racialized) liberal capitalism.[43] My focus, however, is on how Sierra O'Reilly uses this dichotomy as a springboard for seeking out transnational partners and as a foundation for imagining an alternative future for elite Yucatecos in which they are part of a broader community of white elites. Sierra O'Reilly portrays the Caste War as an attack on Euro-Americans and as a battle between civilization and barbarism as a way of not only attracting support from Anglo Americans but also positioning Yucatecos favorably within a transnational framework of race-making and a hemispheric American narrative of progress, freedom, and independence—one that is, however, built paradoxically on the exclusion of racial(ized) others.

Ultimately, Sierra O'Reilly's writings, as well as the strategic coalitions that he imagines through them, speak to a now obscured literary and historical tradition of transnational and intercultural collaboration and coalition-building between Anglos and elite criollos. Like Zavala's travel narrative, Sierra O'Reilly's writings mark another key turning point in the history of Greater Mexico during which multiple futures were envisioned for its inhabitants. They also indicate what has been written out of nationalistic discourses and histories in order to be able to imagine the present-day nation as a cohesive, mestizo whole: racism and internal neocolonialism. Lastly, Sierra O'Reilly's writings reveal both the allure of "modern" republicanism—built on ideas of liberty, equality, fraternity—and, if we read against the grain, the racial, social, and political inequalities constitutive of that republicanism.

Recasting the Caste War in the United States

The Caste War became the linchpin in Sierra O'Reilly's quest for U.S. aid. But there were competing views on how to characterize this war in the United States. Was it a war against outnumbered whites? Was it a justified rebellion against a tyrannical government, from the viewpoint of oppressed Maya Indians? Or was it a civil war between competing political factions—a war in which neither side should be formally recognized or aided until the fighting was really over?

Some U.S. newspaper editors supported the annexation of Yucatán, or at least approved of sending aid to Yucatecos, and agreed that it was a race war led by wild Indians bent on exterminating whites in Yucatán.[44] However, many editors and newspapers opposed annexation for diverse reasons. On the liberal side of the political spectrum, some felt that the Caste War was a just rebellion of oppressed Indians against a nondemocratic government.[45] Others considered Sierra O'Reilly a representative of an illegitimate government, since the opposing political party in Yucatán refused to officially recognize his party.[46] Still others worried that a type of slavery of indigenous people existed in Yucatán.[47] Conservative papers in the United States, on the other hand, often rejected Sierra O'Reilly on racial grounds, seeing him as a representative of a weak and effeminate race that they felt was undeserving of the aid of civilized nations.[48] For both liberal and conservative newspapers in the United States, it seems, Yucatecos were either not quite liberal enough or too inherently barbaric to be worth saving.

Sierra O'Reilly was very aware of these competing views of the Caste War and the role that newspapers had in swaying public opinion about Yucatán and Yucatecos. In his diary entry from March 7, 1848, he laments the power of this negative press and the polarization of his mission to the United States:

> Mientras me pongo en más contacto con los hombres que hacen y dirigen aquí la política, me alarmo más y más sobre el porvenir de Yucatán. Y luego para aumentar más mis mortificaciones, un maldito periódico español de Nueva Orleans, llamado *La Patria*, me ha tomado de su cuenta: hoy he leído un furioso artículo contra mí. . . . ¡La política! ¡Maldita sea la política y más de la manera miserable y raquítica en que la entienden ciertos hombres! (*Diario*, 22–23)

> [As I put myself in further contact with the men who make and lead politics here, I become ever more alarmed as to the future of Yucatán. Then if only to increase my mortification, a damned Spanish newspaper from New Orleans, called *La Patria*, has paid special attention to me. Today, I have read a furious article against me. . . . Politics! May politics be damned, and even more in the miserable and squalid way that certain men understand it!]

Faced with such contentious versions of the Caste War and his mission in the United States, Sierra O'Reilly realized soon after arriving that he would have to portray both Yucatecos and the Caste War in a specific way if he was going to obtain aid or, later, realize the annexation of Yucatán.

In order to gain support from Anglo Americans, Sierra O'Reilly portrays the Caste War in two ways: as a war against whites on the verge of possible extermination and as a war between the forces of civilization and barbarism. Sierra O'Reilly thus attempts to appeal to the U.S. government and the U.S. public on racial as well as political terms while at the same time eliding a history of systematized oppression of Maya Indians by portraying criollos as the community truly in need of aid. In an April 1848 letter to James Buchanan, then secretary of state and Sierra O'Reilly's main contact in the U.S. government, Sierra O'Reilly describes the dire situation of the white community ("la población blanca") in Yucatán: "El país [de Yucatán] está yendo a la ruina y su población blanca está a punto de ser exterminada por los salvajes, a menos que reciba la simpatía, protección y ayuda de las naciones civilizadas" (*Diario*, 99) [The country (of Yucatán) is going to ruin, and its white population is on the verge of being exterminated by the savages, unless it receives the sympathy, protection, and help of civilized nations]. He appeals to Buchanan on racial terms; Anglo Americans in the United States would, Sierra O'Reilly seems to hope, be unnerved by this violence against fellow whites. He was surely aware of the ways in which the Haitian Revolution, which encapsulated fears of the racial other gaining power through violence, haunted whites in the United States throughout the nineteenth century. But when he requests the aid of the United States as a "civilized nation," he also appeals to Buchanan, the U.S. government, and the Anglo American public through the rhetoric of civilization and progress, which is also inextricable from conceptualizations of whiteness. Sierra O'Reilly assumes that fellow civilized nations, in their dedication to and promotion of civilization and progress, are committed to protecting other civilized peoples and communities from noncivilized or noncivilizing forces.

During his time in the United States, Sierra O'Reilly learned that he had to appeal to Anglo Americans on more than just the grounds of racial (white) solidarity, because that was turning out to be far more slippery ground than he had perhaps originally anticipated. In the nineteenth century, cultural and ancestral links to Spain were often viewed as links to whiteness, or at least European-ness, in Yucatán and other parts of Spanish America. But while Sierra O'Reilly perhaps regarded the historical and cultural connections between Yucatán and Spain as links to civilization and Europe, some U.S. Americans, such as Sierra O'Reilly's racist opponents in the U.S. press, saw these connections instead as links to degeneracy and barbarism, part of the legacy of the Black Legend, which, as I have already shown, painted Spain as a decadent and backward empire rather than a progressive civilization. In the nineteenth century, U.S. Americans began to imagine their expanding nation (or "anti-empire," as María DeGuzmán phrases it) as a foil to the barbarous, degenerate, and "black" Spanish empire.[49] Because Spanishness could be understood as a link to both biological/ancestral whiteness and "off-whiteness" in the U.S. context, Sierra O'Reilly had to rely on other commonalities besides just race/whiteness that would possibly substantiate the links between elites in Yucatán and those in the United States.

Thus Sierra O'Reilly focuses on civilization, progress, and freedom as key elements of the white Yucatecan identity and experience that link Yucatán to other fellow American countries such as the United States and differentiate white Yucatecos from Maya Indians.[50] According to Sierra O'Reilly, the Caste War, then, is not just a war between races; more precisely, it is a war between civilization and barbarism, "la guerra de los bárbaros, la salvaje y atroz guerra" (Diario, 98–99) [the war of the barbarians, the savage, atrocious war] against a "civilización de trescientos años" (Diario, 98–99) [civilization of three hundred years]. Since even elite Yucatecos were "not quite" white or were not considered pure white by many in the United States, Sierra O'Reilly also connects Yucatecos and Anglo Americans through the common narrative of civilization and progress. His use of the civilization/barbarism dichotomy can thus be understood in part as a rhetorical device designed to elicit support from Anglo Americans in the United States. But the fact that he writes about this in his private diary also suggests that his belief in this dichotomy was not solely strategic rhetoric.

A call for a simplistic racial solidarity between fellow Euro-Americans would not be sufficient to make all Anglo Americans want to support or annex Yucatán, since Spanish blood or ancestry was not necessarily understood as being equally white in Anglo America. Sierra O'Reilly thus substantiates his claim for whiteness and European connections by portraying criollos in Yucatán as tied to freedom, civilization, and progress. He works to demonstrate that Yucatán is indeed, or at least was before the Maya rebellion, a civilized community interested in these shared republican values. In his February 15, 1848, letter to Buchanan, he describes Yucatán and its politics and culture, stating that "noble, filantrópica, liberal y amplia ha sido siempre la política que ha dominado en Yucatán" (Diario, 81) [noble, philanthropic, liberal, and generous have always been the type of politics that have dominated in Yucatán]. A bit further along in that same letter, he laments what is happening in Yucatán and describes his homeland as "aquel infortunado país, envuelto como está ahora en . . . complicaciones y dificultades, a pesar del hecho de que es uno de los más industriosos, más ilustrados y más liberales de los Estados que formaban la antigua Confederación Mexicana" (Diario, 86) [that unfortunate country, shrouded as it is now in . . . complications and difficulties, despite it being one of the most industrious, most illustrious, and most liberal of the States that formed the old Mexican Confederacy]. In this letter Sierra O'Reilly argues that the reason that Yucatecos have lost control of the country to the rebelling Maya is not because this is an uncivilized country or people but because Yucatecos have been too progressive and too liberal and have believed too strongly in republicanism:

> Nuestra política ha sido siempre la de aligerar la condición social de los indios; mejorándola por medio de la instrucción civil y religiosa y extendiendo entre todos ellos los beneficios de la civilización, de la misma manera y en la misma medida en que lo han permitido sus recursos a favor de los de nuestra raza. Muchos de ellos han sido llamados a ocupar puestos en la vida pública, quienes han conseguido deshacerse de la estupidez habitual, que ha sido y es su característica. Y tan buenos resultados ha producido esta política, en un punto de vista, que finalmente hemos sido víctimas del odio, la envidia y la ferocidad salvaje de los indios orientales, que nos han declarado una guerra de exterminio. (*Diario*, 81)

> [Our policy has always been that of easing the social condition of the Indians; improving it by means of civil and religious instruction; and extending to all of them the benefits of civilization. This has been done in the same way and by the same means as resources have permitted, to help those of our race. Many of them have been called to occupy posts in public life, those who manage to shake off the habitual stupidity that has been and is characteristic of them. This policy has produced such good results, from one point of view, that we have finally become victims of the hatred, jealousy, and savage ferocity of the eastern Indians, who have declared a war of annihilation against us.]

Sierra O'Reilly here rebuts the idea that the Caste War is a just war on behalf of oppressed Indians. In his eyes, Maya Indians are not oppressed; rather, they have been given too many of the rights and "benefits" of civilization and democracy.[51] He also simultaneously reinforces the widely held belief that there are intrinsic differences between civilized Yucatecos and Maya Indians, whom Sierra O'Reilly depicts as inherently incompatible with civilization and progress. He places Yucatecos on the side of civilization and progress, imbued with republican values such as freedom, once again linking Yucatecos to their fellow republicans in the United States.

Sierra O'Reilly establishes a narrative of progress and a history of civilization for Yucatán, just like the United States, and appeals for help for Yucatecos as like-minded peers and members of the same American family, joined together by uniquely American republican values. This trope appears throughout his diary and frequently in his letters to Buchanan. The family ties he creates between American countries are not strictly biological, in this sense, but rather cultural-political ties. Although Anglos and Yucatecos might not be connected by ancestral ties (i.e., common ties to England and northern Europe), he shows that other ties, such as a commitment to republicanism, progress, and independence, could be just as powerful in binding them together. Worried about Yucatán's relationship with Mexico in the aftermath of the U.S.-Mexican War, Sierra O'Reilly repeatedly calls on the United States to help its sibling country, Yucatán, in its negotiations with Mexico. Writing to Buchanan in February 1848, he questions the relationship between the United States and Yucatán:

¿Y cómo pueden los Estados Unidos dejar de reconocer los sacrificios hechos por una nación a la cual está ligada por lazos de hermandad, principalmente porque es débil e indefensa, entregándola a su propia suerte, de modo que un implacable enemigo pueda maltratarla y hasta destrozarla? ¿Es esto compatible con la justicia de un gobierno liberal o con la generosidad de una nación libre y magnánima? (*Diario*, 91)

[And how can the United States fail to recognize the sacrifices made by a nation to which it is bound by links of siblinghood, mainly because it is weak and defenseless, thus handing it over to its own fate, in such a way that an unforgiving enemy might mistreat or even destroy it? Is this compatible with the justice of a liberal government or with the generosity of a free and magnanimous nation?]

The fraternal metaphor, which Sierra O'Reilly uses here and in several other letters to Buchanan, connects Yucatán with the United States as members of the same American family. They are linked together in their political struggles as independent young nations, "aquellos países americanos que están tratando de arrojar de sí el yugo de la dependencia europea" (*Diario*, 81) [those American countries that are trying to throw off the yoke of European dependence]. They are connected through their shared history of European colonization, but more importantly through their commitment to progress and civilization in the Americas. If the United States is truly devoted to the ideals of liberalism and progress, Sierra O'Reilly argues, then she will support her fellow American countries, which are struggling for those same lofty ideals. If they cannot connect as racial equals, at least they can connect in political terms, as fellow Americans.

Following in this vein, Sierra O'Reilly also invokes the Monroe Doctrine as something that binds together the sibling countries of the Americas—Yucatán and the United States—in opposition to European powers such as Spain and England. As Gretchen Murphy explains, one of the central goals behind the Monroe Doctrine was to map "the political binary between Old World tyranny and New World democracy to a spatial construct that divides the globe into two hemispheres."⁵² In his letter to Buchanan on April 3, 1848, Sierra O'Reilly contemplates the options for Yucatán and the future relationship between it and the United States according to the Monroe Doctrine:

> El pueblo de Yucatán no puede permitir que se le mate y destruya sin emplear todos los medios que están a su alcance para evitarlo. Debe, por lo tanto, hacer un llamamiento a alguna potencia extranjera, invocando en su favor los derechos de Humanidad y simpatía que un pueblo ilustrado y civilizado debe tener para otro de la misma clase; ¿y a qué nación podemos llamar, si no es a la poderosa República que se halla a la cabeza de la civilización americana, que tenemos en tanta estima y de la que esperamos derivar nuestra futura prosperidad y adelanto? . . .
>
> Hay una declaración hecha por Mr. Monroe, Presidente de los Estados Unidos, . . . en diciembre de 1823, en la que se establece que el Gobierno americano considerará cualquier medida por parte de las potencias europeas para intervenir en los asuntos de las naciones independientes de América, . . . como dañosa y perjudicial a la seguridad y a la paz públicas. . . . Si, pues, tal intervención tuviese lugar como es más que probable que suceda, Yucatán quedará envuelto en dificultades y su condición sería infinitamente más infortunada que ahora. (*Diario*, 100–101)

> [The community of Yucatán cannot allow itself to be killed or destroyed without employing all the means at its disposal to avoid this. It should, therefore, call out to some foreign power, invoking on its own behalf its Human Rights and the sympathy that a civilized and enlightened people should have toward those of the same class. And to which nation can we call, if not to the powerful Republic that is found at the head of American civilization, for which we have such esteem and from which we hope to derive our future prosperity and progress? . . .
>
> There is a declaration made by Mr. Monroe, President of the United States, . . . in December of 1823, in which it is established that the American government will consider any action on behalf of the European powers to intervene in the affairs of the independent nations of America . . . as harmful and dangerous to public security and peace. . . . If, then, such intervention were to take place, as is more than likely to occur, Yucatán will remain enshrouded in its difficulties, and its condition will be infinitely more unfortunate than it is currently.]

Following the Monroe Doctrine's principles, Sierra O'Reilly connects Yucatán with New World democracy and progress (the United States) rather than Old World tyranny (Spain and Europe), thereby geographically, culturally, and politically mapping Yucatán onto the same Western Hemisphere as the United States. He ends this discussion of the Monroe Doctrine by returning to the metaphor of fraternal relations: "No puedo convencerme de que los Estados Unidos, obrando además por otros motivos más nobles que los de la política, no se apresuren a proteger a sus hermanos de Yucatán y redimirlos de la miserable condición en que están sumidos" (*Diario*, 101) [I cannot convince myself that the United States, acting out of any other motive more noble than that of politics, would not hurry to protect its brothers in Yucatán and retrieve them from the miserable condition in which they are now submerged].

Sierra O'Reilly uses the Monroe Doctrine to position Yucatán and the United States as peers rather than the much more paternalistic attitude that the United States would eventually take in its own rendering of the Monroe Doctrine. In that same April 3 letter to Buchanan, he begins his discussion of U.S.-Yucatecan political relations:

En ocasión anterior, ... invoqué a favor de mi país los sagrados nombres de Humanidad, Libertad y Civilización, sentimientos todos que caracterizan al pueblo de los Estados Unidos. Vuelvo, señor, a invocar aquellos nombres y además el de Justicia. ... Solicito la intervención formal, la activa y eficiente cooperación de los Estados Unidos a consecuencia de la guerra sangrienta, la más cruel que sufre el pueblo de Yucatán. (*Diario*, 98)

[On a previous occasion, ... I invoked, to the benefit of my country, the sacred names of Humanity, Liberty, and Civilization; all feelings that characterize the people of the United States. Again, Sir, I invoke those names and furthermore that of Justice. ... I seek formal intervention, and the active and efficient cooperation of the United States in response to the bloody war, the most cruel one from which the people of Yucatán are suffering.]

Even when requesting direct intervention from the United States, Sierra O'Reilly positions Yucatán and the United States as peers working in cooperation toward the greater goals of "Humanity, Liberty and Civilization" (*Diario*, 98). According to Sierra O'Reilly, the United States and Yucatán, as members of the same family and as fellow civilized nations, have a duty to support one another. The United States, as the leader of progress and civilization in the Americas, should be devoted to protecting and cultivating the delicate growth of these cherished values in its fellow (fraternal) countries.

Through his invocation of the Monroe Doctrine, Sierra O'Reilly also attempts to connect Yucatán and the United States by distancing Yucatán from Spain and Spanishness, thereby placing Yucatán squarely in a new and distinctly American geographic and cultural context. As already discussed in chapter 1, this was a common rhetorical move for early nineteenth-century liberals in Spanish America. The enemies here are European empires. Sierra O'Reilly was intent on establishing a meaningful connection between Yucatán and the United States, and to do so, he also had to distance Yucatecos from their cultural and historical ties with Spain. Sierra O'Reilly here accomplishes a deft sleight of hand: he rejects Spanish colonialism, which is decadent and corrupting, yet he portrays elite Yucatecos as the owners and promoters of civilization and progress—a discourse and narrative that justified and legitimized Spanish colonialism and that was a product of Spanish colonialism. In this way, he recycles a Spanish colonialist narrative but also, in his assertion that American nations naturally share this impetus toward civilization, erases its connection to Spanish colonialism and, ironically, uses it as a means to link Yucatecos to a *new* type of colonialism encapsulated in the Monroe Doctrine.

While Sierra O'Reilly's rejection of Spain in favor of the United States might seem odd, especially given that the United States—not Spain—was the most recent aggressor against Mexico, the move to distance Spanish American history and culture from Spanish history and culture is actually quite characteristic of the Spanish American experience in the nineteenth century. Rupture and discontinuity were key aspects of Spanish American writers' depictions of their newly emerging national identities as countries that were independent from Spain. After the wars of independence from Spain, Spanish Americans had to reconceptualize Spanish American identity "as founded on a break with Spain and, more specifically, with Spanish history."[53] They had to envision American history not as an unbroken continuum, as it had been imagined before independence, "but as a series of purposeful ruptures and other instances of change and transformation."[54] Sierra O'Reilly, like other Spanish American authors and cultural workers, was interested in establishing a uniquely and broadly American identity for his homeland; this was certainly part of his mission in establishing a Yucatecan literary and historical tradition. His turn to the United States and the Monroe Doctrine emphasizes Yucatán's foundation as a new American country, like the United States, defined by its break from Europe (Spain) and intent on maintaining its independence from European powers.

By distancing himself from Spain and invoking the Monroe Doctrine in a plea for help from fellow American countries (sibling countries, significantly), Sierra O'Reilly indicates that civilization could have a future in Yucatán if it is protected from savage Indians and given the chance to prosper outside of the influence of the degenerate Spanish race. Through his attempt to create a sense of racial solidarity and an alliance between sibling nations similarly invested in the promotion of civilization, freedom, and progress, Sierra O'Reilly opens up the possibility of an intercultural coalition between Anglo Americans and Yucatecos. He in fact attempts to write that coalition into existence and pushes to reinforce political ties, pointing out their similarities as civilized American countries joined by a shared colonial history and present/future (anti)empire of civilization and progress.

(Neo)colonial Formations in Yucatán

Sierra O'Reilly and his supporters in the United States envisioned this coalition in more than abstract terms. As he notes in several diary entries from April 1848, he initially received a good number of letters from Anglo Americans who were interested in organizing volunteer regiments that could be sent to Yucatán to fight the Maya rebels.[55] On April 26, 1848, he writes that he has spent a good portion of his day answering "cartas que he recibido de numerosas partes en que me hacen proposiciones de levantar tropas y colonos para ir a Yucatán" (*Diario*, 34) [letters I have received from numerous parts in which they make proposals for raising troops and colonists to go to Yucatán]. Ultimately, though, Sierra O'Reilly was not authorized and did not have the necessary funds to organize such military regiments. Eventually, Sierra O'Reilly realized that a military expedition to Yucatán, especially a voluntary or privately funded one, would be difficult if not impossible for him to implement. Moreover, he decided that a temporary military expedition would not solve the "problem" for white Yucatecos. In his May 8, 1848, diary entry, he mulls over the problem as well as his proposed solution:

> Tengo que sostener una larga correspondencia con periódicos y otros que me han hecho proposiciones para levantar voluntarios. Esto es, en verdad, lo que más importa a Yucatán y esto es, precisamente, en lo que menos han pensado nuestros hombres pensadores. Para que Yucatán se salve, no es bastante que vaya temporalmente una expedición de los Estados Unidos; es preciso que arbitre medios de tener permanentemente una población blanca. (*Diario*, 41)

> [I must maintain a lengthy correspondence with newspapers and others who have made proposals to me for the recruitment of volunteers. This is, truthfully, what matters most to Yucatán, and yet it is precisely this which our wise men have considered least of all. In order for Yucatán to be saved, it is not enough for there to be a temporary expedition from the United States. It is necessary that they decide upon the means for permanently establishing a white population.]

Sierra O'Reilly envisions and even starts to actively plan a different way for Anglo Americans and others to support white Yucatecos in their campaign for civilization: increased white immigration and settlement of Yucatán. In another diary entry later that same month (May 15, 1848), he again speaks about his idea for "saving" Yucatán with "un plan de colonización en grande a fin de atraer extranjeros a Yucatán que es lo que más nos importa para hacer de ese país un pueblo grande y poderoso" (*Diario*, 45) [a fully elaborated plan of colonization so as to attract foreigners to Yucatán, which is what is most important in order to make of this country a great and powerful people].

The new type of colonialism that Sierra O'Reilly is planning in his last few months in the United States centers around the idea of a transnational white community that functions as a civilizing force. By spring 1848, Sierra O'Reilly saw U.S. intervention and foreign (white) immigration as the only solutions to what he envisioned—or at least portrayed—as the imminent annihilation of civilization and the white race in Yucatán. On May 18, 1848, he wrote in his diary, "No hay más esperanza que el auxilio de los Estados Unidos; no hay más remedio de salud que provocar la inmigración extranjera. Nuestra pobre sociedad necesita de una completa regeneración" (*Diario*, 49) [There is no other hope than the aid of the United States. There is no other remedy for our health than the solicitation of foreign immigration. Our poor society is in need of a complete regeneration]. Not only would foreign immigration and settlement increase the number of civilized whites in Yucatán, but it would also, in Sierra O'Reilly's eyes, be regenerative for the weakened white community that currently lived there. The transnational racial coalition envisioned by Sierra O'Reilly and, presumably, his Anglo American supporters in the United States would be composed of modernizing forces that would do away with backward, barbarous Indians and decadent remnants of Spanish colonialism. This new type of colonialist power would "beneficently" work toward progress and modernization—even if that progress could only be achieved through the extermination of Indians. Sierra O'Reilly thus once again recycles a Spanish colonial discourse in a new colonial arena.

Sierra O'Reilly's writing indicates that when faced with the choice of joining either the United States or Mexico, at least some white Yucatecos favored union with the United States over Mexico. The shared commitment to progress and civilization seems to trump the other social and cultural traits that Yucatecos shared with other Mexicans. For example, he explicitly contrasts Yucatán's possible connection to the United States as a fellow civilized American nation with Yucatán's relationship to Mexico—another American nation, obviously, but not necessarily at the same level of civilization. In addition to recognizing that Mexico looked at Yucatecos as enemies for their refusal to support Mexico during the U.S.-Mexican War,[56] Sierra O'Reilly also writes about his perceptions of Mexico in another letter to Buchanan from earlier that year (February 24, 1848):

> Yo no me detengo a pensar en el hecho de que no existe en México un Gobierno constitucional; que la República está en un estado de gran disolución; que está dividida en facciones, las cuales, en su frenesí y delirio, están peleando por conseguir los últimos despojos del país que ellas han deshonrado y calumniado; que la Representación Nacional no ha sido oída, ya que ni se ha reunido en Congreso ni ha sido elegida por la voluntad del pueblo, ni ha sido consultada para nada. (*Diario*, 89–90)

[I will not dwell on the fact that a constitutional Government does not exist in Mexico; that the Republic is in a state of great dissolution; that it is divided into factions, which, in their frenzy and delirium, are fighting to grab the last spoils from the country that they have dishonored and slandered; that our National Representation has not been heard, since they have not met in Congress, nor have they been elected by the will of the people, nor have they been consulted in any way.]

The Mexico portrayed by Sierra O'Reilly is not the civilized and modern nation that elite Yucatecos hoped to join. He seems to echo Zavala's take on the shortcomings of republicanism in Mexico: politics as practiced in Mexico offers merely the resemblance of democratic institutions, but with no actual implementation of the ideals that are theoretically foundational to such republican institutions.

Sierra O'Reilly's writings illuminate a moment when national identity in Mexico was still in flux, when regional affiliations generally superseded any broader (national) affiliations. But perhaps more importantly, his writings bring to light a moment when colonial affiliations (e.g., *hispanidad* or *latinidad*) were not always viewed as *the* defining aspect that could unite people of different geographical and political spaces. His diary and letters reveal an alternative way of conceiving of "America." His is an America in which at least some Yucatecan elites could envision Yucatán as more closely connected to the United States by fraternal ties and political goals than to central Mexico or Spain. A common sense of (past) coloniality (and rejection of this, even if only superficially) could be part of a shared and new forward-looking American identity.

A Failed Future

Ultimately, Anglo Americans decided that they did not want to annex Yucatán, at least partly because they perceived Yucatecos as racially and culturally inferior. Despite Sierra O'Reilly's best efforts, enough Anglo Americans could not be convinced that political-historical ties—to Europe, civilization, and progress—were more important than perceived biological-racial and phenotypical differences. His failure in the United States is indicative of one of the many contradictions of the Monroe Doctrine: even though it divided the world into two hemispheres, with the New World on the side of democracy and progress, this binary was troubled "by the doubt often expressed in the United States that South Americans [and Spanish Americans, more broadly,] were racially incapable of democratic self-rule."[57] While Sierra O'Reilly uses the Monroe Doctrine to establish Yucatán and the United States as siblings and equal peers, the United States would ultimately use it as a legitimization of a paternalistic attitude that allowed and reinforced its strategic assumption of power over the American hemisphere.

The Caste War was thus a watershed in U.S. foreign policy and a turn toward informal neocolonial formations. Kazanjian explains that although "the peculiarity and ambiguity of racial and national formations in Yucatán soured Congress on occupation and annexation, the U.S. aid that did arrive helped to turn the tide of the war in the Creoles' favor, and laid the groundwork for U.S. neocolonialism, or an imperialism freed from permanent military and settler occupation."[58] U.S. government and U.S. businesses turned to informal aid and private investment instead of more costly and formal methods of colonization and military occupation; the Caste War thus served to teach "U.S. capital the advantages of neocolonial development over colonial development."[59]

Sierra O'Reilly was vilified for his role in the disastrous expedition to the United States, and he returned to Yucatán a changed man. His views on the Maya, for instance, were radically altered. Prior to his trip to the United States and the devastation of the Caste War, Sierra O'Reilly's view of Indians, as evidenced in his early journalistic writing, was paternalistic and akin to Rousseau's idea of the *bon savage*; he presented the Maya as "docile, thrifty, frugal, and law abiding. . . . [but also] degenerate, weak, and ignorant."[60] His writings from 1847 and later, however, reveal a marked contrast from his earlier beliefs about Indians. In his diary entry from April 18, 1848, he himself remarks on his change in views:

> Yo siempre he tenido lástima a los pobres indios, me he dolido de su condición y más de una vez he hecho esfuerzos por mejorarla, porque se aliviase de unas cargas que a mí me parecían muy onerosas. Pero ¡¡los salvajes!! Brutos infames que se están cebando en sangre, en incendios y destrucción. Yo quisiera hoy que desapareciera esa raza maldita y jamás volviese a aparecer entre nosotros. Lo que hemos hecho para civilizarla se ha convertido en nuestro propio daño y es ciertamente muy sensible y muy cruel tener que arrepentirse hoy de acciones que nos han parecido buenos. ¡Bárbaros! Yo los maldigo hoy por su ferocidad salvaje, por su odio fanático y por su innoble afán de exterminio. (*Diario*, 30)

> [I have always felt sorry for the poor Indians whose condition has pained me, and more than once I have made efforts to improve it, by means of relieving them of burdens that appeared oppressive to me. But what savages!! Vile brutes that fatten themselves on blood, fire, and destruction. I wish today that this cursed race would vanish and never again appear among us. That which we have done to civilize them has only served to harm us, and it is certainly very cutting and very cruel to have to repent today for actions that had seemed good to us. What barbarians! I curse them today for their savage ferocity, their fanatic hatred, and their shameful zeal for extermination.]

Starting in 1847, he sees and portrays Indians not as noble savages but as barbarians, "esa raza maldita" (*Diario*, 30) [that cursed race], bent on exterminating the white race in Yucatán.

Upon returning to Yucatán after his failed mission to the United States, Sierra O'Reilly became obsessed with three themes that he would pursue throughout the rest of his life: "The Indians' savage ferocity, their fanatic hatred of the whites, and their desire for the extermination of civilization."[61] His campaign to create and record a Yucatecan historical and literary tradition continued, but he now had an additional pursuit that framed his writing: a "journalistic campaign aimed at the extermination of the Maya Indians, a genocidal project that was largely responsible for immediate changes in government policies regarding the indigenous populations in the peninsula," such as the covert sale of Maya Indians to Cuba as slaves.[62]

The story of Sierra O'Reilly's failed mission to the United States and the proposed annexation of Yucatán has made it into few history books. By August 1848, Yucatán had once again been incorporated into Mexico. As Mexico worked toward national consolidation, moments of internal disintegration, such as Yucatán's secession, were dismissed as singular instances of treason or confusion in a longer narrative of national(istic) cohesion. Even by 1848, Yucatecos would not necessarily have wanted to remind Mexico of their lack of loyalty during the U.S.-Mexican War. Criollos in Yucatán were still fighting the Maya uprising and needed the help of the Mexican military, so they certainly would have wanted to assure Mexico of their renewed loyalty.

Second, this history has been swept under the rug in Mexico as an aberration of an otherwise cohesive national narrative of mestizaje. As literary critics and historians have clearly established, over the course of the nineteenth century, mestizaje and the mestizo became foundations of Spanish American identity.[63] Sierra O'Reilly, on the other hand, contemplates the similarities between white Yucatecos and Anglo Americans and rejects racial or cultural mestizaje as part of Yucatecan identity. His writing does not fit into the narrative of mestizaje that would be cemented in place as a foundation of Mexican identity by the early twentieth century. His history is thus that much easier to discard as an abnormal, racist deviation from an otherwise stable national narrative of cohesive racial mixing. It is discarded because memories of racism itself are discarded from Mexican history through the dominant nation-building narrative of mestizaje.

Lastly, the Caste War is often overlooked as less important than other conflicts in nineteenth-century American history, such as the U.S. Civil War, the Mexican Wars of Reform, or the U.S.-Mexican War. It is frequently viewed as a local or regional conflict rather than an event with international origins or (inter)national significance. Kazanjian, however, argues that the Caste War was a "transnational flashpoint that had two crucial effects on U.S. citizenship: it transformed U.S. imperialism from white settler colonialism to neocolonialism, and it produced white, Indian, Mexican, and, eventually, Chicano racial formations that blended the assimilative mode of civilization policy with the eradicative mode of removal policy."[64] While Kazanjian, in *The Colonizing Trick*, focuses on the import of the Caste War for the United States, my reading of Sierra O'Reilly's diary in this chapter focuses on what a deeper examination of the transnational connections between the U.S.-Mexican War and the Caste War reveals about the communities of Greater Mexico. By looking at the connections that elites imagined, and sometimes actively worked to realize, between criollos and Anglo Americans, we are able to see the diversity of perspectives and experiences of Mexicanos, the violence and conflict that occurred within the communities of Greater Mexico, and the ways in which past colonialist racial and cultural formations impacted how Mexicanos imagined themselves within a newly emerging colonialist system (the United States). Reading a history like Sierra O'Reilly's in tandem with more canonical histories of the U.S.-Mexican War reveals the complex cultural and racial negotiations and formations that were taking place in the mid-nineteenth century in both the United States and Mexico.

Sierra O'Reilly imagines an alternative geopolitical configuration of Yucatán and the borders of the Mexican nation and, more importantly, an alternative cultural configuration of inter-American alliances. It is important to point out that this was a configuration that only certain communities and certain groups of people in Spanish America could imagine as a possibility. For the most part, only light-skinned elites who lived in communities that had experienced little direct military aggression from the United States (a dwindling minority by the end of the nineteenth century) could envision this type of relationship. Nonetheless, rather than dismissing Sierra O'Reilly's diary and other writings as anomalies, we may see how Sierra O'Reilly's writings fit into a much larger and longer conversation about intercultural collaboration between Hispanos and Anglo Americans. His writing evokes a period when national identity in America was still being contested and nations were still being mapped—culturally, politically, and geographically. A nonteleological history such as this one can serve as a way of examining and bringing to light the silences, repressions, and anxieties about race and community that are part of a shared, broadly American history. This history is evidence of an alternative imagined community, one not based on the nation as we know and recognize it today.

The Return of the Repressed and a
Return to Paseo de Montejo

The Monumento a la Patria, dedicated to the Mexican nation, is perhaps the most eye-catching monument along the Paseo de Montejo—the stately boulevard in Mérida, Yucatán, described at the beginning of this chapter. The massive monument depicts a mixture of pre-Hispanic indigenous figures and iconography, as well as key historical scenes and actors from independence through the Mexican Revolution.[65] Unveiled in 1956, it presents Mexico as it was envisioned by the mid-twentieth century: a centralized and unified nation that writes out fragmentation and difference even as it celebrates mestizaje. A statue of an eagle devouring a serpent while sitting atop a cactus is one of the most striking details of the monument. This eagle is also the emblem on the Mexican flag and is part of the founding mythology of Tenochtitlan— the Mexica capital on which Mexico City, the symbolic center and capital of present-day Mexico, was subsequently built.[66] This statue is therefore particularly laden with meaning for *central* Mexico—but it does not necessarily have the same significance for Yucatecos, and especially for indigenous communities in Yucatán. The image of the eagle devouring a serpent while perched on a cactus was part of Mexica foundational mythology, but it was not part of any foundational mythology for the Maya, the predominant indigenous group in Yucatán. Moreover, Yucatán has a long history of separatism, including, as we have already seen, secession from central Mexico. The prominent position of the eagle, in combination with the other components of the Monumento a la Patria, however, reminds observers—and particularly Yucatecos—that Yucatán, too, is Mexico. The Colombian sculptor (in yet another great irony, he was not Mexican) of the Monumento a la Patria, Rómulo Rozo Peña, himself reflected on the monument's significance, stating, "Es un altar a la patria para borrar del espíritu nacional las ideas sobre el separatismo yucateco. La patria es todos y para todos"[67] [It is an altar to the fatherland to erase from the national spirit ideas about Yucatecan separatism. The nation is everyone and for everyone]. As the mixture of European, indigenous, and mestizo iconography similarly attests, everyone is hypothetically included in this mestizo nation, but they are first and foremost Mexicans.

A more probing look at and comparison with the other monuments spread along the Paseo de Montejo, however, reveals dimensions to this supposed shared history and culture that are not adequately addressed or represented in the Monumento a la Patria. This monument dedicated to the nation(al) in fact masks a hidden history of division, fragmentation, and internal colonization. The alluring image of an inclusive and harmonious Mexico, represented through the incorporation of Maya and Aztec iconography celebrating the nation's indigenous past, is undercut by the history of the boulevard and two monuments that stand at the opposite end of the boulevard from the Monumento a la Patria: the monument dedicated to Justo Sierra O'Reilly and a new monument erected in 2010 in honor of Francisco de Montejo, the first governor of Yucatán, and his son, Francisco de Montejo "el Mozo" (the Younger). These two monuments and the street itself speak to the forgotten parts of the history of Greater Mexico that are eclipsed by celebratory narratives of national union and mestizaje, such as the one seen in the Monumento a la Patria. They ask us to consider how histories are told and retold and what is left out of those retellings. When read against the grain, these memorials, like Sierra O'Reilly's diary and letters, document very different stories about the internal colonization and repression of indigenous communities and racial(ized) others in Greater Mexico, regional divisions within Greater Mexico, and the cultural and political exchange between elite Yucatecos and elite Anglos in the United States.

The Montejos (father, son, and nephew) were the first conquistadors of the Yucatán peninsula. The monument depicting Francisco de Montejo and his son and the boulevard named for them memorialize the conquistadors who brutally and violently conquered the indigenous communities of Yucatán.[68] In addition to being named for the Montejos, the street was built largely with money from the henequen industry, which depended heavily on coerced labor—primarily indigenous Maya, who were bound to a nearly inescapable system of debt peonage that many historians have described as akin to slavery.[69] In fact, to this day, "Yucatecos remember this time [of the henequen boom] as the 'Age of Slavery' (*la época de la esclavitud*)."[70] Moreover, as historian Allen Wells has shown, the success of the henequen industry, which made Mérida so prosperous for a time, was made possible in part through the collaboration between local elites and the U.S.-based International Harvester Company.[71] This collaborative relationship serves as a prime example of a new type of "invisible" or informal empire based on economic infiltration and domination.[72] The plaque on the monument, "A la memoria de los ilustres Sres. don Francisco de Montejo, Adelantado de Yucatán y de su hijo, don Fransisco, El Mozo" [To the memory of the illustrious gentlemen, don Francisco de Montejo, governor of Yucatán, and his son, don Francisco, the Younger], indicates that this monument is intended to celebrate the two men, who are considered founding fathers of Mérida. The statue and the street thus serve as reminders of Mérida's past, but with little recognition of the violence encapsulated in the images of these two men or the coerced labor of indigenous Maya on the henequen haciendas and the transnational networks of capitalist exploitation and informal imperialism that made the building of this avenue possible.

Completely lacking in self-awareness, this statue, which was erected in 2010, enacts further symbolic violence against present-day indigenous Maya in Yucatán by invoking this shared history and simultaneously concealing the violence that is an inseparable part of it. Although the Monumento a la Patria, sitting just a few blocks farther down the street, is intended to represent "everyone" and be "for everyone," as the sculptor claimed, the statue of the Montejos looking out over the boulevard reveals the mestizaje celebrated in the Monumento a la Patria to be a fiction that flattens a complex history of ethnic and racial violence. This violence, which continues today in systematic if not outright violent ways, is particularly aimed at indigenous communities.[73]

This flattened history is reproduced yet again through the statue of Justo Sierra O'Reilly. As already discussed, Sierra O'Reilly's seeking of annexation in the United States reflects the deep racial and ethnic divisions within Yucatán. Yet as with the Montejo monument, the history of regional and ethnoracial divisionism is not the aspect that is usually emphasized or widely circulated in the narratives created and told about Sierra O'Reilly.[74] Yucatecos today still understand and portray him as a founding father of whom they should be proud.

A more pointed assessment of the men memorialized on the Paseo de Montejo reveals, therefore, the intimate connection between the celebratory, inclusive mestizaje of the Monumento a la Patria and the histories of racism and colonialism encapsulated in the statues of the Montejos and Sierra O'Reilly. Together with the presence of international businesses such as the McDonald's and Walmart along the Paseo de Montejo, they draw attention to a long tradition of *trans*national economic and political community building that has been written out of national(ized) Mexican and U.S. histories. And they also reveal the racial, ethnic, cultural, and socioeconomic hierarchies and divisions that made the imagining of these sorts of transnational communities possible—and that were similarly erased from narratives of Greater Mexico as this community moved toward consolidation.

Economic imperialism is often seen as a relatively recent phenomenon, something that starts in the twentieth century. Sierra O'Reilly's writings, however, indicate that this is not the case. Although Sierra O'Reilly never realized his vision for a new sort of "benevolent," civilizing, and whitening imperialism, his writings index the power and longevity of this discourse in Greater Mexico and, more broadly, Spanish America.

The Monumento a la Patria, with its effusive celebration of Mexican nationalism and mestizaje, thus writes over a much darker history of Yucatán and Greater Mexico—one in which elites worked to establish their position in an international community at the expense of racial(ized) others. At the same time, however, the Monumento a la Patria might also be understood as standing in defiance against the Walmart and McDonald's—to new forms of imperialism. Metaphorically, this monument, like Sierra O'Reilly's writings, thus represents the complexities and ambiguities of nationalism in Greater Mexico. It contests U.S. imperialism, but it does so on sometimes problematic and exclusionary grounds by writing over many other divisions and histories of violence *within* Mexico in order to present a unified front. The nation, as seen here and through the writings of Sierra O'Reilly, is being constantly negotiated and rewritten. It can be, and is, both a source of liberation and a mode of oppression.

The Paseo de Montejo and its monuments—the 2010 monument dedicated to the Montejos, the statue of Justo Sierra O'Reilly, and the Monumento a la Patria—demonstrate the different sorts of colonization and also collaboration that are part of the history of Yucatán. They are a reflection not only of historical experience but also of how that experience has been recorded/ remembered—or forgotten. My analysis of Sierra O'Reilly's diary, jointly with this examination of the modern-day boulevard, brings to light the types of collaboration and negotiation that were, and are, taking place among elites from multiple locales throughout Greater Mexico and the Americas. It speaks simultaneously to the expansive limits of "Greater Mexico" and how the local was, and is, influenced by the transnational—how local elites could conceive of themselves as white because of broader American discourses. Although Sierra O'Reilly's hopes for a transnational coalition ultimately never came to fruition, a glance down the Paseo de Montejo shows that this early attempt would not be the last.

3

A Transnational Romance

María Amparo Ruiz de Burton's *Who Would Have Thought It?*

Writing in 1860 from Norwich, Vermont, to her good friend, the wealthy *ranchero*, politician, and former military commander of Alta California, Mariano Guadalupe Vallejo,[1] María Amparo Ruiz de Burton reflected with melancholy on her past year spent on the U.S. East Coast: "Cuántos cambios en el corto espacio de un solo año ¡Una sola vuelta alrededor del sol y es tan penosa la vista retrospectiva, que no quiero mirarla! Qué mentira es esa de llamar 'memoria feliz' la facultad de no olvidar a pesar de uno mismo!" (*Conflicts*, 240) [How many changes in the short space of only one year. One single spin around the sun and the retrospective view is so sad that I don't even want to look at it! What a lie it is to call "happy memory" the inability to forget, despite oneself].[2] In 1859, she had moved from her native California, away from her friends and family, into a completely different culture and environment in the eastern United States.

But it was not just the last year that had been full of changes for Ruiz de Burton. Born in Baja California (Mexico) circa 1832, María Amparo Maytorena Ruiz immigrated to Alta California (which later became the U.S. state of California) in 1848.[3] Under the provisions of the Treaty of Guadalupe Hidalgo, she became a U.S. citizen, and in 1849, shortly after her move from Baja to Alta California, she married Henry S. Burton, a captain in the U.S. Army who had commanded soldiers in Baja California during the U.S.-Mexican War. As the wife of an active U.S. military commander, she traveled extensively throughout the United States, especially the East Coast, thus allowing her ample opportunity to reflect on the differences between Mexico and the United States and her experiences living between and within both Anglo and Mexicano cultures.[4] Thus her life, in many ways, encapsulates the immense changes and uncertainty that Mexican Americans experienced in the decades following the end of the U.S.-Mexican War in 1848 as they grappled with what it means to simultaneously identify with more than one country, culture, and language. As she traveled through and learned about the United States, Ruiz de Burton, like other Mexican Americans, was exposed to new ways of organizing society—a binary (black/white) racial hierarchy into which Mexicanos did not easily fit and a government that professed to uphold republican values of freedom and equality but in practice denied many of those rights and privileges to those deemed racially suspect or undesirable.[5]

In that same letter from June 23, 1860, Ruiz de Burton nonetheless entreats her friend, Mariano, to come visit her in the "Yankee nation," and she comments on how her time in the eastern United States has prompted her to make comparisons between the two countries in which she has lived:

> Ud. también es necesario que se venga a dar una paseada, que pase un invierno en Washington, y vea qué gran humbug es esta Yankie nation. Un humbug tan sistemado [sic] y bien sostenido que aun ellos mismos casi lo creen. Mucho hay que ver en E.U. y mucho que hace pensar, particularmente si uno empieza a hacer comparaciones. Realmente para apreciar bien una cosa es necesario mirar bien otra. (*Conflicts*, 244)

> [You need to come and visit here, spend a winter in Washington, and see what a great humbug this Yankee nation is. Such a great and sustained humbug that even they themselves almost believe it. There is so much that needs to be seen in the U.S. and much that makes one think, especially if one starts to make comparisons. To really appreciate a thing fully, it is necessary to look closely at another.]

Her description of the eastern United States as a great "humbug"—a "thing which is not really what it pretends to be," or a type of deception, pretense, or sham—but one that must be nonetheless seen and experienced, emphasizes her fascination and also disenchantment with a confusing and perplexing new country and culture that seemed to deceive her and everyone else, including Anglo Americans.[6] As her letter indicates, the decades following the U.S.-Mexican War were another period of transition and immense change, of uncertainty but also possibility for Mexicanos from throughout Greater Mexico as they determined their relationship within this new, foreign, "humbug" nation.

Although the U.S.-Mexican War is often viewed as *the* defining moment for Mexican Americans and, more broadly, Greater Mexico in the nineteenth century, this tendency to focus on the war itself overlooks how grappling with the *aftermath* of war—the experiences that Ruiz de Burton documents in her letters and other writings—entails perhaps an even greater transformation of individuals and the society in which they live. In this chapter, I examine how Ruiz de Burton's first novel, *Who Would Have Thought It?* (1872), reimagines the possibilities for transnational and intercultural collaboration between Mexicanos and Anglos in the second half of the nineteenth century during this period of uncertainty. Like the other authors I have discussed so far, Ruiz de Burton similarly relies on diverse discourses of civilization and whiteness, contrasted with discourses of barbarism and blackness, as a way of linking elites from across the Americas. In the novel, Ruiz de Burton returns in time to two recent and pivotal moments in American history, the French Intervention in Mexico (1861–1867) and the U.S. Civil War (1861–1865), in order to show how elite Anglos and Mexicanos share similar European roots and a similar capacity to overcome barbarism in the future.

While reflecting on these two past moments of change, Ruiz de Burton also speculates about the present and future of Greater Mexico and the place of Mexicanos in a hemispheric, cosmopolitan, modernizing project—but one that is built on its own imperialist and racist foundations. Her trafficking in social and racial hierarchies is an attempt to navigate the uncertain times for Mexicanos following the U.S.-Mexican War, just as her parodies of New England culture are similarly invested in working through the turmoil of Reconstruction in the United States. When understood as a novel in conversation with discourses in Greater Mexico and Spanish America, not just as a U.S.-centered novel, it can be seen that *Who Would Have Thought It?* relies on and upholds many problematic racial and social hierarchies that placed elite Mexicanos at the top at the expense of African Americans in the United States and indigenous communities within Greater Mexico. *Who Would Have Thought It?*, a text that travels between and across borders of many different sorts, speaks to the obscured literary and cultural tradition that I have highlighted in previous chapters—a tradition that sought out and worked to establish affinities between elites in Greater Mexico and the United States, but on problematic and ever-shifting grounds of inclusion and exclusion. I begin this chapter with a discussion of the literary, historical, and cultural contexts in which Ruiz de Burton was writing and living, as well as an assessment of the novel's place within the Latino and U.S. American literary canon. I then consider the use of the captivity narrative in the novel as a commentary on the multiple and overlapping histories of colonialism in Greater Mexico and as a means by which Ruiz de Burton establishes both the elite status and, paradoxically, the victimhood of Mexican Americans such as Lola. I subsequently explore Lola's position within competing racial hierarchies and how Ruiz de Burton envisions Mexican Americans' elite position in both U.S. and Mexican structures. And

I end with a consideration of the ways in which the novel links Mexicano and Anglo elites through similar histories of fragmentation and potential future unions, thus speculating on the limits and shortcomings of republicanism as well as the possibilities of transnational and collaborative networks of belonging for elite Americans.

The Politics of Novel-Writing

The second half of the nineteenth century witnessed several moments of profound instability in Mexico, most notably the War of Reform (1857–1860), which was essentially a civil war, and the French Intervention and Second Mexican Empire (1861–1867), which returned monarchy to Mexico. Mexicans ousted the French and restored republican governance in 1867, but nearly fifty years of political infighting, economic collapses, foreign invasions, massive losses of territory, and civil war had left Mexico and Mexicans anxious and self-reflective about the future of their nation.[7]

This was also a particularly uncertain time for those Mexicanos living on the U.S. side of the newly redefined border. As a member of the Californio[8] elite, María Amparo Ruiz de Burton witnessed firsthand the social, cultural, and political transformation of Mexicanos within the U.S. political system after the U.S.-Mexican War.[9] Newly part of the United States, at least nominally, Mexican Americans like Ruiz de Burton found themselves thrust into a black/white racial binary that was not designed to accommodate the complex racial and cultural hierarchies with which Mexicanos identified.[10] In the United States, politicians and the dominant Anglo American public debated how to incorporate a population that was "not quite white," even when often legally defined as white, into the country during and following the U.S.-Mexican War.[11] These debates reflect the anxieties in the United States (and the Americas) about racial contamination and the limits of U.S. citizenship when it came to groups and individuals who were considered racially suspect. During Reconstruction after the U.S. Civil War, racial categories became perhaps even more important and more policed in a society trying to reassert and maintain racial divisions in a new postslavery context.[12]

In that same 1860 letter in which Ruiz de Burton describes the United States as a "great humbug," she also considers the best method or vehicle for reflecting on the great changes she has experienced, the problems she has observed in the United States, and the differences she has noted between Mexico and the United States. She ponders her options and finally declares to her friend Vallejo that "Creo que lo mejor que yo puedo hacer es escribir un libro. ¿Qué tal? ¿No lo leería? ¿No quiere que lo haga uno de mis héroes?" (*Conflicts*, 244) [I think the best thing I can do is write a book. What do you think? Wouldn't you read it? Would you like me to make you one of my heroes?].

It is significant that she recognizes that writing a book is the best way for her to reflect on these changes, because it is in the second half of the nineteenth century when the novel gains popularity and prestige as a literary form.[13] And as numerous scholars of U.S. and Spanish American literature and culture have shown, it is precisely in this period that the novel establishes itself as a key vehicle for commentary on and creation of national identities in the Americas.[14]

More than ten years after writing this letter, with her husband dead and her finances in shambles, Ruiz de Burton returned to her native California, where she did in fact write and publish two books, the novels *Who Would Have Thought It?* (1872) and *The Squatter and the Don* (1885), which draw heavily on her familiarity with both California and New England (and *The Squatter and the Don* does indeed contain a heroic character modeled after her friend Mariano Guadalupe Vallejo).[15] Her novels, written in English, allow her readers to explore the people and the culture of the newly acquired Southwest territories and reflect on Anglo American culture and U.S. politics through both direct and indirect comparison with Greater Mexico. They also offer a window into this period of immense change and anxiety for Mexican Americans and serve as a meditation on their changing relationship with both Anglo America and Mexico.

As the wife of a high-ranking army officer, Ruiz de Burton was an insider to mainstream Anglo culture in the United States, gaining access to elite circles in the government. However, as a Mexican American, Catholic, and woman, she was at the same time perpetually an outsider.[16] She was a lifelong critic of the U.S. government and never felt truly "at home" in Anglo society, identifying as a native of California and Mexico first and foremost.[17] While Lorenzo de Zavala and Justo Sierra O'Reilly traveled the United States as political exiles or government appointees, Ruiz de Burton was a traveler of a different sort, living in a sort of self-imposed exile while still maintaining ties to both Greater Mexico and Anglo America.

Ruiz de Burton's work represents a shift in how political and cultural work could be done and by whom—not just men but also women. Her work in shaping and commenting on her community of Greater Mexico is realized through the genre of fiction rather than through the political essay, travel narrative, or official governmental work. In the latter half of the nineteenth century, writers from throughout the Americas, especially women, became astutely aware of the political power of the novel and its potentially broad reach in society. One need look no further for evidence than *Uncle Tom's Cabin*, which readers gobbled up in all parts of the United States and abroad.[18] The novel was deemed so powerful, in fact, that it was banned in many U.S. Southern states after it was credited for encouraging slaves to run away and inducing white readers to spontaneously emancipate their own slaves.[19] Particularly following periods of internal conflict, such as civil wars or rebellions, novels also offered a mode of metaphorical reconciliation for diverse communities.[20] For women, who in both Latin America and the United States could not directly influence public opinion through voting or running for office, writing a novel was a way to comment on items of national concern and insert themselves into national and international debates about social and political matters.[21] The novel, particularly the sentimental or domestic novel, genres with which Ruiz de Burton engages in both of her novels, was a genre more open to and more acceptable for women, as both readers and writers.[22] Indeed, in the United States, women dominated the popular reading public for much of the nineteenth century—so much so that Nathaniel Hawthorne once infamously lamented to his friend and publisher, William Ticknor, that "America is now wholly given over to a damned mob of scribbling women, and I should have no chance of success while the public is occupied with their trash."[23]

Ruiz de Burton was extremely well read and multilingual and stayed abreast of current political issues in the United States, Mexico, and abroad.[24] She was also an avid writer in both public and private mediums. She maintained long-term correspondence with individuals across the country in both Spanish and English, published newspaper articles, and wrote at least two plays and even a legal brief, in addition to her two novels.[25] Through her written work, she helped construct an identity for her community, but she also saw herself as representing her culture and her people for an international community. Her choice to write her novels in English, for instance, could be understood in part as an attempt to educate others outside of Mexico or California about the positive attributes of her community and culture, thus combatting negative stereotypes of Mexicanos.[26] Ruiz de Burton was a type of what Kirsten Silva Gruesz calls an "ambassador of culture."[27] As Gruesz explains, "ambassadors of culture" were concerned with "translating" their ideas for a broad, transnational audience; they helped create connections, coalitions, and points of common ground across national and cultural borders. As part of the Californio elite and the wife of a U.S. Army officer, Ruiz de Burton had to negotiate the differences between diverse cultures and languages. She also quite literally crossed multiple borders as she traveled between Mexico and the United States, carefully navigating between Anglo and Mexican cultures, even within her bicultural and bilingual family household. In 1859, she moved with her family to the East Coast, where her husband served in the Union Army during the Civil War. She changed residence frequently with her children in order to be close to her husband as he was transferred to different military camps throughout the East. In fewer than ten years, Ruiz de Burton lived in Rhode Island, New York, Washington, D.C., Delaware, and Virginia. After her husband's death in 1869, she and her children moved back to San Diego, although she continued to travel throughout the United States and Mexico until her death in 1895.[28] Ruiz de Burton was thus intimately familiar with both East

Coast Anglo America and the Mexican American communities that she writes about in her novels.[29]

Her first novel, *Who Would Have Thought It?* (1872),[30] mimics her own biography as it tells the story of transnational travelers, cultural negotiation, and intercultural collaboration. Many of the characters in *Who Would Have Thought It?* are cultural workers and international travelers, just like Ruiz de Burton.[31] They travel to multiple locales in the United States, Mexico, Europe, and Africa. Although the narrative does not describe the characters in every destination they visit, we do see them in a plethora of very distinct locations: the U.S. Southwest, New England, New York City, Washington, D.C., central Mexico, and several different places in the U.S. South.

The novel opens in the years preceding the U.S. Civil War. Dr. Norval has just returned to his New England home after a four-year absence in which he has been in the newly acquired territories of the U.S. Southwest looking for mineral and geological samples for his collections of scientific specimens. Upon his homecoming, his very proper Protestant wife and daughters are shocked to find that he has brought to their home a "specimen" of the animal sort: a dark-skinned ten-year-old girl whom Mrs. Norval quickly labels a "little girl very black indeed."[32] Although Mrs. Norval calls herself an abolitionist, she is disgusted by the blackness of the girl and angry with her husband for having brought a black child into her home. As the story unravels, we find that Lola, the child, is actually not of African or Indian descent but a Mexican of "pure Spanish blood."[33] During his expedition to the Southwest, Dr. Norval encountered a group of Indians who had been holding captive a Spanish woman and her daughter for ten years. Through a series of flashbacks, we learn that Lola's mother begged Dr. Norval to take her daughter away from the Indians, attempt to find the child's father, and take charge of Lola's Catholic education until the girl's family could be found or until Lola came of age to marry. In return for his help, Doña Theresa Medina (Lola's mother) offered Dr. Norval a handsome percentage of a large fortune of gold, diamonds, and other precious jewels she had collected while in captivity.

The rest of the novel narrates events that take place during the Civil War (1861–1864). Lola lives under the cruel gaze of her pseudostepmother, Mrs. Norval, who barely tolerates Lola's presence. Lola's blackface turns out to be a dye that the Indians had forced Lola and her mother to wear in order to conceal their true, non-Indian identities. As it fades, she is described as becoming more and more beautiful, eventually winning the heart of Julian Norval, the oldest son in the family. Because of political pressures for his criticism of the Civil War, Dr. Norval leaves the country in a type of semivoluntary exile, heading to Africa for another field expedition. However, when news comes back that Dr. Norval is missing and presumed dead, Mrs. Norval relocates herself and her daughters to a posh New York City mansion, where they use Lola's inheritance to fund their luxurious lifestyle. Mrs. Norval clandestinely marries Reverend Hackwell, the supposedly pious but actually corrupt preacher who attempts to trap Lola into marriage. Lola's father is finally located in Mexico; Dr. Norval returns, alive, from Africa; and Lola narrowly escapes the clutches of Reverend Hackwell to join her father in Mexico. As the novel closes, Mrs. Norval is ill or has gone mad upon the news of her husband's unexpected return, and Lola and Julian will reunite in Mexico, marry, and begin their life there, together with Lola's wealthy father and her own immense fortune.

Rosaura Sánchez and Beatrice Pita, leading Hispanic literary recovery project scholars, have astutely interpreted *Who Would Have Thought It?* as a "parody of both the early sentimental novel and the mid-nineteenth-century novel of domesticity."[34] Ruiz de Burton is indeed very concerned with the role of U.S. domestic culture and its relation to the foreign. Through her satire of corrupt politicians, immoral Protestant leaders, and greedy and intolerant women who supposedly represent the epitome of republican motherhood, Ruiz de Burton voices a strong critique of Anglo American values as represented in East Coast society. Lola, for example, provides a means for the Norval women to advance in society and become part of modern New York City and its culture. The Norval women are able to participate in "modernity," largely represented by popular fashions and expensive clothing, by exploiting Lola's financial reserves—in this case, quite literally the resources and riches pilfered from the U.S. Southwest, which was once a Mexican territory. As Sánchez and Pita observe, Lola's story thus "constructs an allegory of the modernization of the U.S. attained through plunder, corruption, and war."[35] Ruiz de Burton makes it clear to her readers that the United States has benefited at the expense of others, most notably Mexicanos. Her critique of the United States goes deeper than just an anti-imperial impetus, though; she ridicules nearly every aspect of her contemporary U.S. society, that vast "humbug" nation.

From this disparagement of U.S. empire and Anglo American society, a number of literary critics have concluded that Ruiz de Burton speaks for a subaltern "other" who subverts Anglo American hegemony through its construction of an oppositional Latin American community.[36] For these critics, Ruiz de Burton thus becomes a voice of the underrepresented and a subversive voice within U.S. politics, culture, and society. My examination of *Who Would Have Thought It?*, however, builds upon more recent criticism that has begun to problematize the view of Ruiz de Burton as a subaltern figure or a voice for a cohesive Latin American / Latino community.[37] The idea of a unified pan-Latino community that stands in subversive defiance to Anglo America is certainly alluring.[38] But although critics have repeatedly mentioned the significance of a pan-Latino community and the creation or existence of a transnational *latinidad* in *Who Would Have Thought It?*, most critics nonetheless focus on the novel within a U.S. American context, with much attention given to Ruiz de Burton's critique of U.S. empire and Lola's relationship to Anglo American society and Anglo American characters in the novel—and very little attention given to Lola's relationship to Mexico, Greater Mexico, or the Mexicano or indigenous characters in the novel.[39]

Lola, born in 1847, during the U.S.-Mexican War, in the U.S.-Mexican borderlands, and with a Mexican mother and an "adoptive" Anglo American family, certainly symbolizes a new Mexican American community that must fight against the prejudices and ignorance of Anglo Americans as they search for their place in a new social, cultural, and political context post-1848.[40] But she also represents a contemplation of the new and changing relationship between Mexican Americans and Mexico (and perhaps the rest of Latin America). In my reading of the novel, I examine how Ruiz de Burton engages with and imagines this broader hemispheric community of elites in her novel, with a focus on Greater Mexico and the Mexican side of the border. Ruiz de Burton and her novel speak to an alternative imagining of community rooted in deeply hierarchical and problematic notions of race and culture that at this time are perhaps just as powerful as notions of national identity. Her novel exposes the fractures and divisions within the communities of Greater Mexico and also who is left out of this imagined cohesive community. This alternative imagining of a transnational community of American elites, once a possibility for writers and cultural workers such as Ruiz de Burton, has now largely been forgotten, but to remember it is to recognize the different forms of violence, coercion, and internal fragmentation that were an essential part of life in Greater Mexico and the Americas.

Colonialism(s) in *Who Would Have Thought It?*
Lola and *Latinidad*

Anglo America is definitely a central object of critique for Ruiz de Burton in *Who Would Have Thought It?* Yet this novel is not just about the Anglo side of the border. To begin with, it was written by a woman who was born on the Mexican side of the borderlands. Furthermore, the seed of the novel starts in the borderlands region with Lola and her mother's captivity; much of the novel is told from the perspective of Lola, whose family comes from Mexico; and the events in the novel take place in multiple locales, including Mexico, not solely in New England or the northern side of the U.S.-Mexican border. As I will show, *Who Would Have Thought It?* depicts multiple types of colonialism. Through Lola and her family, the novel contemplates the place of elite Mexicanos within both Mexican and U.S. racial, cultural, and social hierarchies. When we examine *Who Would Have Thought It?* and the spaces and people it depicts on or from both sides of the border, Lola, as an embodiment of a new Mexican American community, represents both a remnant of an old social order (in Mexico) and a harbinger of a new imagined hemispheric social order in which Lola is also part of the white elite colonizers. Through the character of Lola and her stories of captivity, Ruiz de Burton shows the cultural, social, and ethnoracial schisms that were a part of the communities of Greater Mexico on both sides of the border.

To start, we should consider how the novel itself begins: with a captivity narrative. Captivity was a common trope in borderland or frontier literature in both Spanish America and the United States. Captivity narratives almost always share a common general scheme. As Robert McKee Irwin explains, there is almost always a "fair white maiden being abducted by barbaric indigenous American captors."[41] Lola's story follows the formula quite well. These types of narratives in turn "fed racial tensions among whites by portraying indigenous Americans as dangerously violent, animalistically irrational, and with a propensity to rape helpless females."[42] As numerous literary critics have established, captivity narratives helped justify the conquest of new lands and the elimination of Indians, who posed a threat to the sexual and racial purity of the nation, embodied by the virtuous white woman.[43] The captivity narrative in *Who Would Have Thought It?* thereby highlights Lola's whiteness by contrasting her with the barbaric indigenous "other" from whom she must be rescued if she is to preserve her racial and sexual purity.[44]

But Doña Theresa and Lola's captivity also serves as a reminder of how whiteness worked within Greater Mexico. Indigenous groups were considered the barbaric and dangerous "other" not just in the United States but also in nineteenth-century northwestern Mexico. If Lola represents Greater Mexico on some level, as I and other critics contend, then the captivity narrative in the novel highlights how a large portion of the population of Greater Mexico is not included in the concept of community encapsulated in the figure of Lola. For example, when Dr. Norval comes upon Lola and her mother in the Southwest, Doña Theresa arranges Lola's escape with the doctor, remarking, "Thank God, Lolita is away from those horrid savages!"[45] Later in the novel, reflecting on Doña Theresa's fate, the narrator remarks that the kidnapping of people like Doña Theresa would not be possible if "Mexico were well governed" and protected its frontiers.[46] The narrator concludes, "When it is a well-known fact that savages will devastate towns that are not well guarded, is there any excuse for a government that will neglect to provide sufficient protection?"[47] The so-called savages are viewed as the deterrent to civilization and order; they do not form part of the Mexican national community. In fact, they are portrayed as one of the root causes of the breakdown of both the nation and the family unit, and they open up the nation to a new type of savagery: U.S. imperialism, exemplified by the invasion of Mexico during the U.S.-Mexican War and the appropriation of Mexican territories at the end of the war. The narrator's statement also strongly critiques the Mexican government, which is partially to blame for Doña Theresa's kidnapping because it is unable to protect its "civilized" inhabitants or control the "savages" that threaten those inhabitants. The Mexican government and Indians are similarly part of the chaos and disorder that threaten civilization, represented by Lola and her family, as well as the community of elite criollos to which she and her family belong.

Lola's potential elite status and whiteness within the United States are predicated on her assumed position of power within the old Mexican social and cultural hierarchies. Numerous critics have rightly understood Mrs. Norval's coveting and control of Lola's gold and jewels as an allegory for the United States' exploitation and appropriation of Mexicano resources after the U.S.-Mexican War.[48] But it is also important to recognize that Lola's riches actually originate in Indian hands and that Indians were reduced to violent means of self-preservation (kidnapping, theft, ransom, etc.) in order to maintain their autonomy under oppressive forces from Europe, Mexico, and the United States. The novel clearly critiques the U.S. plunder of Mexican lands and resources through the Norval women's appropriation of Lola's riches. However, Ruiz de Burton also, perhaps inadvertently, exposes the pillage of Indian lands and communities at the hands of Mexicans and Spaniards as well as Anglo Americans.[49] Ruiz de Burton thus highlights the overlapping layers of colonial hierarchies that are a part of the history of Greater Mexico and the worldview of Mexican Americans in the nineteenth century. She also depicts Lola as deserving to be at the top of both systems: she is white and elite both in the past context (Mexico) and, therefore, potentially in the future one (the United States).

The captivity of Doña Theresa and Lola therefore should be understood not just as an effort to establish Lola's place as white within a U.S. context. It is also about her place within Greater Mexico and attests to the ways in which her future possibilities are structured on her past status within the old (Spanish-Mexican) colonialist system. Here we have an example of how the histories of two imperial forces overlap. Quite literally, two characters representing their respective colonial/imperial forces—Dr. Norval and Doña Theresa—cross paths and reproduce the multiple colonizations of Greater Mexico. Doña Theresa's acquisition of precious jewels from the Indians reenacts "in miniature the history of Spanish colonization of the Americas."[50] Dr. Norval explains that Doña Theresa was able to accumulate so many riches while in captivity because "the Indians brought her emeralds and rubies, seeing that she liked the pretty pebbles."[51] The infantilized Indians are portrayed as too naive to realize the worth of the diamonds, rubies, and other precious gems. Furthermore, they are portrayed as naturally obeying and actually working to please Doña Theresa, their seemingly natural superior, thus also reinforcing the false notion that Indians have a "natural disposition for manual labor."[52] Doña

Theresa, however, is not depicted as an oppressive colonial force. She is described throughout the book as "self-sacrificing";[53] "pure . . . , high-minded, refined, and delicate";[54] a "martyr . . . [and] an angel."[55] Doña Theresa is portrayed as the victim, not the oppressor. She is also the only one to rightfully identify the supposedly intrinsic value of the gold and other precious jewels, thereby marking herself as the rightful superior to the Indians, who, as their inability to recognize the value of the gold and jewels demonstrates, are not part of the civilized world and incapable of managing their own land and resources.[56]

Reading allegorically, the future—represented through the child, Lola, and also the jewels that represent raw economic potential—is passed from an aging empire, personified through the dying Doña Theresa, to a new imperialist and capitalist empire, represented by Dr. Norval, who colonizes through more covert means, such as "scientific" discovery, encyclopedic classification, and capitalist accumulation.[57] It is his responsibility to watch over the young and naive Lola and protect—not pilfer—her "rightful" riches. But his role is also to bring her into modern capitalist society. For instance, he decides that her gems should be cut and polished in order to be exchanged on the market, thus helping Lola turn her raw goods into currency. Dr. Norval's "benevolent" conquest, which incorporates Lola into civilization and capitalist modernity, goes awry, however, when he leaves Lola and her spoils under the influence of his corrupt(ed) wife.

Mrs. Norval's coveting and, later, outright theft of Lola's jewelry marks her not as a benevolent imperialist like her husband but as an oppressive and savage imperialist. After Mrs. Norval sends the jewelry with her daughters to Europe without the consent of her husband or Lola, Dr. Norval finds out about what she has done and chastises his wife.[58] Even Mrs. Norval knows that what she has done is wrong; she does not really attempt to justify her actions. Rather, her main concern is whether Dr. Norval is going to tell Lola "that she [Lola] is the owner of the money [the Norvals] have been spending, and impress her with the idea that [they] have been robbing her."[59] While Mrs. Norval is labeled a thief who exploits and then undeservedly benefits from Lola's riches, Ruiz de Burton goes to great lengths to show that both Doña Theresa and Lola are the victims—first, at the hands of their Indian captors and then, for Lola, at the hands of Mrs. Norval, the Anglo American aggressor, who keeps Lola and her money hostage in a new type of savage land, New England.[60] Inadvertently, however, the novel also exposes the colonialist systems that doubly disenfranchised indigenous communities in Mexico as well as the United States. Indeed, the disenfranchisement of Indians in Greater Mexico is so complete in the novel that it is represented as neither subjugation nor violence; it appears, paradoxically, only as an absence. Lola and her mother are, in the narrator's view, the rightful owners of the jewels: they are the only ones portrayed as being robbed of their due riches, and they are the main victims in this captivity narrative.

The metaphor is potent: the United States has the potential, under the proper guidance and with the right moral imperialist at the helm (Dr. Norval), to help rather than hinder its fellow struggling American nations, such as Mexico. It could, for example, help Mexico convert its natural resources into economic power on the capitalist market. Moreover, as I will discuss in more detail later, the equitable union of these two nations, the old (Mexico) and the new (the United States), might prove to be beneficial for both countries in the long run. But corruption and greed, embodied by Mrs. Norval, have turned this potentially benevolent conquest into merely more barbaric imperialism—a supposedly modern but also savagely capitalist imperialism.

From Colonialism to Barbarism: American Savagery

Ruiz de Burton's contrast between Indian barbarians and civilized Euro-Americans hearkens back to the dichotomy of civilization and barbarism, which we also saw in my earlier discussions of Zavala and Sierra O'Reilly in the first half of the nineteenth century. Indeed, this was a pervasive dichotomy in the canonical and ephemeral literature of Greater Mexico (and, more broadly, Latin America), such as the travel diaries and narratives of Zavala and Sierra O'Reilly (discussed in chapters 1 and 2). One of the cornerstones of Spanish American literature (still read and taught in schools today), for instance, is Domingo Faustino Sarmiento's *Facundo: Civilización y barbarie* (1845), which represents Argentine Indians and gauchos as the impediments and antitheses to progress and civilization in Argentina. *Who Would Have Thought It?* marks a moment when these discourses were evolving and changing, although not disappearing. The novel contrasts with earlier representations and discussions of this dichotomy in Greater Mexico, which set out a clear binary between civilized Euro-Americans (criollos) and uncivilized indigenous communities. While indigenous groups are certainly still portrayed as the epitome of savagery in *Who Would Have Thought It?*, Ruiz de Burton also brings in two very different notions of civilization: the modern U.S. nation and elite Europeanized communities in central Mexico. Even though the United States enjoys the material comforts of progress (railroads, the telegraph, etc.), it is a morally and politically corrupt society with a shallow and materialistic view of culture. Mexico as a whole, on the other hand, is not portrayed as being materially modern. We do not see an overabundance of signs of progress like we do in the numerous descriptions of trains, telegraphs, and so on in New England. But the novel shows that what Mexico lacks in industrial development, it more than makes up for in the cultural sophistication of its elites. Ruiz de Burton thus anticipates later Spanish American *modernistas* like José Martí and José

Enrique Rodó, who rejected U.S. utilitarian materialism. In his canonical essay *Ariel* (1900), Rodó critiques Anglo American utilitarianism and rejects "nordomanía," the pervasive attraction to U.S. material culture. He proposes instead the cultivation of spiritual, cultural, and artistic innovations as a way of combating U.S. imperialism.[61]

While Ruiz de Burton does not necessarily reject all aspects of material modernity, she speaks to a similar tradition of thought when she highlights the barbarity of modern materialists and the nouveau riche. Her use of the captivity narrative—Lola's captivity in the Southwest and in New England, under the watchful eye of her adoptive stepmother, Mrs. Norval—highlights two different groups of savages who, though different, are nonetheless both threats to Mexicanos (and especially Mexicanas): Indians and Yankees.[62] Ruiz de Burton thus attempts to rework the civilization-barbarism dichotomy with a triangulation among Indians, Anglo Americans, and elite Mexicanos. Indians continue to represent the barbaric side of American culture in every aspect. But while the United States enjoys a level of material success, Ruiz de Burton shows that morally and culturally, the United States is much less civilized than (elite) Mexico. Mexico might not be as materially developed, in terms of industry or technology, as the United States, but the novel shows that its elites embody the true spirit of modernity in other ways—culturally, artistically, intellectually, and morally.

Ruiz de Burton thus critiques the United States on several different levels in the novel. Yet at the same time, she also reinforces the racial and cultural hierarchies that existed in Mexico in the nineteenth century—remnants of Spain's own empire in America. With the captivity narrative in *Who Would Have Thought It?*, we must consider who is left yet further marginalized by the story: in this case, the indigenous communities of the U.S.-Mexico borderlands. The indigenous characters serve seemingly contradictory but actually complementary purposes: they foreground the victimhood of Doña Theresa and Lola while simultaneously establishing their whiteness, civilization, and therefore their justifiable and "rightful" conquest of indigenous communities in the U.S.-Mexican borderlands. As Doña Theresa and the narrator's remarks about the "savages" illustrate, the novel thereby openly shuns indigenous groups and rejects their participation in the nation—be it in Mexico or the United States. The indigenous communities portrayed in the novel are quite literally liminal to the nation. They are nomadic and pass back and forth across the national boundary between the United States and Mexico. In addition, they do not belong to and are not desired as community members in either the United States or Mexico. They are relegated to a politically, ideologically, and physically liminal space.

Race, Culture, and Blackness in *Who Would Have Thought It?*

The new Mexican American community that Ruiz de Burton imagines through the character of Lola embraces neither racial mestizaje nor a multiracial national community, but as I will discuss next, she does envision a place of privilege and power for Mexican Americans within a new hemispheric community of white elites through representations of Lola's rightful place within ethnoracial hierarchies in both Mexico and the United States. When the reader of *Who Would Have Thought It?* first meets Lola, she is essentially wearing blackface. Her skin has been dyed a darker color by her Indian captors. As the black dye wears off, though, the narrator explains that Lola becomes whiter and more beautiful. The use of blackface brings race and racism to the forefront as key points of interest and concern in the novel. Blackness and the instability of whiteness are perhaps the principal anxieties of the novel.[63] As historian Matthew Frye Jacobson explains, the use of blackface highlights the "actor's [own] whiteness in stark relief" to the blackface of his character.[64] In other words, when white characters dress in blackface, they call attention to the difference between their "true" skin color and that of the black character being played, thereby affirming their own whiteness. In the context of *Who Would Have Thought It?*, Lola's blackface serves a similar purpose: her whiteness and European features are so prominent that her Indian captors must dye her skin so that strangers cannot immediately recognize her for what she is: non-Indian and white. The only way for her to pass as an Indian or dark-skinned person is to physically alter the color of her skin, thus actually emphasizing her underlying identity as white.

Mrs. Norval and the rest of the community in New England largely reject Lola when she appears in her initial blackface; they do not treat her as an equal. Her blackface also serves as a marker of the fear of racial contamination. Mrs. Norval is even convinced that Lola's fading blackface, which leaves her temporarily with dark spots on her skin, is evidence of some sort of contagious skin disease and repeatedly refers to her as a "horrible little negro girl."[65] But a few years later, when Lola returns to the Norval household from her stay at a convent where she has been attending school, her complexion has lightened and she has become as white as any of the New Englanders. Indeed, everyone comments on her whiteness—partially because of the radical change in her appearance. By the end of the novel, Lola's beauty as a now fully white Spanish lady outshines that of both of the Norval daughters, and several white Anglo American men vie for Lola's hand in marriage.

This uncovering of masks is yet one more critique of U.S. society: the supposedly freedom-loving, abolitionist New England is in reality quite racist. Mrs. Norval, for instance, is known by her friends and community as "a good abolitionist in talk, . . . [but not] in practice."[66] Although she self-identifies as an abolitionist, her comments about the "horrible little negro girl" reveal that she is in fact bigoted and intolerant.[67] She openly shuns the black characters depicted in the novel, as when she first meets Lola and exclaims, "'How black she is!' . . . with a slight shiver of disgust."[68] Mrs. Norval, like many of the novel's corrupt politicians and immoral churchgoers, does not practice what she preaches. Throughout the novel, there is a disconnect between the ideals of U.S. Americans and their actual practice. In reality, the actions of many characters often undermine the very ideals—such as freedom, equality, and democracy—that those same characters purport to uphold.

It is important that Ruiz de Burton focuses on New England and, later in the novel, Washington, D.C., as her centers of critique because they serve as metonymies of U.S. culture and government/politics, respectively. Washington, D.C., is, of course, the seat of the U.S. government, and New England is associated with the historical roots of U.S. cultural identity. It also came to represent the ideologies of capitalist "free labor" and the self-made yeoman— the republican values on which the country was supposedly founded.[69] Ruiz de Burton disparages New Englanders and politicians in Washington, D.C., and, through their symbolic weight, thereby also critiques the foundations of U.S. cultural and political identity. She shows that this dominant concept of national identity actually springs from a regional Northern outlook. Furthermore, this dominant concept of national identity has been militarily, culturally, and economically imposed on the rest of the United States—and perhaps all of the Americas—as the ideal for which all must strive, despite the flaws and inconsistencies in the practice of those ideals that we see in *Who Would Have Thought It?*

Ruiz de Burton uses characters like Mrs. Norval not only to point out that racism continued to exist in the United States, even in abolitionist communities, but also to critique the hypocritical nature of U.S. Northerners, who embraced abolition as an ideal but rejected African Americans in practice— and then imposed that same ideal on others. Indeed, as I have shown, the novel is not primarily interested in racial equality; rather, it is interested in uncovering the hypocrisy inherent in the very foundations of U.S. culture and politics and questioning the assumed association of civilization, republicanism, progress, and whiteness. Throughout the novel, Ruiz de Burton depicts people from multiple ethnoracial backgrounds in order to play with and expose two different sets of racial hierarchies and also place Lola (and Mexicanos) favorably within both. In the United States, she exposes a hierarchy that includes the categories of black, off-white, and white. In the nineteenth century, although people from certain parts of Europe, such as Ireland (as we see with the Irish maids in *Who Would Have Thought It?*), might not be considered fully white, they still benefitted from a degree of whiteness and often sought to maintain their uncertain whiteness and positions of relative power as free wage laborers through the support of slavery and at the expense of black freedom.[70] And in Mexico, she reveals a hierarchy based on the categories of Indian, mestizo, and criollo (or European-descended). She does not attempt to discard these hierarchies, but she does try to rewrite them in significant ways, with Lola at the top in both.

It is important that Ruiz de Burton chooses a heroine who is descended from "pure" Spanish blood. Dr. Norval explains Lola's blood lineage when he tells the story of the kidnapping of Lola's mother: "[Lola's mother] told us how she was carried off by the Apache Indians and then sold to the Mohave Indians, and how Lolita was born five months after her capture. So you see how Lolita's blood is pure Spanish blood, her mother being of pure Spanish descent and her father the same, though an Austrian by birth, he having been born in Vienna."[71] Ruiz de Burton explicitly links Lola to a Spanish bloodline— and therefore a European racial background. The fact that Lola's father is of Austrian birth makes her connection to Europe—and whiteness—even more concrete for readers, even in an Anglo American context. She is not off-white, as someone from Italy, Ireland, or Spain might be considered in the nineteenth century; she is of Austrian blood, from the very center of Europe. This connection to Austria is also significant because many Spanish Americans believed that the Hapsburgs, from Austria, were the rightful heirs to the Spanish throne (a point to which I will return shortly).

The narrator asserts—quite emphatically—that Lola is not multiracial and not *mestiza*. Indeed, as I have already discussed, mestizaje was not embraced uniformly in Mexico's Northwest borderlands—or even always in central Mexico. In nineteenth-century northwestern Mexico, elites strove to empower themselves by proving their European heritage and denying any indigenous roots; wars and other conflicts with indigenous communities on the frontier further hardened these racial attitudes.[72] Ruiz de Burton's emphasis of Lola's whiteness serves not only to denounce the hypocrisy of supposedly nonracist U.S. society but also to highlight Lola's elite status within Mexico. Lola's racial identity as a white *criolla* serves as a stark contrast to the barbaric indigenous groups living in the borderlands. Lola never even has to defend her claim to whiteness; the readers know her true racial identity from the beginning, and the other characters in the novel are eventually able to recognize her whiteness, a product of both nurture and nature, when they examine her manners and physical features closely.

For example, when ten-year-old Lola first arrives at the Norval house, her manners are already so refined, despite having been raised as a captive among Indians, that she disdains to answer rude questions from the Norval women and prefers to remain silent until she is appropriately addressed as an equal.[73] Similarly, Lola already knows that she is socially and racially above the Irish maids working in the Norval household, who are described as coarse and dirty.

She is so repulsed by their filthiness that she refuses to share a bed with them, preferring to sleep on the hallway floor with the dog, "as far from the Irish-women as possible."[74] As Jesse Alemán astutely notes, the novel implies that "the Irish maids have much to learn from Lola about being white."[75] Even Mat-tie, the youngest of the Norval girls, comments on Lola's beauty when she first arrives, seeing past her blackface and noting "what magnificent eyes she has, and what red and prettily-cut lips," while Lavinia, Mrs. Norval's unmarried sis-ter who lives with them, also recognizes that "negroes' lips are not like those."[76] For the careful observer, Lola's features are distinctly European. Dr. Norval further confirms Lola's racial biology, carefully retelling how she was born five months after Doña Theresa's capture, thus eliminating the possibility that Lola could be the mixed-race child of Indian captors.

Ruiz de Burton reinforces Lola's elite status by highlighting the fact that Lola's family is not from the borderlands but from central Mexico, the civiliz-ing and domestic center of the Mexican nation. As Irwin notes, in the 1800s, the Mexican borderlands were "sparsely populated by a mix of criollo settlers and indigenous peoples, distant from the nation's center in terms of trans-portation, communication, and culture."[77] Central Mexico, in contrast, is a space of civilization and cultured elites. Although the novel does not por-tray central Mexico as a hub of modern industrialization, it certainly confirms the representation of central Mexico (its elite community, at least) as a center of a different sort of civilization based on morality and intellectual produc-tion rather than on material goods. For example, when Isaac, Mrs. Norval's brother, is finally freed from a Confederate prison camp after being captured while fighting for the North in the Civil War, he is "sick of his country and countrymen, for what he thought their heartless ingratitude in leaving him forgotten in a prison" and decides to travel to Mexico "to get away from ingrates."[78] He travels to Mexico City to find Doña Theresa's father and hus-band and deliver to them Doña Theresa's *testimonio*, which he had found by chance while working in the dead-letter office, not realizing the connection between Lola and the letter. He is enchanted by the refined manners of the gentlemen, pleased with their hospitality, and impressed by the food he is served and the "best wine he had ever tasted in all his life."[79] Mexico City is portrayed as a nucleus of refined culture and sophistication. The com-munity to which Lola belongs through her familial ties is an exclusive one that values whiteness and shuns the savage peripheries of the modern nation. Moreover, Ruiz de Burton reinforces nineteenth-century racial hierarchies, in both Mexican and Anglo contexts, and emphasizes the importance of race—specifically, racial purity—in this novel and in her conceptualization of both the Mexicano and Anglo American communities she describes by repeatedly giving evidence for Lola's whiteness, especially in contrast to other off-white characters, such as the Irish maids.

Who Would Have Thought It? critiques the hypocrisy of the racist-abolitionist Northern United States through negative portrayals of New England and Washington, D.C.; however, the novel does not embrace racial equality or imagine a utopia of racial equality in either Mexico or the United States. Lola's blackface, whitening, and position at the top of multiple racial hierarchies function not only to critique Anglo American society and culture but also to question the pervasive dichotomies of the day and the connections among republicanism, progress, civilization, and whiteness. Who is truly civilized? To whom does whiteness belong? Lola's story upsets established U.S. hierarchies by placing a Mexican American woman at the top and by questioning, through her blackface, how whiteness is constructed and defined. But the novel simultaneously works to establish new parameters of belonging in which elite Mexicanos such as Lola maintain a position of power at the expense of other racialized or ostracized groups, such as African Americans, Irish immigrants, and Indians. Her future position as white within the United States is predicated on her past position within Mexico. Lola's evolution over the course of the novel shows that these two ethnoracial hierarchies are in fact quite compatible, as Lola assumes and is eventually recognized in both contexts for what she "truly" is: white and civilized, and more so than many people in New England, supposedly the most civilized and modern part of the United States.

Yankee Despotism and the Limits of Republicanism

As Ruiz de Burton wrote *Who Would Have Thought It?*, she was well aware that the entity "Mexican American" was still very much in the process of being defined—culturally, racially, socially, and politically. The addition of Mexican Americans into the U.S. racial and political system muddied the black/white binary that had dominated U.S. culture and politics for so long. As her letters and other writings attest, she was deeply concerned about the place and role that Mexican Americans would occupy in the United States.[80] Thus it is no stretch to read these concerns into *Who Would Have Thought It?* and understand the novel as participating in and encouraging a discussion about the building of communities and nations as well as concepts of community that go beyond our concept of the nation(al) as we know and recognize it today.

Much criticism on *Who Would Have Thought It?* has tended to focus on the novel's condemnation of U.S. culture, politics, and people, which once again reinforces resistance to Anglo America as a defining characteristic of Mexican American literature, even in an early work like *Who Would Have Thought It?*[81] While these elements are important, the text itself ruminates on transnational and intercultural collaboration rather than on resistance as an option for the future of elite Mexicanos and Anglo Americans. The assertion that Ruiz de Burton's depictions of Anglo American society serve as a foil to the "other" America—*Latin* America—overlooks the intimate relationship between Lola and the Norval men (Dr. Norval, her benevolent protector, and Julian Norval, her lover) and the portrayal of other Anglo American characters, such as Isaac, Mrs. Norval's brother, who is also presented in a positive light and rejects dominant Anglo American culture. As I will show, the sympathy created for these Anglo American characters simultaneously serves to critique republicanism as practiced in the U.S. North and join together elite Mexicanos and Anglos.

The two most sympathetic male characters in the novel, Julian Norval and Dr. Norval, share much in common with Lola and elite Mexico. Julian and Dr. Norval are both oppressed by the U.S. (Union) government because of their political beliefs and their sympathies for the U.S. South. Despite the fact that he has helped fund several regiments for the Union Army, Dr. Norval becomes known in his New England community for his "absurd sympathy and treasonable defense of those wicked rebels."[82] He decides to leave the country before he is arrested on false charges of treason. Julian is treated equally harshly by the same government for which he nearly dies on more than one occasion. He receives word that he is going to be dismissed without trial from military service for supposed disloyalty to the president. Despite repeated attempts to speak to his political representatives and acquaintances, Julian does not have much success in having his dismissal rescinded or even finding out why he is being accused of disloyalty. Not allowed to defend himself in a trial, he eventually goes to the White House to speak in person with President Lincoln, exclaiming in desperation, "Why should I not have a trial? by heavens! why not? Has *might* usurped the place of *right* in this free, beloved land of ours? Am I a free man, or an abject slave?"[83] Later, he becomes more explicit in his criticism of the government. Lamenting his own lack of freedom while he fights for the emancipation of African American slaves, he complains, "I wish to have my freedom. If the negroes have it, why shouldn't I? I did not bargain to surrender my freedom to give it to Sambo."[84] Clearly, Ruiz de Burton is critiquing U.S. politics on several levels, once again pointing out the disconnect between the democratic ideals and the shoddy (at best) implementation of those ideals. On another level, however, the narrative positions characters like Julian Norval as a type of "white slave"—a helpless victim, just like his father and uncle Isaac, of the U.S. government, without rights or privileges. The true slaves in this novel are the white men, such as Julian and Isaac, who are representatives of a cultured and enlightened minority group and slaves of the unjust North.

In a novel set mainly during the U.S. Civil War, the absence of depictions or discussions of (black) slavery is notable and, as numerous critics have rightly noted, "tellingly reveals the narrative's attempts to valorize the South."[85]

Similarly, by portraying whites like Isaac, Julian, and Dr. Norval as having fewer rights and freedoms than the African Americans they are fighting to emancipate in the Civil War, Ruiz de Burton strategically links elite Mexicanos and Anglo Americans, especially Southerners, through a shared history of victimization and whiteness and a rejection of Yankee democracy. Through this critical vision of the U.S. government, which gives rights to some while denying those same rights to others, Ruiz de Burton exposes the divisions and hypocrisy within the country and challenges the idea of a unified or cohesive national community in the United States. However, even as Ruiz de Burton contests this notion of a unified national community, she also connects different regional, national, and culturally distinct groups around the same idea of white slaves or oppressed whites. White Southerners and Californio elites are similarly victims of Yankee imperialistic and corrupt democracy masked as republicanism.

Rather than portraying Mexican culture as the antithesis to U.S. culture, *Who Would Have Thought It?* shows that certain sectors of the population in both Greater Mexico and the United States actually have much in common, largely due to their European roots, their cultural and biological links to civilization and whiteness, and their desire for (what Ruiz de Burton sees as) a more just form of government. Ruiz de Burton in fact goes back in time in her novel to two decisive moments in American history—the U.S. Civil War and Maximilian's Second Mexican Empire (or the second French Intervention) in Mexico—in order to speculate on the future for Mexicanos and their place in an ever-changing America. She returns to moments of national disintegration in order to consider the future(s) for herself and others like her. In the process, she also fosters deeper connections among American elites that speak to a concept of community not based solely on national affiliations.

Who Would Have Thought It? is indeed very interested in what it means to have a fragmented national community and what happens to those fragments in the aftermath of war or economic and political collapse. The novel begins with the unraveling of a "foundational fiction," the union of Lola's parents. Lola's father and mother represent an ideal criollo community, with strong ties, through biology/blood and culture, to both Europe and Mexico. Her father, Don Luis, as mentioned earlier, was actually born in Austria, and her mother, Doña Theresa, is of pure Spanish ancestry, although born in Mexico. Allegorically, they thus form an ideal Mexican community, bringing together criollo (Doña Theresa) and European (Don Luis) elites in Mexico. Rather than a rejection of or distancing from Europe and European influence, a move that was prevalent in novels and rhetoric in postindependence American nations, the union between Doña Theresa and Don Luis suggests that the ideal Mexican community of criollo elites would continue to include and embrace Europe/Europeans. But Doña Theresa and Don Luis are violently separated because of Mexico's vulnerable national borders and ineffectual central government, which was further destabilized by the U.S.-Mexican War. The narrator of *Who Would Have Thought It?* explicitly states that if "Mexico were well governed, if her frontiers were well protected, the fate of Doña Theresa would have been next to an impossibility."[86] Ruiz de Burton's ideal community of European-oriented Mexican elites, represented by Lola's parents, is threatened by disintegration, made possible because of a weak national (republican) government and dangerous racial "others" (i.e., non-Christianized Indians).

As I have already hinted, it is no coincidence that the novel takes place during two later periods of instability and intense uncertainty that caused many Mexicanos and U.S. Americans, as well as outside observers, to question the viability of a nation(al) and a republican government: the second French Intervention in Mexico (1861–1867) and the U.S. Civil War (1861–1865). As we have already seen in my earlier discussions of liberalism and republicanism in Greater Mexico in the first half of the nineteenth century, Mexicans debated and fought over what form of government best suited the Mexican nation for nearly the entire nineteenth century. The French Intervention, however, certainly renewed the controversy and gave it more immediacy.[87] Republicanism was not the only possible form of good government in the minds of elite Mexicans in the nineteenth century. There was a great concern over the *populacho* and whether the commoners and general population were really fit for the task of representing themselves.[88] Historian François-Xavier Guerra points out that there was a view of the masses as "a set of individuals or social groups who did not belong to the world of the powerful, the 'people' in contrast to 'those at the top,' 'patricians,' privileged groups."[89] In other words, elite Spanish Americans were wary of republican forms of government that placed power directly in the hands of the people, or *pueblo*. In fact, for Spanish American elites, the term *pueblo* itself contained a social and cultural inference, as they were considered "the lowest classes in society . . . [with] manners which conflicted with those of the elites, forms of judgement in which emotion of passion played a greater role than reason, and behavior which clashed with conduct considered 'civilized.'"[90]

In *Who Would Have Thought It?*, Don Felipe, Lola's Spanish grandfather, also ponders the possibility of an alternative to republicanism in Mexico, stating, "But if it is positive and certain that the Archduke [Maximilian] will accept the crown in Mexico, I shall be only too happy to be the most loyal of his subjects. And, what is more, not only will I consider such an act perfectly honorable and patriotic, but I would consider it wrong to oppose the re-establishing of a monarchy in Mexico under a Hapsburg, for the Hapsburgs were, and are, the legitimate and lawful heirs of the glorious Isabella and the Great Charles V [of Spain]."[91] The French Intervention entailed a reassessment of the viability of republicanism in Mexico. As the conversation between

Don Luis and Don Felipe implies, the French Intervention also carried with it the potential of a more immediate connection with European cultural and political values, since Napoleon III appointed Maximilian as the emperor of Mexico. Conservatives sought to portray this not as an imposition of foreign rule but as the legitimate reestablishment of the Hapsburgs as rightful heirs to the Spanish crown and the monarchy (the argument being that the colonies never would have sought independence if the Hapsburgs had rightfully remained in control of Spain and its colonies). Ruiz de Burton thus intimates that the future Mexican national community should not necessarily revolve around a republican form of government.

The conversation between Don Luis and Don Felipe further indicates that republicanism, especially the form practiced in the Yankee North, is not necessarily the right—or only—form of government for Mexico. Indeed, the suggestion is that Mexico would not have suffered its territorial losses and would not continue to suffer from weak borders, Indian raids, and so on if it rejected liberal republicanism once and for all. It is particularly revealing that Don Felipe remarks that the choice of a European prince for a ruler should be understood, perhaps contrary to our modern-day understanding of such a choice, as "perfectly honorable and *patriotic*."[92] Ruiz de Burton herself was unambiguous about her support for Maximilian and her sadness after his ousting and execution. In 1867, she wrote (again to Vallejo, with whom she disagreed on many political matters) that "con Maximiliano murió nuestra nacionalidad, allí pereció la última esperanza de México . . . y ahora los Yankies sólo esperan la hora que mejor les convenga para enterrarla para siempre, y pisotear la tierra encima y barrer todo vestigio desagradable después" (*Conflicts*, 271) [our nationality died with Maximilian. There Mexico's last hope perished . . . and now the Yankees only await the hour that best suits them to bury her forever and trample the earth above and sweep away any unpleasant trace afterward]. Although it might appear odd to us that Mexicanos would view a French-imposed monarchy as a better, more patriotic representative of the Mexican nation, elites did not always see American republicanism as the best option. Similarly, elites in Spanish America did not view democracy and aristocracy as being set against each other; they "regarded it as absolutely natural that the people should elect the best, that is to say, themselves [the elites], and in this sense democracy was not set against aristocracy but, on the contrary, led to it."[93] A good democracy, from this vantage point, should essentially maintain and reinforce the old aristocratic order. Guerra explains that a democracy of popular expression, on the other hand, "was regarded as anarchy—a riotous demonstration of the urban riffraff—and, at the same time, as despotism, the despotism of pure numbers."[94]

Ruiz de Burton expresses similar doubts about republicanism and democracy in both her novel and her letters. She indicates that the democracy being practiced in the U.S. North, and thrust on the U.S. South following the U.S. Civil War, is indeed a despotism of pure numbers in which the basest people will rule. In that same 1867 letter to Vallejo, she comments sardonically on the shortcomings of republican forms of governance, which she sees as a detriment to Mexico's progress as a nation:

> En esta era de ilustración la fuerza bruta manda, y tenemos que someternos. ¡Cuánto ha progresado el mundo bajo el impulso de prácticas republicanas! Antes se oprimía en nombre del Rey, y hoy en nombre de "la libertad" ... gran progreso han hecho los políticos ciertamente.... Ciertamente que vale la pena. (*Conflicts*, 271)

> [In this era of enlightenment, brute force commands, and we must obey. How the world has progressed under the impetus of republican practices! Before, they would oppress in the name of the King, and today in the name of "freedom" ... what great progress politicians have truly made.... Truly it is worth it.]

Ruiz de Burton, here in her letter and also with the conversations between Don Luis and Don Felipe in the novel, implies that republicanism, supposedly the most liberal form of government, is not the only choice for Mexicanos. Furthermore, it might not be the *best* choice, and it might, in fact, not equally protect the rights of all citizens; it might not be, in other words, a truly *liberal* choice. Indeed, the truly liberal choice would be to let the people decide their form of government, and as Don Felipe surmises, "The Mexicans did not want a republic; they wanted a good and just prince."[95] He continues, explaining to Don Luis, "A republican form of government is not suited to the Mexicans, and it is well that the chance be made with *their free approval*."[96] Don Felipe also laments the fact that, in his opinion, the United States has foisted its own version of republicanism on Mexico:

> Of course the ideas of this continent are different from those of Europe, but we all know that such would not be the case if the influence of the United States did not prevail with such despotic sway over the minds of the leading men of the Hispano-American republics. If it were not for this terrible, this *fatal* influence—*which will eventually destroy us*—the Mexicans, instead of seeing anything objectionable in the proposed change [to Maximilian's rule], would be proud to hail a prince who, after all, has some sort of a claim to this land, and who will cut us loose from the leading strings of the United States.[97]

Through the conversation between Don Luis and Don Felipe, Ruiz de Burton suggests that the type of democratic republicanism practiced in the Northern United States—in which the majority is not restrained by the inalienable rights of a minority—is just as oppressive as any other form of government, perhaps more so because it pretends to uphold the ideals of equality and liberty even as it imposes those ideals, sometimes through imperialistic conquest, on others.

The novel shows that this type of democratic republicanism not only is poorly suited for Mexico but also does not even seem to work very well in the United States, where it has led to the devastation of the Civil War and the destruction of the U.S. South. The rampant moral and political corruption of the United States is perhaps best exemplified in the novel by the Cackles, aptly named because they deserve to be laughed at but also because there is no content to their character; they are the epitome of "silly chatter," noisy but meaningless or inconsequential talk.[98] The young men of the Cackle family ascend in the military despite (or because of) their stupidity and cowardice. They become rich through war profiteering, lining their own pockets with government payouts, while supplying the Union Army with shoddy or damaged goods. And they rise in politics even though they have no underlying morals or driving political ideologies besides their lust for power and money. Through these characters, Ruiz de Burton warns readers about the chaos of a republican government ruled by the incapable masses—masses who will, we see in the very last chapter, continue to elect bad politicians such as the Cackles. But by showing the corruption and almost criminal inefficiency of the politicians in Washington, D.C., she also asks her readers to question if republicanism is in fact even being practiced in the United States and if democracy is a good form of government. Indeed, it does not seem to be working very well for those characters who begin the novel believing in republican ideals. As we have already seen, Dr. Norval must flee the United States in fear of being tried as a traitor simply because he criticized the war—and despite the fact that he raised money to fund several regiments of the Union Army. Julian is nearly dishonorably discharged for supposed disloyalty as well, even though he served honorably for the Union. And Isaac is left to die in a Confederate prison camp because of a petty personal squabble with a powerful politician in Washington, D.C. Each of these cases shows the corruption and unjust ways in which democracy is practiced in the Northern United States, where honest men like Dr. Norval, Julian, and Isaac suffer injustices while others, such as the Cackles, portrayed as dishonest scavengers, increase their cultural and economic capital at the expense of others and to the detriment of the meaningful functioning of democracy.

The very last lines of the novel serve as a meditation on the dismal future of politics in the United States, as the Cackles, the epitome of everything that is bad about Yankee democratic republicanism—corruption, stupidity, ignorance, frivolity—announce their plans to start a new political movement, "Cacklism." Brook Thomas explains that this is a veiled reference to the rift in the Republican Party during the elections of 1872 and Massachusetts senator Charles Sumner's famous speech "Republicanism v. Grantism," in which Sumner attacked President Ulysses S. Grant and the corruption and incompetence associated with his administration.[99] Ruiz de Burton links Sumner and the liberal Republicans (the "Cackles") with corruption when in reality Sumner had proposed a break with President Grant and the Republican Party because of the corruption associated with Grant's administration.[100] In a feverish speech that enthralls his family and others, Beau Cackle entreats his listeners, "The Democratic party is dissolving. Now is the time for us to catch the falling pieces and join them and shape them into *Cacklism*. If we don't do so, we will be very foolish."[101] Cacklism, in this light, is just about taking advantage of whatever situation presents itself; there is no underlying greater ideology or morality guiding the Cackles besides their own greed and self-promotion. The Cackles (or liberal Republicans) are willing to completely change their political stances and parties if it means that they can rise to the top of the heap. In the end, the Cackles and their "Cacklism," the future of U.S. governance, leave readers with a sour taste about the poor implementation and practice of republican ideals in the United States. On a more profound level, the novel ultimately questions the dominant historical narrative of the Civil War as the triumph of a more egalitarian democracy over illiberal Southern republicanism. In fact, it shows just the opposite: Yankee democracy is more despotic and oppressive than both the slaveholding South's republicanism and Maximilian's monarchy.

Transnational Lola and the Future(s) of Greater Mexico

Who Would Have Thought It? is not just about the potential collapse of governments and communities (represented by the second French Intervention and the U.S. Civil War). In other words, it is not just a foundational fiction "gone wrong." While it certainly laments the current state of culture and politics in both the United States and Mexico, it also looks toward the future—or rather, toward Ruiz de Burton's present, since the novel takes place in her immediate past. Thus a second and equally enlightening way to read this novel is to look at its open ending as part of a successful foundational fiction about the potential for a different type of community that transcends national boundaries: a new transnational and intercultural community of white elites.

The novel ends with the imminent marriage of two sympathetic and morally irreproachable characters—Julian and Lola. Lola escapes from New England and goes to Mexico, where she is reunited with her father and maternal grandfather. After finishing out his service in the U.S. military, Julian Norval also travels to Mexico to marry Lola and presumably start a new life there with her. Through the marriage of these two characters, Ruiz de Burton suggests that certain sectors of the U.S. population and the Mexicano population have a great deal in common. Once again, it is important that Lola is a Mexican American with European origins. Similarly, Julian is portrayed as an American with a European sensibility, with an affinity for foreign, European tastes. Mrs. Norval complains, for instance, that Julian has been "completely ruined by his unfortunate trip to Europe. . . . [and] will never get over his fondness for foreigners."[102] Gretchen Murphy argues that through this appeal to European cultural authority, the novel "emphasizes the larger frame of transatlantic culture in which Ruiz de Burton wants to place the Americas." The novel thus "reimagines the New World as a space of transatlantic cosmopolitanism and renders meaningless the geographical division of the globe into Eastern and Western Hemispheres."[103]

Just as Ruiz de Burton unites the U.S. South and Mexico through a shared history of oppression, she also brings together cosmopolitan sectors of society in the United States with criollo elites in Mexico through their mutual affinity toward and ties to European culture. However, as Murphy explains, this "European cultural authority . . . is also racial authority."[104] Additionally, European culture is tied to whiteness. Murphy concludes that through this emphasis on European cultural authority, "Ruiz de Burton is also correcting a cartography that constructed the Western Hemisphere as an isolated and unified space in order to racially separate Europe from the Americas."[105] Through this linking of groups from multiple nations that look to Europe for cultural authority, Ruiz de Burton imagines a new type of transnational community brought together by an ideal of European blood, whiteness, and elite class status. Ruiz de Burton's new transnational community is embodied in the marriage of Lola and Julian, and Mexico becomes the proposed space for realizing this union.

In the novel, Mexico City is portrayed as both European and distinctly American. For instance, after Isaac's stint in the Confederate prison camp, when he travels to Mexico City to find Doña Theresa's family and deliver to them her final *testimonio*, he is constantly delighted by Mexico, its history, and its culture. As he rides through Mexico City on his first days there, he "enjoys the magnificent scenery on his route, and builds innumerable castles on the classic ground of Montezuma the timid and Cortez the daring."[106] Through this short description, the narrator reminds us that Mexico has a truly "American" history. Histories of and historical novels or romances about the conquest of the Aztecs were very popular in the nineteenth century in both Spanish America and the United States. Writers and audiences looked at events such as the conquest as part of a distinctly American foundational moment.[107] The narrator also uses figures like "Cortez the daring" and "Montezuma the timid" to remind readers about the lasting influence of Spain—and Europe—in Mexico as well as the "natural" inferiority of indigenous peoples.[108] The foundational histories of conquest invoked are American, somewhat paradoxically, because of their link to European empire and history. The "great" American past being described here is not a glorification of an indigenous American identity but a nostalgia for a Europeanized past, for a Europeanized American identity, firmly rooted in the conquest and oppression of indigenous communities. The clash of these two worlds—and the subsequent European domination over them—is what is distinctly American. In the same paragraph, the narrator describes the household of Lola's father and grandfather as a place of knowledge, refinement, and culture: the men sit in their library "by a table loaded with papers, books, reviews, pamphlets, etc.";[109] they are busy "reading letters of great interest. . . . [that] have arrived by the last mail from Europe," written in English, German, French, and Spanish.[110] When Isaac arrives at their house, Don Luis and Don Felipe are hospitable, inviting Isaac to stay at their "handsome and commodious" house, where he enjoys delicious food and wine, as well as excellent treatment by the well-managed household servants.[111] The Mexico described in *Who Would Have Thought It?* is a land of refined intellectuals with a rich history that is explicitly linked to Europe—and whiteness—both in the past and in the present.

The narrator's nostalgic vision of the past Spanish empire forms part of what historian John Nieto-Phillips has termed the "White Legend" of Spanish imperialism. The White Legend was part of a Hispanophilic movement that glorified the Spanish colonial past and Spanish conquistadors and lamented the loss of a preindustrial, but not indigenous, society—the victim of "Anglo American materialism, technology, pragmatism, and individualism."[112] While the Black Legend was still a powerful discourse in nineteenth-century America, the White Legend pushed back against the image of Spain as decadent, ruthless, and barbaric. This was an attempt by Hispanophiles (mostly Anglo Americans enamored of Spanish history and heritage) to transform history—set the record straight, so to speak—by replacing "Black Legend chronicles of carnage, mayhem, miscegenation, and decadence . . . with melancholy tales of dutiful missionaries bringing faith and reason to the Indians, and of knights in armor exploring the farthest reaches of humanity."[113] The narrator's depiction of Mexico reinforces this White Legend: Mexico is a land unspoiled by industry or corrupt modernity. The narrator's descriptions and Isaac's impressions of Mexico thus invoke a sense of nostalgia for a simpler and more refined past linked to Europe by conquest and culture but also by race, because the White Legend is also about racial whiteness.

The new community represented through the union of Lola and Julian is not only American (in the broadest sense possible) but also distinctly transnational in nature. Lola, for example, is raised on the American frontier (the U.S. Southwest). She is both Mexican and European by parental lineage and U.S. American through Dr. Norval's symbolic adoption.[114] Lola is also American according to the geographic spaces she occupies—first the U.S.

Southwest, then New England, and lastly Mexico. Julian is U.S. American by birth but shares an affinity for European culture, and by the end of the novel, his future also appears to be in Mexico. Through Julian and Lola, Ruiz de Burton connects Mexico and the United States to Europe but also situates them spatially in the Americas.

This foundational fiction—Lola's and Julian's—is not primarily about how to incorporate Mexican Americans into the United States; it is an imagining of cultural networks that transcend national and ethnic boundaries. In this imagined community, Anglo Americans and Mexicanos (Julian and Lola) come together, significantly, in (central) Mexico—not the United States. Ruiz de Burton proposes an alternative type of community based on European roots and cultural authority to which certain Anglo Americans and certain Spanish Americans, such as the elite criollo community in Mexico City with which Lola and her family identify, can belong. Lola, as a representative of a Mexican American community (becoming part of U.S. society not through her own choice but only because of the shifting boundaries after the U.S.-Mexican War, whereby she ends up on the U.S. side of the border), ultimately finds that she belongs in Mexico, but not because of an antagonism between Anglos and Latinos or because of a sense of solidarity with a homogenous and egalitarian Latin American community. She belongs in Mexico City because she belongs to a community whose identity revolves around a certain elitist concept of class and race. Just as not all U.S. Americans belong in this elite community, not all Mexicanos belong in this community either. By situating her foundational couple in Mexico City, Ruiz de Burton also indicates that Mexico—and perhaps certain segments of Spanish America—has as much of a claim as Anglo America to belonging to this community—and by extension, to its ideal of whiteness. Mexico City, as seen by Isaac and described by the narrator, is a space of culture and refinement with genuine links to both Europe (the old) and America (the new). It is a transnational space where oppressed whites from all over America can come together, joined by their connection to Europe, whiteness, and civilization. The novel is purposefully open-ended, allowing space for these transnational, intercultural coalitions to take shape.

Beyond the Romance: Colonized Futures and Forgotten Pasts

Ruiz de Burton's novel looks toward the creation of a collaborative, transnational community rooted in a shared sense of whiteness that reinforces the idea of European cultural and racial superiority. While it is tempting to look at works such as *Who Would Have Thought It?* as part of or as a forerunner for a Chicano studies tradition that opposes Anglo domination and neocolonialism, we must remember that in the nineteenth century, resistance and antagonism to Anglo America were not yet cemented in place as a central marker of Mexican American cultural and historical identity. Cultural workers like Ruiz de Burton were still uncertain as to what relationship Mexican Americans would have with Mexicans, Spanish Americans from other regions, Anglo Americans, and Europeans. *Who Would Have Thought It?* highlights a period in American history when Mexican Americans could still conceive of themselves—and fought to portray themselves—as connected to Europe and certain sectors of the Anglo American population through a common history of whiteness and a shared sense of oppression.

Who Would Have Thought It? speaks to the insights that can be gained when we look beyond national boundaries in our analysis of Mexican American, Mexican, and U.S. American texts, especially during the turbulent nineteenth century. Her writing reveals some of the ways in which Mexican Americans fought for a voice within the United States and the Americas but also the problematic grounds on which they sometimes articulated that voice. Her novel, as I have shown, can be understood in part as an argument for intercultural collaboration that moves beyond national boundaries. The novel itself, written in English and published in Philadelphia, is also further proof of the existence of that intercultural collaboration. By writing in English, she attempts to appeal to those Anglo Americans who might look at her novel and its political messages favorably, who might also be critical of their own "humbug" nation and see that they, too, have more in common with elites in Mexico or other parts of Spanish America than with the "Cackles" in the United States.

Under the guise of a romantic or sentimental novel, Ruiz de Burton's work moves beyond the domestic sphere to comment on pressing cultural, social, and political concerns. *Who Would Have Thought It?* is a text with numerous social and political goals. It seeks to educate its Anglo readers about elite Mexicanos and show that Mexican Americans are deserving of the rights and privileges of citizenship within the United States. It also works to reveal the many hypocrisies inherent to U.S. culture and governance and expose the ways in which the imperialist aims and endeavors of the United States are at odds with true republican ideals. The open ending of the novel preserves the possibility of future coalitions between elite Mexicanos and Anglo Americans. Indeed, we are promised that Julian and Lola will marry at the end of the novel, but the fact that we do not witness the actual marriage suggests that the moment for this marriage is *now*, Ruiz de Burton's present. Ruiz de Burton's nineteenth-century readers, she indicates, were in a position to see such a union take shape and perhaps help form and support such a union.

By examining Ruiz de Burton's position not just within the U.S. cultural and political sphere but also in the broader context of Greater Mexico, we can more clearly see how cultural border crossers like Ruiz de Burton fostered connections, imagined communities, and built coalitions that moved beyond national boundaries and linked together multiple geographic and cultural spaces. However, while *Who Would Have Thought It?* should be understood as a transnational text, it is also rooted in the regional experience and individual perspective of Ruiz de Burton. She is able to imagine an intercultural coalition in part because of her class status, her cultural capital (her connections to elite Californio families and her position as the wife of an Anglo American military commander), and her assumed familial and cultural links to Spain and Spanishness. These allowed her to envision a connection between Anglo Americans and elite, light-skinned Mexicanos based at least in part on their shared phenotype and European ancestry. Other Mexicanos with darker skin or from lower classes were automatically excluded from this same sort of proposed linkage.

Similar to the other texts I discuss in chapters 1 and 2, *Who Would Have Thought It?* provides us with an open ending full of uncertainty but also of possibility. When Ruiz de Burton published this novel, she could not have foreseen the ways in which the systematic disenfranchisement of Californios, regardless of their position of privilege before the U.S. conquest of Mexican territories, would leave the vast majority of them destitute, relegated to a lower class, and largely excluded from the category of whiteness—if not always legally, then at least socially. She could not have anticipated that a transnational coalition such as that which she imagines in her novel would ultimately not fully materialize for Mexican Americans outside of the literary imaginary. Nonetheless, her novel serves as a link to another, now forgotten, way of conceiving of the Americas, one that imagined common ground between the United States and Mexico—and one that imagined these connections through problematic concepts of culture, class, race, and belonging that actually excluded large segments of America but should nonetheless be recognized as part of our shared history.

4

Between Two Empires

◄◦►

The Black Legend and
Off-Whiteness in Eusebio
Chacón's New Mexican
Literary Tradition

On October 7, 1897, the newspaper *El Boletín Popular* of Santa Fe, New Mexico, published a poem by a local writer and lawyer, the young Eusebio Chacón (1869–1948). Through extended use of apostrophe, the poem, titled "A la Patria," or "To the Homeland," speaks directly to the poet's homeland, which appears to be Mexico, using the familiar "tú" (you):

> Yo no nací en el nido que formaron
> Las águilas valientes que te hicieron,
> Y aunque mis padres por tu honor pelearon
> Y en tus lides intrépidos murieron,
> Bajo aquellos nací que te humillaron
> Cuando tu frente con su planta hirieron
> Bajo aquellos nací que te han quitado
> La Méjico novel, mi suelo amado. (*Writings*, 234)[1]

> [I was not born in the nest that gave
> Birth to the valiant souls that shaped you,
> Although my fathers fought for your honor
> And died in glorious battle for you,
> I was born under those who humbled you,

Those who placed a boot to your neck
I was born under those who took from you,
Mexico, the land that I love.] (*Writings*, 230–231)[2]

The poet has a bond with Mexico, his "patria" [homeland], but in the very next stanza, he realizes the limits of this bond, describing his experience as one of exile and uncertainty: "Pero afanoso en mi destierro sigo / Incierto el curso que en el tiempo pisas" (*Writings*, 234) [Still, I push forth in my exile / Unsure of the path to come (*Writings*, 231)]. He longs for something he has never really known, a connection that has been broken. *Exile* seems to be the only word that might encapsulate his reality, but even that does not quite capture his experience, according to the poem, as it is an exile from a country in which he was not born and has not lived.

The poem ends by reflecting on the speaker's nostalgia for this lost—or rather, never actually possessed—attachment and his conflicted relationship with both his imagined homeland and his beloved New Mexico, under control of the United States:

Oh, mi patria, ¿por qué yo no he sabido
Lo que es vivir bajo tu suelo hermoso?
¿Por qué me niega el hado endurecido
Beber de tus aguas y aspirar dichoso
Siquiera un día tu aire apetecido
Y ávido hastiarme en su caudal sabroso?

¿Por qué, dime por qué? . . . ¿algún delito
Ha cometido contra ti el proscrito?
Quizá no vuelva mi laúd templado
Una vez más a darte su armonía,
Ni hacia ti llevará el cierzo blando
Los tristes ecos de la trova mía;
Roto el laurel, me alejaré llorando
Llevando con mi inmensa nostalgia
Retoños de dolor que en mi alma crezcan
Y esperanzas sin fin que no florezcan. (*Writings*, 236)

[Oh, homeland, why have I never known
What it is like to live on your precious soil?
My fate is to live without your waters
Never to take in the breath of your air.
What would it be like to take in your life

Giving winds? To avidly drink until full of
Your sweet waters?

Why? Can you tell me? Have I committed
Some crime against you?
Shall it be that my muted lute
Will not give you its harmonies
Nor the gentle north winds carry
The melancholy echo of my song to you;
The wreath is bent, I shall bid adieu in tears
I go forth with such immense nostalgia,
A budding sorrow that grows in my spirit
Deferring hopes and dreams.] (*Writings*, 233)

In this poem, Chacón conveys some of the ambivalences of Nuevomexicanos as the end of the nineteenth century approached: they were both Mexican and U.S. American yet out of place in both contexts.[3] They shared a connection to but also an alienation from Mexico. He lives in a land, presumably New Mexico, that is both familiar and also foreign; it is his ancestral land, but one that has been conquered by an invader, the United States. He yearns for a past and a community that he has never actually experienced or known in the first person, voicing an experience of diaspora.[4]

This poem thus articulates the conflicted position of the Nuevomexicanos of Chacón's generation, "incierto el curso que en el tiempo pisas" (*Writings*, 234) [unsure of the path to come (*Writings*, 231)], who identified at least partially with Mexico while at the same time trying to find a place for themselves in the United States under the people who had conquered and robbed Mexico of the very territories in which they lived. In New Mexico, the 1880s and 1890s were a period of immense change, spurred by the arrival of the railroad, a massive increase in immigration of Anglo Americans to the region, and the end of a long period of isolation that had characterized the New Mexican experience for most of its previous history.[5] This generation of Nuevomexicanos, born after the end of the U.S.-Mexican War in 1848 (and therefore the first generation born under U.S. rule) yet still living in a sort of limbo, as New Mexico had not yet been admitted to statehood, sought to realize their "esperanzas sin fin," or deferred hopes and dreams, within a new social, cultural, and political context. They did so through the written word and, more specifically, through local newspapers and small printing presses.[6] Nuevomexicanos like Chacón saw the press as the means for both educating their people and providing a tangible and recognizable history and literature for their people—forms of cultural capital during a period of intense turbulence and disenfranchisement of Nuevomexicanos.[7]

Chacón was one of the men who spearheaded the efforts of this generation of writers, editors, and other cultural workers to create a "literatura nacional" [national literature], unique to New Mexico, that would combat negative stereotypes of Nuevomexicanos, educate the local populace about their own history and culture, and create a sense of unity and pride in the community.[8] In addition to his poetry, Chacón published essays, articles, and even two short "novelitas," or novelettes, in the local press. These two novelettes, *El hijo de la tempestad* [*The Son of the Storm*] and *Tras la tormenta la calma* [*The Calm after the Storm*], published together in 1892 as one volume by *El Boletín Popular* in Santa Fe, New Mexico, reflect and dramatize the racial, cultural, social, and political tensions that existed in late nineteenth-century New Mexico and provide a glimpse into how elite Nuevomexicanos were reimagining their own national and regional identity and their new and changing connections with Europe, Spain, Mexico, and the United States in the nineteenth century.

Chacón's novelettes provide a window into how Mexican Americans—in this case, Nuevomexicanos—were thinking about race, language, and culture and the limits of both whiteness and blackness as they worked through another moment of uncertainty and transition during New Mexico's long process of appealing for U.S. statehood. Chacón's novelettes, written during the turbulent 1890s, show the ways in which past colonial hierarchies of race and culture influenced how elite Nuevomexicanos saw and portrayed themselves within a new colonial context, as a territory of the United States. This period marks a transition for elite Nuevomexicanos from a position of relative privilege and power (the colonizers) to one of subordination and subalternity (the colonized) within the United States. The 1890s, however, were a brief moment during this generation's lifetime when elite Nuevomexicanos could still conceive of the possibilities of equal inclusion within the United States. However, as Chacón's writings reveal, they were already suspicious of what that inclusion might mean, how it might be achieved, and what losses such inclusion, if only superficial, might incur for their community.

Chacón's work highlights the different strategies used by Nuevomexicanos to position themselves in relation to both Spain and Anglo America while eliding cultural, racial, and political connections with Mexico. On the one hand, he draws on Spanish cultural forms and uses discourses of purity of blood linking Nuevomexicanos to Spanish conquistadors as a means of establishing Nuevomexicano heritage as white and Nuevomexicanos as therefore fit for self-governance. On the other hand, he and his fellow Nuevomexicanos had to maintain a critical distance from Spain and demonstrate their compatibility with Anglo American political principles as they fought for their right to self-governance as a new U.S. state. At the same time, his works seem to jump from one imperial context (Spain) to the next (United States), completely skipping over New Mexico's Mexican history, in an attempt to eschew any connections with the racial miscegenation popularly assumed by Anglo Americans to be an inherent and degenerate/degenerating component of Mexican identity, both culturally and racially. Thus throughout these two novelettes, we can see the ways in which Chacón, like so many of his fellow Nuevomexicanos, was forced to negotiate the fine line between the Old World and the New: his novelettes look toward the Old World (Spain) as proof of European heritage and white-ness while simultaneously shunning the trappings of the "old," "backward," and "barbarous" Spain and moving toward the New—in this case, a new New Mexican literary tradition distinct from both Mexico and the United States. In the process, however, he also contemplates competing concepts of barba-rism and modernity and subtly critiques the barbarity of the United States' supposedly modern government.

Like Lorenzo de Zavala, Justo Sierra O'Reilly, and María Amparo Ruiz de Burton, Chacón and his work form part of an alternative literary and cultural tradition that sought out affinities, rather than hostilities, between (certain) Mexican Americans and Anglo Americans even as his writing exposed the hypocrisies in the United States' supposed promotion of liberty and equal-ity. His work highlights a moment when Nuevomexicanos were fighting to create political coalitions with Anglo Americans while they also worked to preserve their own culture, language, and history and establish a space of agency for themselves within U.S. society. These two goals were not seen as mutually exclusive. Moreover, resistance was not the only or always the most effective way of envisioning the relationship between New Mexico and Anglo America. Collaboration, cultural negotiation, and compromise, as I will show, were also options in the minds of many elite Nuevomexicanos. Seen in this light, Chacón's writings highlight not only the longevity and richness of writings by Spanish-speakers within the United States but also the pervasiveness of the "other" cul-tural and literary tradition of transnational and intercultural coalition-making and accommodation that has, since the nineteenth century, been largely writ-ten out of Latin American and U.S. Latino studies. Lastly, as I will discuss, while Chacón's novelettes and other earlier works explore these possibilities for elite Nuevomexicanos, his later works reveal the limits of this sort of collaborative relationship between Hispanos and Anglos as growing Hispanophobia slowly but surely eroded such options for most Mexicanos by the end of the nineteenth century. Chacón's work thus speaks to a specific moment of transition for elite Mexicanos as they came to grips with their racialization and increasing disem-powerment within American hierarchies of race and power.

A New, New Mexican Literature

Born to a prominent family in New Mexico, Eusebio Chacón spent his life living between southern Colorado and New Mexico.[9] Although he is not an extremely well-known name in Latino literature today, in his own day he was a prominent community leader, lawyer, writer, and advocate for Hispano rights in New Mexico and southern Colorado.[10] Well educated and a gifted writer and orator from an early age, he received a bachelor's degree from the Jesuit Las Vegas College in 1887 and completed a law degree from the University of Notre Dame in Indiana in 1889. Like Justo Sierra O'Reilly, he was also invested in writing and recording the history of his region. He also saw himself as the founder of a new "literatura nacional"—a distinctly regional, original, New Mexican, "national" literature. Yet despite the fact that Chacón has been credited with writing the first New Mexican novel in Spanish, his literary work in particular has remained largely understudied.[11] Francisco A. Lomelí and A. Gabriel Meléndez have written multiple articles focusing on Chacón's connection to an early U.S. Hispanic literary tradition.[12] But in their attempts to rescue Chacón from the discarded archives of U.S. literary history, they have mostly written about the importance of Chacón's two novelettes as examples of an early Hispanic literary tradition in the United States. While this link is obviously important, few literary critics have paid attention to the content of the texts themselves, despite their richness.

El hijo de la tempestad and *Tras la tormenta la calma* have remained critically underexplored, perhaps in part because of the multiple borders—both geographic and conceptual—that these texts straddle. They are not considered "Latin American" literature because they were written in a U.S. territory, New Mexico. Yet they are written in Spanish, situating them outside of the realm of canonical U.S. literature. In addition, although Lomelí and Donaldo W. Urioste "rediscovered" Chacón's two novelettes in 1976, there was no modern edition of the novelettes available until quite recently, with the publication of Meléndez and Lomelí's comprehensive bilingual collection *The Writings of Eusebio Chacón*, which includes all Chacón's known writings.[13]

Chacón's novelettes help record and represent the experiences of Nuevomexicanos during this period. But they also demand attention because they compel us as readers to reconsider how national literary and historical canons are formed, what is excluded from the canons, and what these discarded non-canon-forming texts reveal about the fissures in canons and cohesive narratives of community or nation formation. Chacón's novelettes highlight the convergence of multiple national and linguistic traditions, thus throwing into disarray neat categorizations and periodizations of national(ized) canons. I go back to his texts not because they reveal some linear and most "original" articulation of a Chicano or proto-Chicano identity but because they speak to lost discourses, missed connections, and now forgotten ways of envisioning Nuevomexicanos and their relationship to Mexico and the United States. In other words, they do not reveal the *linear* connections with our present. His work instead highlights a conception of community that existed both within and beyond the nation and thus propels us to consider the limits of the nation—what has been erased from national(ized) narratives of community formation in Greater Mexico and the United States.

The novelettes are two distinct stories, although they share much thematically. The first novelette, *El hijo de la tempestad*, takes place in a fantastic and unnamed setting, thus more easily permitting an allegorical reading of the story. The first scene of the novelette begins with biblical echoes: a man and a pregnant woman lost in a violent storm search for shelter. The couple eventually finds a cave, where the woman gives birth to a son so fierce, according to the narrator, that the mother immediately dies. The next day, the father finds a village, where he asks for help for his son while he goes back to take care of the mother's body. But a Gypsy woman has foreseen the birth of the child and has warned the villagers against helping the man.[14] Because of the superstitions of the villagers, the man finds no one to help him with the child except for the Gypsy woman. He leaves the baby with her and is never heard from again. As the novel progresses, we learn that this adoptive mother of "el Hijo de la Tempestad," as the child is called, is not only a "despised" Gypsy, as the narrator describes her, but also a witch. And her pet monkey is actually just a disguise for the devil himself. After this initial backstory, the plot jumps forward about twenty years. El Hijo de la Tempestad is now the leader of a group of one hundred bandits who terrorize the countryside, pillaging the towns and taking people captive. Among the captured "slaves" is a beautiful maiden and her father. Despite el Hijo's advances, the maiden has retained her honor (virginity), but before her father dies, she promises to her father that she will marry el Hijo and thus preserve her honor. However, just as el Hijo and the maiden are about to formalize their nuptials, a troop of soldiers enters the cave, killing el Hijo and rescuing the beautiful maiden.

The second of Chacón's novelettes, *Tras la tormenta la calma*, takes place in a more realistic and tangible space: Santa Fe, New Mexico. It focuses on a classic love triangle between Lola, an orphan and femme fatale; Pablo, who is poor, but hardworking and honest; and Luciano, the rich student who attempts to seduce Lola away from Pablo. Luciano is so enraptured by the Romantic literature he is reading, which is almost all from Spain or about Spain (Espronceda's *El estudiante de Salamanca* and Byron's *Don Juan* are two of the texts mentioned) that he decides that he, too, as a good student, must search out the amorous adventures he has read so much about; the narrator explains that Luciano "nada creía más propio de la vida Estudiantil que todas aquellas blasfemias, indecoros, inmoralidades y faltas de honor" (*Novelitas*, 38) [came to believe that the life of a student was just about blasphemy, shamefulness, immorality, and breaches of honor (*Writings*, 87)]. Despite an initial rejection, Luciano eventually wins Lola over. Pablo becomes suspicious of Lola's changing attitude toward him and discovers Lola and Luciano in a compromising situation when Pablo and Lola's aunt unexpectedly enter Lola's room one night. Lola's aunt dies from shock and disappointment, and Pablo chases Luciano through the streets of Santa Fe until he eventually catches him, roughs him up, and brings him back to Lola's house, where Lola and Luciano are forced to marry one another.

Although the two novelettes have no characters in common nor any plot continuity, two factors ask readers to make a connection between them. First, and perhaps most obviously, they were published jointly, as a single volume, under the title *El hijo de la tempestad; Tras la tormenta la calma: Dos novelitas originales* [*Son of the Storm; The Calm after the Storm: Two Original Novelettes*]. The titles of the novelettes also create a thematic connection between the two stories, since both titles refer to a storm of some sort ("tempestad" and "tormenta"). Second, Chacón wrote only one very short introduction for the entire book—instead of one for each novelette—indicating that these novelettes are to be read in tandem. In his introduction, Chacón discusses his purpose in writing the stories:

> Sobre el suelo Nuevo Mexicano me atrevo á cimentar la semilla de la literatura recreativa para que si después otros autores de más feliz ingenio que el mio siguen el camino que aquí les trazo, puedan volver hácia el pasado la vista y señalarme como el primero que emprendió tan áspero camino. (*Novelitas*, 2)

> [I dare lay the foundational seed of an entertaining literature on New Mexican soil so that if other writers with a more felicitous talent can later follow the path I hereby establish, may they look back at the past and single me out as the first to undertake such a rough journey.] (*Writings*, 49)

Chacón clearly sees his texts as a starting point for a New Mexican literary tradition, and he is conscious that his novelettes are the "first" in this new tradition. He looks toward the future, seeing himself and his works as paving the way for other writers in New Mexico. Thus in the introduction to his book, Chacón sets up his literary texts as a sort of speculative blueprint for future New Mexican writers—and I would contend, by extension, for New Mexican community identity.

In the nineteenth century, novels about romantic unions served as a space for debating and envisioning the potentialities as well as the pitfalls of a new nation or community. In these novels, romantic and sexual unions—whether frustrated or consummated—functioned as allegories for national consolidation and development. Through intermarriage, these novels lay the foundation for their nations and its citizenry: the ideal national community. Or, in the case of frustrated marriages, they draw attention to the problems that should be avoided if these nations hope to move toward consolidation and productive citizenry. These novels are actively engaged in constructing their nations and envisioning what these nations should or could look like. The fact that both stories end in either frustrated or consummated marriages further encourages readers to understand these texts through the lens of allegory, as foundational fictions. Chacón is writing into existence not just a New Mexican literary tradition but also a specific vision for the future of his New Mexican community.

In New Mexico in the second half of the nineteenth century, newspapers and print publications were avenues for imagining a coherent and unified past, present, and future New Mexican community. As Benedict Anderson has shown, the increasing prestige of print languages and the rapid growth of print technologies in the nineteenth century made it possible for groups to imagine a new political community: an "inherently limited and sovereign" nation.[15] Print technologies enabled communities to construct a common link between individuals and groups and articulate a national consciousness. In response to racist Anglo American attacks that portrayed Nuevomexicanos as morally, socially, and intellectually inferior, Chacón and his fellow Nuevo-mexicanos similarly mobilized themselves against these attacks by turning to the written word—history and literature—as evidence of their intellectual and cultural accomplishments and as an affirmation of a distinctive New Mexican history and culture. As Meléndez explains, after 1848, Nuevomexicanos became aware that "the struggle for the hearts and minds of *Neo-Mexicanos* increasingly became a war of words, an ideological battle that pitted the idea of Anglo-American primacy in the West against the tenacity of *Neo-Mexicano* self-image and self-representation."[16]

In addition to sociohistorical essays, verse, fiction, and oratory, Chacón, not unlike Justo Sierra O'Reilly, was active in publishing and publicizing pre-1848 literary and historical works by Hispanos from his region. Chacón had a clear motivation for doing this: he wanted to make these sorts of historical and literary texts "accessible to the general populace from southern Colorado and northern New Mexico, in order to provide historical substance and some sense of literary and intellectual continuity to Hispanic communities who were otherwise being accosted for supposed backwardness, illiteracy and social inferiority."[17] Thus Chacón was very self-conscious of his role in constructing New Mexican history and a New Mexican community identity through his writing and publishing. He was aware that the written word had power and could be used as a source of agency for Nuevomexicanos. His novelettes should thus also be understood as enmeshed in a push to cultivate a sense of historical continuity for his New Mexican community through the dissemination of both historical and contemporary writings by New Mexican authors (or authors associated with the settlement of that region).

It is also important to note that New Mexico was involved in a particularly intense struggle for statehood during the 1890s, when Chacón was writing these novelettes. As historian John M. Nieto-Phillips explains, at this time there was a growing consensus among Nuevomexicanos that they wanted to be admitted into the union, yet "congressional opposition managed to squelch New Mexico's statehood efforts on five occasions between 1888 and 1895 by invoking overtly racist arguments."[18] Statehood was a way for Nuevomexicanos to regain a voice in national and regional politics; yet forty years after the Treaty of Guadalupe Hidalgo ended the U.S.-Mexican War, New Mexico still had not been admitted as a state.[19] According to Nieto-Phillips, Nuevomexicanos came to understand that "their statehood hopes hinged largely on convincing Washington lawmakers that New Mexico's 'Mexicans' were racially white—or white enough—to merit full inclusion in the body politic."[20] They thus turned to their Spanish heritage as a source of ethnic agency in an attempt to regain control over politics and cultural assets.[21] Redefining themselves as Spanish—or direct descendants of Spaniards rather than racially suspect "Mexicans"—became a way for Nuevomexicanos to empower themselves and to be recognized and possibly included as part of the white U.S. nation.

Wrapped up in Chacón's idea of a new New Mexican literary tradition, then, is also the idea of a new regional identity fraught with contradictions and tensions. Indeed, it is possible to look for the connections between Chacón's writing and the struggle for statehood not just because of his dedication to publishing and publicizing past works by New Mexican authors but also because Chacón was a vocal community member who was concerned about how Nuevomexicanos and his homeland, New Mexico, were being portrayed in literary and political writings in the present. He was deeply distressed about New Mexico's inability to participate in the U.S. government and about the representation and perception of Nuevomexicanos in Anglo America. For example, one of Chacón's most anthologized speeches, "Elocuente Discurso," from 1901, which was later published in local Spanish-language newspapers, defends Nuevomexicanos against racist comments.[22] Chacón advocates for Nuevomexicanos by asserting their Spanish American ("hispanoamericano") identity and by explicitly linking them to Spanish blood and ancestry:

> Yo soy hispanoamericano como lo son los que me escuchan. En mis venas ninguna sangre circula si no es la que trajo don Juan de Oñate, y que trajeron después los ilustres antepasados de mi nombre. Si en alguna parte de las Américas españolas, o lo que antes fueron dominios españoles, se han conservado en su pureza los rasgos fisionómicos de la raza conquistadora, esta ha sido en Nuevo México. Mezcla alguna ha habido, sí, pero tan leve y en tan raros casos, que el decir que somos, como comunidad, una raza mixta, ni está comprobado por el hecho histórico, ni se resiste al análisis científico. (*Writings*, 195)

[I am a Spanish American like those who are listening to me. No other blood
runs in my veins than the one brought over by don Juan de Oñate and later by
the renowned ancestors bearing my name. If there is any place in the Spanish
Americas, or what was once under Spain's rule, where the purity of physical features of the conquerors have been preserved it has been in New Mexico. Some
mixture has occurred, of course, only slightly and rarely, but to claim that we are
a community of mixed peoples does not stand up to historical or scientific
analysis.] (*Writings*, 188–189)

Chacón's speech indicates that he is aware of the ways in which ideas about
racial degeneration and racial mixing have been used against Nuevomexicanos
to deny them power and representation in the United States.

As María DeGuzmán points out, while Old World Spain and Spaniards
were certainly viewed and portrayed in the popular Anglo American imagination as barbaric, culturally degenerate/degenerating, and racially suspect (and
therefore slightly "off-white"), Spanish American countries were equally seen
as "a site and sign of miscegenation and contamination rather than regenerative hybridity."[23] In fact, contact and exchange with African slaves and Native
Americans in the New World—the intermixing that Chacón denies and down-
plays in his fellow Nuevomexicanos—marked Spanish Americans as even
more racially mixed and therefore more degenerate than their already racially
suspect Spanish ancestors. Chacón's definition of Nuevomexicano identity in
this speech thus works to link Nuevomexicanos biologically and racially to
Spain and Spanish roots through references to the purity of the Spanish blood
circulating in Nuevomexicanos as well as their shared "rasgos fisionómicos de
la raza conquistadora" [physical features of the conquerors]. Spaniards might
have been considered slightly off-white to many Anglo Americans, but they
were closer to whiteness than mestizo Mexicans.

Chacón explicitly addresses New Mexico's frustrated pleas for statehood at
the end of this speech, concluding,

Volvemos hoy con el ahinco de los que no conocen otra patria ni otra bandera
que la americana, a pedir, quizá por la vigésima vez, esta tan deseada admisión a
la soberanía de estado para probar que somos dignos de las libertades republicanas, y aptos para asumir las responsabilidades que acarrean. (*Writings*, 199)

[We can now return with the zealousness of someone who knows no other
country or flag than the United States to demand, perhaps for the twentieth
time, our much desired admission into a sovereign State, proving that we are
worthy of republican liberties and capable of assuming the responsibilities that
that implies.] (*Writings*, 192)

In this speech, Chacón defines his racial identity, and that of other Nuevo-mexicanos, as Spanish. Likewise, he implies that Nuevomexicanos are capable of governing themselves because of their Spanish heritage—because they are distinct from Mexicans and those with mixed blood. Thus even as Chacón charges the U.S. government with many shortcomings, he still seeks to be included as a member of that nation and simultaneously reproduces the same type of racist logic that denies him and other Mexican Americans entry as full citizens into the nation. He elides any connection between Nuevomexicanos and Mexican roots, which would link them, according to the logic of U.S. racial hierarchies, to even more pronounced levels of perceived racial misce-genation and contamination, thereby marking Nuevomexicanos as unfit for self-governance. Historian Ramón Gutiérrez explains that after 1850 in New Mexico and other regions of the U.S. Southwest, longtime Hispanic residents sought to distinguish themselves from defeated and stigmatized Mexican nationals, as well as the large numbers of more recently arrived Mexican immi-grants whom they perceived as lower class and of dubious racial origins.[24] In order to differentiate themselves from these other groups of Mexicans, Nuevo-mexicanos returned to old ethnic categories stemming from Spain's old *sistema de castas* and began calling themselves Spaniards (*españoles*) or Spanish Ameri-cans (*hispanoamericanos*).[25] These terms of self-identification were so power-ful because they immediately signaled a set of privileged identities: "Christian, romance language speaker, a culture and ancestry that originated in Rome, European legal institutions, and a Caucasian racial origin."[26] Thus "when oper-ating in the English-speaking world, ethnic Mexicans sought this status as a sign of respect and superiority over Mexicans."[27]

Although labeling themselves as Spanish or Spanish American was a way for Nuevomexicanos to assert their connections to Spain and to mark themselves as white—or at least whiter than Mexicans—this whiteness was still marginal at best in the context of Anglo America. Spain and the Spaniard had long been marked in Anglo American popular consciousness as "off-white"—a shadowy vestige of the Black Legend, which painted Spain and Spaniards as barbarous, morally black, and culturally degenerate. In Anglo American discourse, Spain was sometimes considered part of southern Europe, but Old World Spain also "conjured fantasies and anxieties about strange and volatile mixture, purging and contamination, attributed to and provoked by the traces and remnants of the Muslim Conquest, the Christian Reconquest, and the Inquisition."[28] Thus by the nineteenth century, the "blackness" of the Spaniard was increasingly "not only a religious, ethical, and historical issue, but a racial one as well."[29]

So although Chacón relies on connections to Spain and Spanishness as a link to racial purity rather than miscegenation, he also works to distinguish Nuevomexicanos politically from Spaniards when he engages with questions of statehood and attests to Nuevomexicanos' loyalty to the United States and its republican values. He reminds his listeners that Nuevomexicanos "no conocen otra patria ni otra bandera que la americana ... [y] somos dignos de las libertades republicanas" (*Writings*, 192) [know no other country or flag than the United States ... [and] are worthy of republican liberties (*Writings*, 199)], thus situating Nuevomexicanos firmly within an American hemispheric community and within the U.S. national and political body. Unlike "backward" Spaniards—supposedly tied to both monarchy and Catholicism—Nuevomexicanos are suited for "American" forms of governance such as republicanism.

Obviously, Chacón was aware of and engaged with the debates and discussions revolving around the questions of identity and statehood in New Mexico in the 1890s (and later). Indeed, the ongoing debates about statehood and citizenship in New Mexico illuminate the tensions present in Chacón's novelettes. In order to appreciate the richness of Chacón's novelettes, we must also explore not only the ways in which these foundational fictions sow the seeds for a new literature but also the ways in which they were in dialogue with—or at least reflected on—the ongoing debate surrounding the struggle for statehood and a "new" New Mexican identity. In this moment of ambivalence, on the precipice of potential change, Chacón uses his writing to imagine and speak to his community of Nuevomexicanos—a community that engages with Anglo Americans through multiple and overlapping discourses of empire.

Spanish New Mexico

In *El hijo de la tempestad* and *Tras la tormenta la calma*, Chacón negotiates between two competing visions of the Spanish past and present. On the one hand, he engages with a narrative, shared by many Nuevomexicanos, that imagines and portrays Spanish ancestors as white conquerors and representatives of (past) Spanish greatness, as well as proof of Nuevomexicanos' ability to self-govern. On the other, he responds to the pervasive Anglo American conceptualization of the Spanish past and present, which sees and portrays those same Spanish ancestors—and, by extension, Nuevomexicanos—as linked to the Black Legend, to brutality and degeneracy (both moral and racial), marking Spain and all its progeny as off-white and of questionable racial origins and therefore unfit for self-governance. Chacón thus contends with both the negative connotations associated with the Spanish colonial past and the more socially and politically "desirable" associations with Spanish ancestry. As Nuevomexicanos fought for statehood, they also had to face these tensions, exorcising the "barbarities" of Spanish history, shunning the "backwardness" and "degenerative" racial mixings of imagined Spain, and highlighting only the culturally and racially valued attributes of their Spanish ancestors.

Although Chacón marks his novelettes as foundational for an original New Mexican literary tradition, he chooses to reuse well-established literary genres and explicitly link his work to a European literary and cultural tradition. In both novelettes, we can see traces of the captivity narrative and the banditry trope but also the *novela ejemplar*[30] and the *comedia*[31] (both from the golden age of Spanish literature), the theme of honor (also harkening back to Spain's golden age), Spanish stock characters such as the Don Juan and the Don Quixote figures, and of course, the overt reference to Shakespeare's *The Tempest*.[32] It is possible to view Chacón's many references to Spain and Europe as an attempt to establish the literary tradition in New Mexico— much like the regional identity—as explicitly tied to Spain and Europe and thus a type of whiteness, even if marginally classified as such. Chacón rests his literary authority, at least in part, upon his use of well-known tropes, stock characters, and themes common to the Spanish literary tradition. This is especially evident in his second novelette, *Tras la tormenta la calma*, with its direct references to Spanish literature and its similarity to a *novela ejemplar*, as well as its use of the Don Juan and Don Quixote characters, both embodied in Luciano. Like Don Juan, Luciano feels it is his duty—and his position in life—to seduce Lola away from Pablo, even though Luciano is not in love with Lola, nor does he intend to marry her. And like Don Quixote, Luciano originally gets his ideas for the "conquest" of Lola from the books he is reading. He is so impressed by the Romantic figure of Don Juan that he decides he, too, must become a Don Juan figure and begin his seduction of young women.

A closer inspection of the novelettes also reveals the striking similarities between Chacón's introduction to the novelettes and Cervantes's prologue to his *Novelas ejemplares*. In his prologue, Cervantes writes, "Yo soy el primero que he novelado en lengua castellana"[33] [I am the first to have written novels in the Castilian tongue], emphasizing the newness of this literary form. Chacón similarly comments on being the first to write in a new literary tradition, "la semilla de la literatura recreativa" (*Novelitas*, 2) [the foundational seed of an entertaining literature (*Writings*, 49)]. Cervantes points out the originality of his *Novelas ejemplares*, claiming that "las muchas novelas que en ella [la lengua castellana] andan impresas, todas son traducidas de lenguas extranjeras, y éstas son mías propias, no imitadas ni hurtadas; mi ingenio las engendró, y las parió mi pluma, y van creciendo en los brazos de la estampa"[34] [the many novels that are currently in print (in Castilian) are all translated from foreign languages, and these are my very own, neither copied nor stolen; my imagination conceived them and my pen birthed them, and they continue to grow in the arms of the printing press]. Chacón similarly remarks on the originality of his own novelettes: "Son creación genuina de mi propia fantasía y no robadas ni prestadas de gabachos ni extranjeros" (*Novelitas*, 2) [These novels are a genuine creation of my own fantasy and not stolen or borrowed from Anglos or foreigners

(*Writings*, 49)]. Taking Chacón's words at face value that his writings are neither stolen nor borrowed from "gabachos" (a pejorative term for Anglo Americans) or "foreigners" (which in New Mexico in the late nineteenth century was used in opposition to the term *nativo*, "reflecting the strong ancestral identification of Nuevomexicanos with their homeland"), and considering Chacón's obvious and almost direct imitation of Cervantes's prologue, then Spaniards must not truly be foreigners in New Mexico.[35] Instead, these references highlight the cosmopolitan qualities of Chacón's new *literatura nacional*. Furthermore, as John Alba Cutler argues, they show that "Chacón's quest to produce an authentic national literature . . . does not require a divorce from other national literary traditions."[36] Spanish literature and culture, in this light, are an integral part of the New Mexican literary and cultural tradition and do not detract from the originality or authenticity of his new national literature.

With these multiple references to the Spanish literary tradition, Chacón once again aligns himself with Spanish cultural authority. Through the use of themes and explicit textual imitations of canonical Spanish literature, his texts look to Spain for authority even as they strive to be something completely new and authentic ("genuina"). Just like the New Mexican community they are working to establish and describe, these texts are simultaneously connected to and also cut off from their Spanish past; they are new and culturally distinct from their Spanish predecessors, yet the Spanish influence can still be very clearly detected and provides some source of cultural capital.[37]

Spanish Gypsies and Blackness in New Mexico

In much the same way that these texts negotiate their connection with a Spanish literary tradition and their creation of a new one distinct from Spain, when Nuevomexicanos looked toward Spain as proof of their whiteness in a racist and racialist hierarchy within the United States, they also had to be careful about identifying too closely with Spain. They had to portray themselves as different from Spain and truly American. In the United States in the late nineteenth century, Spain was still a worrisome enemy with a long history of empire in the New World. Spain certainly was a concern to the U.S. government at the time that Chacón was writing these novelettes—just six years before war would break out (in 1898) between the United States and Spain over Cuba, Puerto Rico, Guam, and the Philippines. During this period, many Anglo Americans remained unsure of Nuevomexicanos' loyalty to the United States and were worried about Nuevomexicanos' possible allegiance to Spain and Spanish ancestors.[38] Thus Nuevomexicanos had to walk a fine line between their identification with Spanish culture and history on the one hand and their rejection of present-day Spain on the other—while also eschewing links to Mexico and Mexicans. Nuevomexicanos, similar to Ruiz de Burton, had to strategically position themselves as both outsiders and insiders in the context of U.S. politics and culture.

Erlinda Gonzales-Berry discusses this dual positioning of Nuevomexicanos, explaining that they "frequently referred to New Mexico as *nuestra patria* (our homeland), thereby revealing a collective sense of unity and separateness vis-à-vis the new colonialists, even as they spoke of themselves and their people as loyal citizens of the new [United States] hegemonic state."[39] As insiders, they worked to establish themselves as loyal citizens who should be allowed to participate in the new, Anglo-dominated political sphere. As outsiders, they simultaneously worked to fashion their community as culturally— and perhaps ethnically—distinct from Anglo Americans. Chacón's statement, for instance, that his novelettes are not stolen from "gabachos" highlights that his new literary tradition is also distinct from the Anglo American literary tradition (*Novelitas*, 2). It is uniquely New Mexican.

Chacón and other Nuevomexicanos would have been acutely aware that Spanishness as European or white was not the only way in which Spanish identity was being imagined or constructed in the nineteenth century. As DeGuzmán explains, in the United States in the nineteenth century, an Orientalizing vision "dominated as the major mode through which Spain, Spaniards, and 'Spanishness' were made to signify. . . . [thus casting] Spain in an ultimately inferior or subordinated position, however romanticized or alluring."[40] The U.S. "anti-empire," as DeGuzmán phrases it, was constructed, through literature and images, as a foil to the barbarous, degenerate, and black Spanish empire associated (sometimes explicitly) with the Black Legend. Economic and religious enemies of Spain propagated the Black Legend in the sixteenth and seventeenth centuries by centering their narrative of Spanish history on the brutalities and violence that accompanied both Spain's conquest of indigenous communities in the New World and its religious Inquisition in the New World as well as the Old. The image of Spain as barbarous and cruel—as the antithesis to the United States' supposedly benevolent and civilizing empire— was still alive and well in the imaginations of writers and others in the United States in the nineteenth century. In fact, this image was being kept alive as a mechanism of self-identification for Anglo Americans; the black and barbaric Spanish empire served as a mirror or an inversion against which Anglo Americans could contrast their own righteous empire.

Although Chacón relies heavily on the positive image of Spain and the corresponding Spanish literary/cultural traditions in his novelettes, the negative image of the blackened, decadent Spain also appears in the figure of the adoptive Gypsy mother of el Hijo de la Tempestad in the first novelette. Not only is the Gypsy "sucia como todos los de su raza" (*El hijo*, in *Novelitas*, 4) [as slovenly as any of her race (*Writings*, 50)], but she is also evil (her pet monkey is, after all, the devil in disguise) and a type of sorceress. The association between the Gypsy and Spain was well established by the late nineteenth century throughout Europe and the Americas, where the Spanish Gypsy was made famous with the figure of the Gypsy femme fatale Carmen from Prosper Mérimée's novel (1845) and Bizet's opera (1875), both titled *Carmen*. The figure and the story of Carmen "helped to make Andalusia, the tobacco factory and Spanish Gypsy quarter in Seville, the Gypsies as a romanticized group, bull-fighting, guitar music, and bold seductive dance movements typical of Spain as an imagined whole."[41] Through representational practices such as the story of Carmen and popular paintings of Spanish Gypsies, "Spain and the Spanish empire were typed as Moor, Indian, or . . . Gypsy, and thus implicitly fated as corrupted and decaying."[42]

The discourse that viewed, understood, and portrayed Spain, Spaniards, and ultimately Spanish Americans as linked to degeneracy—and that was increasingly, throughout the nineteenth century, a *racialized* degeneracy—was not limited solely to Anglo America, although it was perhaps most strongly and enthusiastically articulated there. The figure of Carmen and the trope of the black Gypsy (and her problematic connection to but also ostracization from Spain) was present in Spanish and Spanish American cultural spheres as well.[43] As Hispanic literature scholar Alejandro Mejías-López reveals, the "simultaneous process of demonization and romanticization that Spain underwent in the nineteenth century northern European imaginary, rendering it a backward and primitive country," also became an internalized discourse for Spaniards and Spanish Americans by the nineteenth century.[44] Indeed, the "pervasiveness of nineteenth-century racial categories and their strong association with the new concept of modernity"—a modernity from which Spain and its colonies were largely excluded, at least rhetorically—led Spanish Americans and Spaniards alike to become obsessed with what they were lacking and why they had come to be viewed as racially, culturally, and politically degenerate and backward.[45] The figure of the Gypsy—represented and popularized on both sides of the Atlantic by Carmen—was part of a narrative of racial, economic, and cultural backwardness and degeneration linked to Spain, Spaniards, and Spanish Americans.

The fact that the Gypsy has a monkey as a pet also summons an association between monkeys and Africans / African Americans. According to popular nineteenth-century Western scientific and evolutionary racial theories, Africans (and mixtures with African blood) were located on the bottom rungs of the evolutionary racial hierarchy, connected most closely, of all races, to apes and the animal kingdom.[46] The monkey thus invokes another link between Spain/Spanishness and blackness, perhaps as a reference to the African influence in Spain or the proximity of Spain to Africa. A popular notion under serious consideration in the 1890s was that Africa really started at the Pyrenees in northern Spain rather than at the Strait of Gibraltar, which separates southern

Spain from Morocco.[47] The gypsy's close relationship with the monkey further highlights the connection between moral degeneracy (since the monkey is merely the devil in disguise) and racial degeneracy (since he also represents a connection to Africa and blackness).

The Gypsy in *El hijo de la tempestad* thus encapsulates the tensions between the two competing images of Spain and Spanishness circulating in Chacón's time. Chacón and other Nuevomexicanos rely on Spanish culture as a link to Europe and whiteness; yet at the same time, that alliance with Spain could also bring Nuevomexicanos' whiteness and fitness for self-government into question if they were associated too closely with the dark side of Spain's history (the Gypsy) and the racial hybridity associated with Spain's past. These discourses were certainly prevalent in Anglo America, but as Mejías López's work demonstrates, they were also circulating within the Hispanic transatlantic world and were indicative of an obsession with an internalized sense of racial, political, cultural, and/or economic inadequacy in Spanish America.

The image of the Gypsy as a mother figure, then, is quite important when reading *El hijo de la tempestad* as an allegory for New Mexican community formation (past, present, and future). Given the close association between Gypsies and Spain, it is hard not to read the Gypsy mother as a representation of New Mexico's mother country, Spain. The apparent triumph of the law and the banishment of the Gypsy mother at the end of *El hijo de la tempestad* point to a desire to purge the negative association of Spain from the culture and traditions of New Mexico. After el Hijo is killed, the Gypsy woman lives in isolation in the mountains, returning as a ghostlike figure to the cemetery on stormy nights: "Decíase tambien que en las noches borrascosas bajaba de la montaña una vieja encorvada en compañía de un feroz mono, y se dirigían al cementerio donde se hartaban de osamentas humanas" (*El hijo*, in *Novelitas*, 28) [It was said as well that on stormy nights an old stooped woman in the company of a fierce monkey came down from the mountain, steering themselves into the cemetery where she took her fill of human bones (*Writings*, 65)]. The Gypsy and her evil monkey become a sort of local legend of the past evils of the town—a haunting of the Spanish imperial past as well as an oblique reference to its links to Africa and blackness. The narrator notes that eventually "se llegó un día en que la vieja no hizo su excursión nocturna y ya no se la volvió a ver más" (*El hijo*, in *Novelitas*, 28) [a day came in which the old woman did not make her nocturnal excursion and was never seen again (*Writings*, 65)]. Presumably, the Gypsy, too, has finally died, thus ending the novelette. Significantly, el Hijo's legacy and the fear it inspires in the local community do not fully dissipate until the Gypsy, the final remnant, dies.

If the Gypsy woman does represent the dark side of the Spanish past, perhaps *El hijo de la tempestad* is an attempt to exorcise that past, to show that it does not belong in New Mexico or in this community. The Gypsy, after all, is isolated from any community by the end of the story. Ironically, in Chacón's attempt to exorcise the black side of Spain from New Mexico, however, he simultaneously writes the Gypsy *into* the New Mexican literary tradition by writing her into his foundational text. Chacón's use of the Gypsy figure speaks to the ways in which, somewhat paradoxically, the Gypsy, a figure who was marginalized within Spain and slated to be eliminated from the nation, became a symbol of that nation.[48] In the Spanish American context, these symbolic operations, by which the ostracized and subaltern—Jews, Gypsies, Moors, Africans, and Native Americans—came to represent Spain and Spanishness, had even more serious consequences for "those in subaltern positions within Hispanic societies . . . who found themselves twice removed from power as subalterns of subalterns."[49] As Mejías-López explains, they "often became the scapegoats of Spain's and Spanish America's conflicted new positionality with respect to modernity, a modernity that increasingly in the nineteenth century became associated with the 'Anglo-Saxon race.'"[50] Chacón's Gypsy figure therefore might be understood as both a projection of Nuevomexicanos' *own* fears about miscegenation and hybridity and a scapegoat for any perceived degenerative or backward qualities that continued to affect how Nuevomexicanos and their culture were understood by others.

Banditry and the Modern Nation

In this foundational allegory, the Gypsy's (read Spain's) influence has been almost entirely negative and destructive. Under her tutelage, el Hijo became a bandit, an example on the most basic level of lawlessness and moral degeneracy. Banditry was indeed a ubiquitous trope loaded with significance in nineteenth-century Latin American politics and literature. Latin American literature scholar Juan Pablo Dabove thoroughly examines the figure of the bandit and banditry in *Nightmares of the Lettered City: Banditry and Literature in Latin America, 1816–1929*. As he explains, the bandit trope is "both the product of and the arena for the struggles between the lettered city and the various social sectors that challenged its dominance."[51] The real-life bandit as well as the literary figure can thus be understood as a way of debating the shape of the nation and voicing concerns about and critiques of the forming nation. In the case of the real-life bandit, these critiques often take the form of physical violence. Chacón, as a voice of the lettered elite in his New Mexican community, similarly uses the banditry trope to discuss and evaluate the formation of his community. El Hijo, the central figure of banditry, is quite literally the embodiment—or displacement—of Chacón's own anxieties about the New Mexican past and present. He represents many of the elements that Chacón is trying to write out of New Mexican history and culture: he is the outlaw, the ill-bred, orphaned, and degenerate side of the New Mexico's past.

Chacón's banditry narrative follows many of the characteristics outlined by Dabove. It is written during a moment of "generalized crisis (e.g., revolution, war, or dynasty change) in the legitimacy of an established order."[52] In Chacón's case, the old Spanish-Mexican colonialist system has disintegrated, and Nuevomexicanos are fighting to be included in a new order—U.S. society and government. Dabove also explains that banditry was "key in the definition of some of the founding paradigms in Latin American national development . . . such as barbarism versus civilization, chaos versus order, and modern liberalism versus colonial corporatism."[53] In this reading of the bandit in Latin America, the bandit represents the barbaric, chaotic, and degenerate result of Spanish colonialism—something that the nation, whether Mexico or New Mexico, and the productive citizen must fight to suppress. Considering this moment of crisis and the role that banditry has traditionally played as a site for debating the nation but also establishing paradigmatic views of the nation and its citizenry, the ending of the story is especially important. With the death of el Hijo and the Gypsy at the end of the story, Chacón attempts to place New Mexican culture and history within the arc of modernization, civilization, and order, which is associated with the United States' "benevolent" empire of progress and enlightenment. El Hijo, as a bandit, a figure of lawlessness and a result of the Gypsy's (or Spain's) miseducation, cannot form a part of this new community in New Mexico. If Nuevomexicanos want to be admitted as a part of a new state, with full rights as U.S. citizens, Chacón allegorically indicates that they need to be modern, lawful, and civilized citizens—similar rhetoric to that used by Anglo Americans to legitimize their own (often militarily enforced) right to govern over "uncivilized" countries and communities. Neither the bandit nor the Gypsy mother belongs in Chacón's imagining of New Mexico.

However, although *El hijo de la tempestad* seems to reject Spain and its degenerating influence on Nuevomexicanos allegorically through the figure of the Gypsy mother, the novelette is not overly optimistic about the future of New Mexicans within the new U.S. imperial system either. When el Hijo is finally killed at the end of the story, it appears that law and order triumph. Yet the last page of *El hijo de la tempestad* leaves careful readers wondering if a type of barbarism lingers on, though now under a different colonial ethos. On the very last page of the novelette, an anonymous military captain answers questions from curious campesinos who are gossiping about the disappearance of the old Gypsy woman. The captain jokingly responds to their questions: "¿Os interesais en la vieja alcahueta, picarillos? Pues sabed que se la llevó el diablo, á lo más profundo de los infiernos, ja, ja, ja! Tiénela allí, barriendo el aposento que deben ocupar ciertos politicastros que traen á la patria muy revuelta, ja, ja, ja!" (*El hijo*, in *Novelitas*, 28–29) [You're interested in the old pimp, you rogues? Well, knoweth that the devil took her to the deepest pit of all Hell, ha, ha! He has her there sweeping the chamber that should be occupied by certain petty politicians who keep our country in upheaval (*Writings*, 65)]. Implicitly, it would seem that the "politicastros," or "petty politicians," mentioned by the captain are the Anglo politicians who control New Mexico without giving Nuevomexicanos a voice in the governance of their own state, or "patria." Because New Mexico was not a state, New Mexicans (both Anglo and Nuevomexicano) had little autonomy or control over local land, resources, and political offices even though men who were legally defined as white, which included many Nuevomexicanos, technically had federal citizenship. As federal citizens, Nuevomexicanos were protected by the rights of the U.S. Constitution, but they had no political rights. They had no elected representative in the federal government, as they were only allowed to elect a nonvoting delegate to Congress.[54] And in local territorial politics, Nuevomexicanos also had little control, since the U.S. president appointed territorial officials, including the governor, and these officials were overwhelmingly Anglo Americans.[55] Nuevomexicanos were thus largely excluded from national politics and also marginalized from local politics, which were controlled by Anglos on the East Coast who had little knowledge of or interest in local New Mexican politics—perhaps those "politicastros" to whom the narrator refers.

Moral degeneracy of the sort that deserves an eternity in hell therefore continues to haunt the characters in this story. But the Gypsy, the figure associated with (or scapegoated as the representative of) all the negative aspects of Spain's colonial endeavor in the New World, is replaced by a new figure: the Anglo American politician who colonizes through covert methods such as supposedly modern and modernizing laws that are just as oppressive as formal colonialist systems. It is the United States' supposedly modern and egalitarian system, in fact, that has allowed the lawlessness of el Hijo's banditry to flourish in the first place and has created, instead, what Cutler calls a "vacuum of good government."[56] Ultimately, this critique of U.S. politicians and governance makes readers consider "how the distribution of the benefits of modernity has always been unequal" in the United States.[57] Some places, such as New Mexico, on the margins of the nation, do not seem to ever be included in the modern nation or receive any of its benefits. Echoing Ruiz de Burton's pointed criticism of corruption and poor leadership in the U.S. government, as we saw in her novel *Who Would Have Thought It?*, Chacón similarly questions whether democracy, as practiced in the United States, is really the most modern and civilized form of government for all people who live within its borders.

Unlike the bandit, who exists outside of the law, the politician is created by and legitimized through the law. Through the figure of the Gypsy woman, Chacón ponders the lasting and perceived degenerative effects that associations with Spain and Mexico could have on the New Mexican community, but he also ends this novelette by questioning whether the new system under the

U.S. government is really any more forward-thinking than the past one. The banditry trope is particularly well suited for just this type of political/social commentary because at the core, banditry and bandits question state authority. Banditry was so powerful and perhaps so prevalent and dangerous in Latin America in the nineteenth century in part because it was also a symbolic challenge of (state) power. As Dabove explains, in "its most developed forms, banditry did not challenge a law or a right but rather the state as law-giver and ultimate source of legitimate violence."[58] The anonymous captain at the end of the story compares the Gypsy and the bad politician and determines that they should both end up in the same place, thus encouraging readers to question the differences between one colonial power (Spain) and the next (the United States).

Because Spain was ubiquitously portrayed as barbarous (and the Gypsy, in particular, represented the epitome of degeneracy) in the nineteenth century, Chacón's decision to place the Gypsy and the modern politician on par with one another is particularly striking. Even as Chacón attempts to write Nuevomexicanos into the modern era with his rejections of banditry and associated barbarism in this foundational text, his story is equally ambivalent about the supposedly modern U.S. political system. He calls into question whether Anglo America should indeed be called modern or civilized when its representative—the bad politician—is just as backward as one of the most denigrated and racially suspect emblems of both Spain and Spanish culture, the Gypsy. Indeed, as Cutler also argues, this novelette shows us a world in which "the rule of law has broken down, calling attention to the lawlessness of US rule in the Southwest and describing an American modernity that is rendered incompletely and unequally."[59]

El hijo de la tempestad thus questions many of the very dichotomies that Chacón is hoping will simultaneously serve Nuevomexicanos in their bids for statehood and all the rights that would entail. The end of *El hijo de la tempestad* in particular disrupts the well-established and interlocked nineteenth-century binaries of white versus black, civilization versus barbarism, and modern versus degenerate by calling into question whether modern U.S. politics is really any more civilized or any different from the past Spanish colonial system or the "racially degenerate," and therefore politically suspect, Mexican nation. While the Spanish colonial and Mexican national systems may have produced bandits who prospered outside the law, like el Hijo, modern U.S. politics have also nurtured bandit-like figures, politicians, thereby introducing a new and even more troubling level of degeneracy because they are created and legitimized by the law, which should theoretically be (and was viewed and popularly portrayed as) a civilizing force, according to the narrative of the benevolent U.S. antiempire. His novelettes thus thread a fine line between attempting to locate Nuevomexicanos favorably within these dichotomies and highlighting the inconsistencies and contradictions within these very same dichotomies.

Chacón's portrayal of Anglo Americans as representative of a different sort of *modern* barbarism that corrupts people and culture speaks to a vision of Anglo American culture that would become a pervasive discourse in Spanish American *modernismo* by the end of the nineteenth century. Spanish American writers responded to racial discourses that portrayed Spain and Spanish American countries as backward and underdeveloped "by writing of their northern neighbors as overtly materialistic, a culture of consumers rather than thinkers, and ultimately the antithesis of the true modern spirit."[60] Chacón, like Ruiz de Burton before him, questions what it truly means to be modern, who is included in modernity, and the grounds for that inclusion. Like Ruiz de Burton, he sets the stage for later Spanish American and Mexican American writers who would capitalize on this discourse and widen an already perceptible fissure between Anglo and Hispanic cultures, which came to eventually be seen not just as different but as antagonistic to one another, locked in a battle over the meaning and practice of modernity itself.

Captivity Narratives and Race in New Mexico

While Spain—or figures of Spain and Spanishness—is presented in Chacón's two novelettes in sometimes contradictory ways, there are also a few glaring absences in these two novelettes. The first novelette, *El hijo de la tempestad*, also contains a captivity narrative—the beautiful maiden, captured by el Hijo, is eventually rescued at the end just as she is about to be forced into marriage with him. But there is something strange about this captivity narrative. As I noted in my discussion of the captivity genre in the previous chapter, American captivity narratives follow the "general scheme of fair white maidens being abducted by barbaric indigenous American captors."[61] In *El hijo de la tempestad*, the fair white maiden is obviously present, but the indigenous captors are nowhere to be found. There is no mention of el Hijo—or any other character, for that matter—having any indigenous ancestry.

As numerous critics have explained, the captivity narrative of the white woman with a male Indian captor and a white male rescuer helped construct and cement discourses of racial difference and white femininity.[62] Rebecca Blevins Faery explains, "Stories of whites captured by Indians, especially those involving women, helped in significant ways to produce the difference, at first cultural but eventually racial, in which stories of contending 'red' men and 'white' men were grounded and which became the rationale for European conquest and the emergence of a nation founded on white male supremacy. These stories, then, were a significant element in the construction of discourses of racial difference and racial categories of 'red,' 'white,' and 'black.'"[63] Faery ultimately sees the captivity narrative as leading to the construction of a (U.S.) nation based on racial difference and white male supremacy. As numerous critics have shown, captivity narratives frequently emerge and become popular at moments of crisis in the national imaginary, especially those that are racially charged. Andrea Tinnemeyer goes a step further to argue that the captivity narrative is essentially a "genre of racial encounter and border crossings" rooted in the "panic produced by the destabilization of whiteness and U.S. citizenship."[64]

Given the important role that race plays in a traditional captivity narrative, the absence of any racial difference in *El hijo de la tempestad* is particularly striking. In fact, when one looks closely at the text, the racial category of all the main characters—with the exception of the Gypsy—is not entirely clear. Chacón never explicitly defines their racial identities. Race thus appears in this text, somewhat paradoxically, more as an absence (again with the exception of the Gypsy woman). However, this absence of race is just as revealing as any more open discussion of race.

On a basic level, Chacón perhaps simply does not want to engage with the subject of indigenous influences or mixing of blood—even if it is metaphorical or even if the marriage between the maiden and el Hijo at the end of the story is ultimately frustrated. As Robert McKee Irwin also explains, *fronterizos*—those Mexicans living in the borderlands between Mexico and the United States—were very conscious of the negative ways in which they were portrayed in the United States, as "dark-skinned, uneducated, uncultured mongrel peasants."[65] In an attempt to create an image of themselves as "ethnically different than other Mexicans," Northern elites often denied any indigenous roots or racial miscegenation, once again highlighting their "pure" European pedigree.[66] Although Irwin focuses on Mexicans living in the northwest borderlands of Mexico, Chacón's "Elocuente discurso," as mentioned earlier, speaks to these same preoccupations. In fact, he delivers this speech as a defense against just these types of accusations; in his words, he is defending his community against the racist idea that "los hispanoamericanos son una gente sucia, ignorante y degradada, mezcla de indios e iberos" (*Writings*, 194) [we Spanish Americans are a dirty, ignorant, and inferior people, a mixture between Indians and Iberians (*Writings*, 187)]. But he also strategically links Nuevomexicanos to Spain and whiteness through an emphasis on the purity of their shared Spanish blood.

Legally governed by the United States but still unable to fully participate in their own governance due to their status as a territory rather than a state, Nuevomexicanos knew that their bid for statehood rested largely on their ability to convince lawmakers that they were, as a community, white enough—that is, *not* indigenous, mestizo, or black—to be included as a state. Nuevomexicanos and Anglo Americans in New Mexico who were proponents of New Mexican statehood therefore worked to portray Nuevomexicanos as Spanish and not Mexican. Many local governmental leaders insisted that the Mexicans in New Mexico were really just Americans of Spanish descent, and as the "groundswell for statehood intensified, leaders of the movement tried to vanquish all 'Mexican' impressions of these 'Spanish' Americans."[67] The word Mexican was tied to the indigenous, the "mongrel" races, and miscegenation— all of which were to be avoided if New Mexicans (both Anglos and Nuevo-mexicanos alike) wanted to gain their right to self-governance in a state with a Hispano majority. In their attempt to receive political recognition within the U.S. system, Nuevomexicanos had to deny any possible connections to sub-jects (Mexicans, Indians, mestizos) that might further mark them as racially off-white and therefore possibly unfit for self-governance. So on a basic level, perhaps Chacón does not want to associate himself, New Mexico, or the New Mexican literature he is creating with indigenous influences in any way, and he thus avoids using an indigenous captor in his otherwise fairly typical captivity narrative.

In *Tras la tormenta la calma*, there is a similar absence of racial differ-ence. Gonzales-Berry has an excellent allegorical reading of the love triangle between Lola, Pablo, and Luciano. She reads Pablo, the working-class hero of (possibly) mestizo origins, as a displacement of Chacón's anxieties about how to incorporate the unwanted indigenous other into his foundational text. She explains that "Chacón's solution to this conundrum was to create a space for the indigenous other within the trappings of a mestizo identity dis-course. Hence, when Pablo, the bronze-faced, working-class mestizo forces the fair-headed boy of the *nuevomexicano* elite . . . to join the mestiza commoner Lola in matrimony, Chacón's all-embracing ideal of a *nuevomexicano* cultural nationalism appears on the narrative palimpsest. The 'all-embracing' nature of the enterprise is of course relative since it excluded Indians *as* Indians from Chacón's imagined nation."[68] As Gonzales-Berry points out, Chacón denies space in his story for the indigenous other. Mestizaje is ambiguously present in the novel: none of the characters is explicitly labeled as mestizo, but Pablo is described as having "la color del rostro algo quemada" (*Tras la tormenta*, in *Novelitas*, 33) [the skin of his face . . . somewhat burned (*Writings*, 84)], and Lola is repeatedly labeled as "morena" (*Tras la tormenta*, in *Novelitas*, 33), or dark skinned. But this ambiguous mestizaje becomes, somewhat paradoxically, a way of erasing an indigenous presence and thus whitening through mestizaje.

The use of mestizaje as a whitening or homogenizing discourse has a long history in Spanish America and especially in Mexico, where the mestizo was officially embraced by the state in the late nineteenth and early twentieth cen-tury as the ideal citizen and a central figure in the national imaginary, inaugu-rated perhaps most clearly by Benito Juárez's ascendency to power as the first self-identifying indigenous Mexican president and the Mexican government's official embrace and promotion of mestizaje and indigenous culture as integral parts of the Mexican nation during and following the Mexican Revolution. Carrie C. Chorba, for example, notes that the Mexican state "not only touted the figure of the mestizo as the emblematic Mexican but also celebrated mestizo identity as a way of assimilating different sectors of society into a mainstream [nonindigenous] national culture."[69] But Chorba also explains that "as a totalizing vision, this mestizophile identity discourse reduced society to a single racial and ethnic essence, thus subordinating—if not denying—the heterogeneous reality of the country . . . [and sidestepping] the thorny issue of race."[70] Hispanic cultural studies scholar Joseba Gabilondo further explores the centrality of the mestizo figure to Spanish American nationalisms, explaining that in the second half of the nineteenth century, writers and intellectuals in Latin America "asumirán el problema de la raza como central a la constitución de cada república y, por eso, pasarán a hablar de 'nuestra/la raza' y del 'mestizaje' como procesos centrales de la construcción nacional"[71] [would assume the problem of race as central to the constitution of each republic, and because of that, they would proceed to talk of "our/the race" and "mestizaje" as central processes of national construction]. In other words, in the second half of the nineteenth century in Spanish America, mestizaje became a way of both talking about national identity and, paradoxically, *avoiding* discussions about racial difference and racial violence. Mestizaje was thereby positioned as an essential component of national identity, something that equalized all citizens and was a shared feature of all citizens, thus erroneously positing that racial difference and racial(ized) violence are not part of Spanish American culture or history. Following this logic, the racially marked individual—namely, the indigenous or Afro-Latino—must abandon the concept of racial difference in order to be included as part of the mestizo nation.

Chacón therefore may be signaling that there are no racial others in these stories because he wants his readers to see that there are no racial problems in New Mexico. Certainly, as we have already seen, Nuevomexicanos were striving to show lawmakers that New Mexico was a territory of descendants of Spaniards. Avoiding the issue of race or of racial difference could also be seen as a way of whitening his text; race is not an issue in New Mexico, according to this logic, because racial difference does not exist. Gabilondo explains how new constructions of mestizaje and race as central to national imaginaries and discourses of citizenship in Spanish America actually created an "absenting" of race or a move to deracialize people and communities that had previously been marked by racial difference:

En el discurso del mestizaje, el estado es la institución que reconoce el individuo racialmente marcado como sujeto puramente político y, por tanto, no marcado racialmente. Así, el estado termina por legitimar el racismo como problema

políticamente inexistente y que, por tanto, emigra al ámbito de la "cultura" y del
"arte." Es decir, el discurso del mestizaje oscilará entre la denuncia de la explo-
tación racial y la legitimación del control estatal del individuo racialmente marcado que pasa a ser sujeto político no marcado racialmente.[72]

[In the discourse of mestizaje, the state is the institution that recognizes the
racially marked individual as a purely political subject and, therefore, not racially
marked. Thus the state qualifies racism as a nonexistent political problem, causing it to emigrate to the realms of "culture" and "art." That is to say, discourse
around mestizaje oscillates between a denunciation of racial exploitation and
the legitimation of state control of the racially marked individual who becomes a
nonracially marked political subject.]

Gabilondo looks at José Martí's ideas about mestizaje and the mestizo as an
example of this transformation of race and racial ideologies in Latin America.
While Martí has been applauded for his egalitarian and progressive stances on
race and mestizaje in Latin America, Gabilondo argues that

lo que interesa a Martí no es la celebración del mestizaje como nueva realidad
y teleología racial de Latinoamérica, sino precisamente la desaparición del
problema racial bajo la nueva equiparación del individuo mestizo con la [equi-
paración] de sujeto de estado . . . , por lo cual simultáneamente el problema
racial se afirma en su universalidad de ciudadanía y se niega como particularidad
histórica. . . . A partir de la universalización natural del mestizo como único
ciudadano de la república latinoamericana, Martí pasa a negar la historia particular del conflicto racial en Latinoamérica y, consecuentemente, convierte esta
negación en teleología e ideología racial.[73]

[what interests Martí is not the celebration of mestizaje as a new Latin American reality and racial teleology but rather precisely the disappearance of racial
problems under the new equivalence of the mestizo individual with that of the
subject of the state . . . , through which the racial problem is simultaneously con-
firmed in its universality as citizenship and negated as a historical peculiarity. . . .
From this natural universalization of the mestizo as sole citizen of the Latin
American republic, Martí goes on to deny the peculiar history of racial conflict
in Latin America and, consequently, transforms this denial into racial ideology
and teleology.]

Although Gabilondo is speaking particularly about Martí's views on race, his
larger argument is that this conceptualization of race—this erasure of racial
difference and racial conflict as part of national histories and imaginaries—is
actually characteristic of national(ist) racial discourses of citizenship and

belonging (such as mestizaje). In a similar way, by grouping all Nuevomexicanos into one homogeneous racial category that is able to go unmarked and
unnamed, Chacón attempts to deracialize New Mexico while simultaneously
writing indigenous people out of his foundational texts. In Chacón's two novelettes, New Mexico is not a region of racial others or dangerous racial mixings but rather a region with no racial problems, where race does not need to
be defined, contested, or even contemplated because it appears that everyone
has assimilated to the Hispanic norm. Even those who might be labeled biologically mestizo have lost all cultural traces of indigeneity. Indeed, it is interesting that the only racial other explicitly mentioned in these two novelettes
is the Gypsy—someone not from the New World but a remnant of the Old—a
ghost of the Spanish imperial past. In Chacón's New Mexico, it seems that
there are no racial others precisely because there is no racial difference. Even
if we consider Pablo and Lola as mestizo figures, as Gonzales-Berry does, the
type of mestizaje embraced here is the type that homogenizes and whitens
through assimilation to the dominant hispanized culture. In Chacón's foundational fictions, racial conflicts do not need to be resolved through marriage
because these conflicts do not exist.

Although Chacón knew Nuevomexicanos would have to prove their whiteness in order to be included within the racist U.S. nation, he also saw how the
racial hierarchies within which he was enmeshed could be used against Nuevomexicanos if this "proof" of whiteness ultimately failed to be recognized.
Once again, Chacón walks a fine line between two discursive modes. On the
one hand, he looks at the mixing of races in the Gypsy as dirty and degenerative; he does not want to associate himself with racial miscegenation of any
kind, lest Nuevomexicanos be viewed as off-white or not fully white. On the
other hand, he seems to deny the very existence of race or racial identities at all
by refusing to racially define his characters (except the Gypsy). As Chacón and
his fellow Nuevomexicanos moved toward statehood, they continually had to
confront this same dilemma: they were forced to construct their racial identities within a discourse of racial difference even as they fought to show that
there was indeed *no* racial difference in New Mexico—it was not a territory
of indigenous, Mexicans, and mestizos but rather a region of Nuevomexicanos
and descendants of pure Spaniards, a space where race does not matter and
histories of racial conflict have been erased.

Ambivalent Endings: The Language of Subalternity

One of the only markers of difference in these novelettes is language. Chacón
writes exclusively in Spanish in the novelettes. He seems to be using language
not as a racial marker but as a cultural one, identifying his audience as Spanish speakers—a culturally but not necessarily racially distinct group within an

English-dominant country. When Chacón writes these novelettes, the imagined community he is writing to and for consists of his fellow elite, Spanish-speaking Nuevomexicanos. These stories are their histories: reminders of the degeneracy they have overcome, warnings about the difficulties and possibilities that lie ahead, and lessons about how to portray themselves if they wish, as he certainly does, to be included in U.S. politics and society. Even as he attempts to find a space for Nuevomexicanos within a racist Anglo America through his erasure of Indians and indigeneity, he also simultaneously marks his community as distinct from Anglo America (and from Mexico or Spain, for that matter). They are Spanish speakers, with their own history and literary tradition distinct from "gabachos" and "extranjeros" (*El hijo*, in *Novelitas*, 2). He strives to show that Nuevomexicanos are white enough to be included in the U.S. nation, but he also attempts to create a space for New Mexican literature and culture that is simultaneously separate from—but not necessarily antagonistic toward—Anglo America. He carves out a space for Nuevomexicanos that is simultaneously incorporated within but also distinct from the U.S. national imaginary. However, Chacón's decision to use Spanish for his novelettes is probably one of the main reasons they have remained so understudied and peripheral to the U.S. literary canon. In this way, the continued marginalization of his writing also speaks to the transformation of Spanish from a hegemonic language of power within the Spanish colonies and Mexico to a subversive and also subordinate language within the English-speaking, dominant context of the United States. His texts thus anticipate the ways in which the Spanish language would become a marker of cultural and racial difference within the United States.[74]

Chacón's novelettes meditate on the new regional and national identities being contested and created in New Mexico in the late nineteenth century. Ultimately, in these two novelettes, he offers us a glimpse of the many contradictions and tensions that elite Nuevomexicanos had to navigate in their move to articulate their own unique identity as a community during this moment of immense change, as they transitioned from a position of colonizer to colonized. Chacón looks to Spain and the Spanish literary tradition as a way of linking Nuevomexicanos to the Old World, Europe, and through a shared similar sense of whiteness, Anglo America. At the same time, however, Chacón's texts seek to be a voice of a new literary tradition in New Mexico. Even as Chacón—and other Nuevomexicanos like him—looks to the Old World for legitimacy within the racist U.S. system, he simultaneously situates himself and his literature within the New World, within New Mexico, as part of a completely new identity—Spanish and broadly American but, above all, uniquely New Mexican.

Chacón's novelettes and especially his introduction to them build up his literature as foundational for not only New Mexican literature and culture but also, allegorically, the New Mexican community imaginary. Similar to the texts I have examined in previous chapters, this little book highlights a period in the nineteenth century when different colonial affiliations (e.g., being a former Spanish colony) and languages (Spanish versus English) did not prevent Nuevomexicanos from imagining a space for themselves within the U.S. nation. The novelettes thus speak to a history of Hispano-Anglo cultural and political relations that sought out affinities rather than antagonisms between certain segments of the Anglo and Hispano populations in the Americas even as they also question, albeit more subtly than the works of Ruiz de Burton or Zavala, the limitations and inconsistencies of U.S. governance. Chacón nonetheless proposes a way for Nuevomexicanos to enter U.S. politics through a strategic positioning of Nuevomexicanos as white (enough) and civilized. This evocation of whiteness should not be understood as a type of assimilation to Anglo America, however. Rather, it is one component of a racial and ethnic identity that has, according to Chacón, always been present in New Mexico. At the same time, he also fights for a uniquely New Mexican linguistic and cultural tradition that is distinct from both Mexico and Anglo America. The community he envisions is very specific to the local—New Mexico. It might be understood as intercultural in the sense that it is enmeshed within U.S. politics and seeks to be included as part of that nation—though simultaneously as a distinct community with its own unique linguistic and cultural tradition.

Like Sierra O'Reilly's and Ruiz de Burton's works, Chacón's novelettes also highlight the ways in which the prior Spanish-Mexican colonialist status of borderland elites continued to inform and influence their position and imagining of themselves within a new empire (the United States). Prior colonialist systems of domination, whereby indigenous communities were often violently stripped of rights, properties, and other social and physical goods, still impacted the ways in which communities and individuals in New Mexico—and the rest of Greater Mexico—saw themselves and others, especially in terms of race, culture, and politics. Chacón is able to write these types of stories and imagine a space for Spanish-speaking Nuevomexicanos in the U.S. nation in part only because of his position of (relative) power within the still-visible and influential Spanish-Mexican colonialist system. Certain individuals and communities in the borderlands—those with darker skin, manual laborers, and those with less clearly visible ties to Europe, Spain, modernity, and civilization—would have doubtless found this a much more difficult if not futile task.

Chacón's writings also bring to light, somewhat paradoxically through silence, the racial "others" who have been omitted from a cohesive narrative of nation or community formation in parts of Greater Mexico. They have been silenced—through whitening, exclusion, or outright violence—first within the Spanish-Mexican colonialist system and then later through a racist legal system and social hierarchy under the U.S. government. If this is a foundational text, as Chacón argues, then the foundations of New Mexican literature and culture are built, to a certain extent, upon the erasure, repression, and silencing of racial others within the New Mexican community.

Indeed, it seems particularly fitting that Chacón himself writes that these novelettes are foundational New Mexican texts, the "semilla de la literatura recreativa" (*Writings*, 2) [seed of an entertaining literature (*Writings*, 49)], because this highlights how Mexican American identity, particularly in the case of New Mexico, has *not* always been premised upon antagonism toward Anglo America. His writings demonstrate that in the nineteenth century, many Nuevomexicanos sought to work with and within Anglo American politics and society—and some, like Chacón, in fact saw intercultural coalition-building between Anglos and Mexican Americans as foundational to their future identity as a community. Yet his critique of the ways in which the United States has unequally meted out the benefits of modernity and his defense of his community as a distinct entity—legally part of the United States but also culturally and linguistically distinct—also indicate the limits to such a tradition of collaboration between Anglos and Mexicanos.

His work, in this sense, marks a moment of transition when some Mexican Americans still saw the possibility of a future for themselves within the United States. But we can also see how he, like many other Mexican Americans, begins to question whether that shared future was one he should desire, whether it was one in which Mexican Americans would ever be included as equals or whether they needed to create their own community, separate from mainstream Anglo America. His poem "A la Patria," mentioned at the beginning of this chapter, reflects the preoccupations of Mexican Americans like Chacón as the century closed: What is their "patria"? Where do they belong? Or why don't they belong? Whether that "patria" is located in the United States or Mexico, Chacón's poem is unequivocal in its ending: "Roto el laurel" [The wreath is bent], he writes, and "me alejaré llorando" [I shall bid adieu in tears]. As the century closed, Mexican Americans increasingly said goodbye not just to their past identities as Mexicans but also to the idea that they might have and sustain a relationship of collaboration and cooperation with Anglos in the United States. While Chacón's earlier work, these novelettes, examines the possibilities for inclusion within the United States, his later work became much more pessimistic about the prospects for Nuevomexicanos in the United States and much more strident in its attack on the dominant U.S. Anglo American culture.

Conclusion

◄◇►

Remember(ing) the Alamo:
Archival Ghosts, Past and
Future

In the final days of the siege of the Alamo (February 23–March 6, 1836), a turning point in the Texas Revolution (1835–1836), General Santa Anna, the leader of the Mexican army, famously ordered his men to take no prisoners, despite the fact that the rebel Texans were greatly outnumbered and almost certain to lose the battle. This battle has gone down in Texas lore as one in which brave Texans, including such legendary names as Davy Crockett and Jim Bowie, fought valiantly for Texas independence to their very last breath.[1] But it also served as an example, according to this same folklore, of Mexicans' barbarity and ruthlessness. Following this vein of thought, only a truly savage people would so mercilessly mow down so many men without offering any conditions of surrender.

In 1836, the phrase "Remember the Alamo!" quickly became a rallying cry for rebel Texans, and news of the crushing defeat, contrary to Santa Anna's predictions, actually attracted new recruits to the Texas cause from throughout the United States. But the Alamo and how it was remembered also reinforced the belief among Anglo Americans that Mexicans were uncivilized and cruel—an inferior race, distinct from Anglo Americans—and that the conquest of Mexican territory was therefore not only justified but ordained by God, part of the manifest destiny of the United States. In U.S. popular culture, the Alamo thus came to symbolize the heroism and patriotism of freedom-loving Texas Anglos as well as the cruelty and savagery of Mexicans. It has also come to encapsulate the fierce antagonism between these two cultures and countries and, for many Mexicanos, their oppression by Anglos. The Alamo itself, as a space of public memory, has come to be revered as almost holy ground for many Texans and remains today the most visited tourist attraction in the state.[2]

For most of the nineteenth century, however, the physical space of the Alamo had remained mostly forgotten, used for various purposes, such as "a grain facility for the U.S. Quartermaster's Depot, a supply store, and a whiskey house."[3] It was not until the turn of the twentieth century, in fact, that the Alamo really became celebrated as a site of public culture with national significance in the United States.[4] The Alamo returned to the public eye nearly seventy-five years after the Battle of the Alamo when two women fought what historian L. Robert Ables termed the "second battle for the Alamo."[5] These women were Clara Driscoll, the wealthy daughter of a prominent Texan family with a multimillion-dollar empire in ranching, banking, and commercial developments; and Adina De Zavala, an ardent patriot of Texas, defender of Texas history, and the granddaughter of Mexican statesman and the first vice-president of Texas, Lorenzo de Zavala. This second battle for the Alamo took place not on the battlefield but in the public arena—in sensational newspaper articles and Texas courtrooms—as the two women and their supporters fought over how the Alamo should be preserved and who should be the guardian of the site. It was a battle of words instead of weapons over what the Alamo meant and would mean and how that history would be written.

These two "battles" for the Alamo—or over how the Alamo would be remembered—reveal the power of narrative in constructing and writing national(ized) histories. But they also demonstrate how resistance and antagonism would come to be seen as the essential and dominant discourses for understanding U.S./Mexican and Anglo/Hispano interactions. As the nineteenth century closed, this second battle of the Alamo spoke to the ways in which the discourses I have highlighted in *Forgotten Futures*—the discourses of transnational collaboration, intercultural negotiation, and hemispheric solidarity, as well as the internal fragmentation and hierarchies of power that supported such transnational and intercultural endeavors—would indeed become almost entirely forgotten and erased from national(ized) memories.

The second battle for the Alamo was in some ways a contest over the physical space of the Alamo. De Zavala, for example, at one point barricaded herself inside the Alamo and refused to leave for three days, effectively "under siege," as the sheriff cut off electricity and forbade anyone from bringing her food or water.[6] But it was also a dispute over the meaning of the Alamo and the way that history is written. Two cohorts of women, one led by De Zavala and the other by Driscoll, were both part of the Daughters of the Republic of Texas (DRT), an organization that worked (and still works today) to research, preserve, and protect the history of the Republic of Texas.[7] The two factions of women within the DRT disagreed, however, about exactly *how* the Alamo should be preserved and what parts of the site deserved preservation.

De Zavala and her supporters wanted to preserve the Alamo as it had stood from its early Spanish mission days, including the convent/barracks; she also believed that the convent/barracks had been where most of the fighting had taken place during the 1836 battle. Driscoll and her contingent wanted to demolish the convent/barracks portion of the property in order to build a more eye-pleasing park surrounding the mission chapel; in doing so, they would be able to make the revolutionary battle, not its history as a Spanish mission, the central focus of the site, since they felt the chapel was the site of most historical significance related to the battle of 1836.[8] The two women and their groups also disagreed about who should be the guardian of this hallowed site. De Zavala had initiated the DRT's involvement with the Alamo and dedicated her life to researching and recording Texas history and therefore wanted her chapter of the DRT to be in charge of the site's maintenance, but Driscoll had fronted most of the money to purchase the property and therefore felt her chapter should be the guardian.

Following her "siege" in the Alamo, De Zavala and her followers were ostracized from the rest of the DRT. In 1910, her chapter was legally disaffiliated from the DRT and lost control of and any rights to the custody of the Alamo.[9] In 1911, Governor Oscar B. Colquitt decided that the convent/barracks portion of the Alamo should be preserved and renovated—a victory for De Zavala and her supporters, who continued to operate as a group despite being officially disbanded from the DRT. But just two years later, while Colquitt was out of state, his lieutenant governor ordered the demolition of the upper-story walls of the convent/barracks.[10] For most of the twentieth century, the DRT failed to recognize De Zavala for her role in the preservation of the Alamo.[11] Driscoll, on the other hand, was long lauded as the "savior" of the Alamo.[12]

De Zavala nonetheless continued to dedicate her life to the preservation of Texas history. In 1917, she self-published a book, *History and Legends of the Alamo and Other Missions in and around San Antonio*. The culmination of more than twenty years of research on Texas history and folklore for De Zavala, this slim volume is a polyphonic collection that mixes together history, legends, folklore, poetry, diaries, and other archival documents. As a whole, the different histories, stories, and excerpts in her collection explore and comment on the Battle of the Alamo and, more generally, the history of early Texas. But perhaps more importantly, *History and Legends of the Alamo* contests a certain vision of history—encapsulated in the phrase "Remember the Alamo!"—that has pitted U.S. Anglo Americans and Mexicanos against one another. Instead, her book "remembers the Alamo" in a different way—as a place that represents the multilingual, multiethnic, and transnational origins of Texas and the United States.

At the beginning of the section "Legends of the Alamo" in *History and Legends of the Alamo*, De Zavala inserts a poem by Grantland Rice, an early twentieth-century U.S. writer best known for his sports writing. The poem, "Ghosts of the Alamo," begins by alerting readers to the ways in which the past still haunts the present at the Alamo:

> There's the tramp of a ghost on the low winds tonight,
>   And echo that drifts like a dream on its way;
> There's the blue of the specter that leaves for the fight,
>   Grave-risen at last from a long vanished day;
> There's the shout and the call of grim soul unto soul
> As they rise one by one, out of death's shadowed glen
>   To follow the bugle—the drum's muffled roll,
>   Where the Ghosts of the Alamo gather again.[13]

The poem goes on to say exactly who those ghosts are: Davy Crockett "leaps from the dust," Jim Bowie "caresses a blade red with rust," and Lieutenant Colonel William Travis calls "the roll of his men / And a voice answers 'Here!'"[14]

But if De Zavala starts her book by invoking, through the inclusion of Rice's poem, these now famous U.S. folk heroes, many other moments in *History and Legends of the Alamo* subtly contest this one-sided version of Texas history, which begins, supposedly, with the Battle of the Alamo. She includes popular folktales and legends from the Tejano community, and she also incorporates Spanish documents from the early Spanish settlers, excerpts from church records of Spanish missionaries, and artistic renderings of the early missions from Mexican sources.[15] Thus her text highlights not just the Anglo contributions to Texas history—those of Crockett, Bowie, and Stephen Austin, for example—but also the ways in which Tejanos contributed to the early settlement of Texas and the Texas Revolution, thereby also bringing to light the Spanish and Mexican history of Texas.[16] De Zavala's book, in other words, shows that there are other ghosts haunting the Alamo: the Tejanos, for instance, who are not even named or included in a poem such as Rice's (except, perhaps, as adversaries to the "true" Texan heroes) but played an important role in Texas history.

De Zavala's entreaty during her "battle" with Driscoll to save the convent/barracks portion of the Alamo from demolition mirrors her dedication to writing about and documenting all parts of the history of the Alamo and of Texas—its Spanish and Mexican history as well as its U.S. American history. Yet even her rendering of Texas history contains its own gaps and shortcomings. *History and Legends of the Alamo* often romanticizes and extols the grandeur of the Spanish mission past with little regard for the violence against indigenous communities that is an essential part of that history.

The first battle for the Alamo, in 1836, was a military battle over national boundaries. The second was a legal and rhetorical contest over a site of national and regional symbolic importance. I bring up both battles here, albeit briefly and a bit superficially, because they demonstrate the ways in which history is being nearly constantly (re)written, remembered, constructed, and manipulated in order to fit the needs of different communities. The objects that we use to record history and culture—whether a diary, a popular legend, or a monument—are sites of constant revision and negotiation.

It is significant that the battle of the Alamo has traditionally been portrayed in the United States as "us" versus "them," with a fairly clear line between Mexicanos and Anglo Americans. In this representation of the Alamo as the crucible for Texan identity, the Alamo reinforces the idea that Texas was made by and for Anglos and "serves mythologically as a second birthplace for the [U.S.] American, who undergoes a regeneration in the sacrificial death inside the Alamo image."[17] Tejanos and Mexicanos, according to this mythology of the Alamo, are not part of this origin story—except as antagonists. De Zavala, on the other hand, highlights the contributions of Tejanos, like her grandfather, to the Texas Revolution. Her book and her dedication to and interest in preserving Spanish mission sites similarly shows that Texas has long been a region of linguistic, cultural, and ethnic diversity and that the origins of Texas begin not with the Alamo but rather much earlier, with the Spanish settlement of the region. Furthermore, this "second battle of the Alamo" reveals how these sorts of narratives about national consolidation are constructed only after the fact—in this case, nearly seventy-five years after the original battle.

De Zavala's text thus meditates on how history is written and what gets left out after something like the Battle of the Alamo becomes enmeshed within national(ized) histories. Even as De Zavala celebrates Texas's history, she also suggests that it is impossible to understand the Alamo, or Texas, without also considering the multiethnic, multiracial, multilingual, and transnational roots of its community and without considering the intimate connections between Anglos and Mexicanos.

In *History and Legends of the Alamo*, De Zavala turns to the past to show how the histories of Mexico and the United States were densely intertwined, and not always in antagonistic ways, thus speaking to the discourses I have uncovered in earlier texts by Mexicanos throughout the nineteenth century. Yet her book was not just about the past. It was also about her present and future, just as historic sites, monuments, and sites of public memory such as the Alamo remain battlegrounds over the present and future identities of our community. Anthropologist Holly Beachley Brear explains that these sorts of contested sites "are still where we fight the social and political Other, but with images and words rather than guns."[18] It is through these sites, she continues, that "we create boundaries between 'us' and 'them' with identities born from historic individuals, identities inherited by entire groups in current society. Our battle sites, in being the origin of these images, become our most hallowed ground and the object of patriotic pilgrimages."[19]

History and Legends of the Alamo, seen in this light, might be understood as a response to the debate with Driscoll about the Alamo and an attempt to include that part of the Alamo—the Spanish mission history, not just the Texas Revolutionary history—that had been at least partially demolished, literally and figuratively. Because the Alamo is supposedly the origin of Texas society and identity, "claiming its past is a principal means of establishing groups and individuals as being heirs to the present."[20] As Brear explains, "Those who control identities born at the Alamo receive ancestral ties to the past, ownership to the present, and, if calls to 'Remember the Alamo' remain intact, inheritance rights to the future."[21] In this sense, De Zavala's book is about the past, but it is also about the role that the past has in our present and, significantly, our future. It is about how we construct our communities and who gets to be considered a member, with the past serving as a form of legitimacy for inclusion in the present and future.

Although De Zavala, like her grandfather before her, shows many of the connections between Mexicanos and Anglos during the nineteenth century, her vision of the past would ultimately be silenced—just as she herself would remain during her life largely unrecognized by Anglo-centric mainstream Texas for her role in the preservation of the Alamo and just as her grandfather's contributions to the Republic of Texas would be largely erased from U.S. American history.

I chose to conclude with a discussion of Adina De Zavala in part because I started this book in chapter 1 by talking about her grandfather, Lorenzo de Zavala; the contrast between how the discourses of transnational and intercultural collaboration are voiced in the two texts and the historical contexts is striking. Lorenzo de Zavala, writing in 1834, explicitly discusses the future of Mexico as well as Mexico's potential to work alongside the United States in their joint battle for republican values such as liberty and equality. He is somewhat ambivalent about what this will mean for Mexicanos, but it is nonetheless a possibility—and one that he sees materializing, significantly, in the future. It is fitting that the very last line of his travel narrative is written in the future tense, as he postulates that "el sistema americano obtendrá una victoria completa aunque sangrienta" (*Viage*, 368) [the American system will obtain a complete though bloody victory (*Journey*, 195).]

Adina De Zavala, on the other hand, writing in the early decades of the twentieth century, engages with this same discourse of collaboration not by imagining a future collaboration between Anglos and Mexicanos but by recuperating a usable past—a past that would legitimate her and other Tejanos as truly part of Texas and the United States. For Adina, it appears that this discourse of collaboration and intercultural negotiation, even when attempting to work toward a new future for Tejanos and Mexicanos, could only now be envisioned in the past. It is fitting, in fact, that De Zavala's book includes so many ghosts and stories about haunted spaces. Adina De Zavala, her history of the Alamo, and her fight to preserve the Alamo speak to and mirror the different cultural dynamics and historical discourses I have uncovered throughout *Forgotten Futures*, but her method of portraying them—in the past tense, as a haunting, rather than in a speculative future—indicates a significant change in the ways in which these discourses might be used and articulated. By the beginning of the twentieth century, a period that witnessed the growth of segregation of Latinos in the United States as well as their racialization and expulsion from the category of whiteness, this discourse of collaboration between Anglos and Mexicanos could only be voiced as such—as ephemeral and ghostlike, as a haunting of the past that could only be dimly perceived. The fact that she ultimately lost her battle for the Alamo indicates just how much power this discourse had also lost by the beginning of the twentieth century. It reflects how discourses of resistance and antagonism were becoming the dominant ways of viewing interactions between the United States and Mexico and between Anglos and Mexicanos. Rather than understanding the Alamo as a space that demonstrates the convergence of different cultures and nations and the shared history of different communities, the U.S. public would ultimately come to interpret the Alamo, as Driscoll and others desired, as a site of U.S. nation-making and as a site that speaks to the antagonism and differences between Anglos and Mexicanos.

In *Forgotten Futures* I have sought to reexamine these forgotten discourses of transnational collaboration, hemispheric solidarity, and intercultural negotiation, but not necessarily to celebrate them, for, like De Zavala's portrayal of savage Indians and gentle missionaries—which imagines a version of Texas history in which not Anglos but Spaniards are the first "true" Texans, thus simultaneously erasing the indigenous presence—they are constructed on their own deeply problematic grounds. Yet to ignore these unpleasant dimensions of the history of Greater Mexico serves as a way of whitewashing history and functions as a type of historical color blindness. It renders incomplete and fragmentary an incredibly complicated picture of the past. Although these discourses are no longer the dominant ones in Greater Mexico today, they reveal important insights about the experiences of nineteenth-century Mexicanos, how they saw themselves in a hemispheric context, and the sorts of internal schisms and violence that would eventually need to be strategically forgotten in order for them to come together as a community. Racism, classism, sexism, and other forms of marginalization continue to exist in Greater Mexico—as they do everywhere. To recognize this history, as well as its attempted erasure, is therefore also a way of acknowledging its pervasiveness and its continuation into the present. It is a way of recognizing how we are all, in our present, haunted by this shared past.

Acknowledgments

I have been thinking about the topics and the people in this book for nearly a decade. Over that period of time, many people have helped me along the way and improved this book in ways almost too numerous to count, but I will do my best to acknowledge them here.

First, I am grateful for the guidance I received as a graduate student at Indiana University, where I first started thinking and writing about the ideas contained in this book. Deborah Cohn, my advisor, helped make my writing better and my critical analysis sharper. She was a generous and thoughtful mentor in both intellectual and practical matters. Alejandro Mejías-López and Kathleen Myers opened me up to new and exciting ideas through their teaching and research and our personal interactions. My book is greatly informed and inspired by their research and approaches to Latin American literature and culture. Lastly, I am grateful to John M. Nieto-Phillips, who is not only a first-rate scholar but also a great mentor, colleague, and friend. John introduced me to the vibrant field of Hispanic recovery work.

Numerous people have read drafts and different versions of parts of this book, and I am thankful to all of them. Silvia Roca-Martínez read various versions of my book chapters and patiently responded to my sometimes-tedious questions, especially about minutiae related to translations. I am appreciative of her patience, critical eye, and camaraderie. I have had several long-distance writing partners who provided valuable feedback to me at critical moments as I developed my book: thank you to Elise Bartosik-Vélez, Nicholas E. Bonneau, Kelley Kreitz, Jared Patten, and Emily Tobey. Through the National Center for Faculty Development and Diversity, I met other long-distance colleagues, including Tyson Brown, Candace Kaleimamoowahinekapu Galla, and Ray Block. Although they are in different fields, their support was critical as I worked to complete this book. I was also privileged to be able to share portions of my book at several different conferences and seminars in which senior colleagues provided useful feedback on my project. Kirsten Silva Gruesz, Anna Brickhouse, Theresa Delgadillo, and John Alba Cutler provided insightful suggestions and encouragement in such instances. I also thank the other participants in the Newberry Library Seminar on Borderlands and Latino/a Studies for their comments and questions on an early version of chapter 2 and the participants in the C19 Seminar "The Hemispheric South and the (Un)Common Ground of Comparability," who helped me think through many of the theoretical questions that I engage with throughout this work. Lastly, I thank the two anonymous readers who read my manuscript and book proposal for their insightful comments and suggestions.

When I was just starting the research for this book, Gabriel Meléndez and Francisco Lomelí sent me an advanced copy of their (then forthcoming) manuscript, *The Writings of Eusebio Chacón*, which was immensely important for my research. Without their generosity, I would have certainly been much delayed in completing this book.

I would also like to express my appreciation to the Instituto Franklin for allowing me to reprint my article "Race, Slavery, and Liberalism in Lorenzo de Zavala's *Viage a los Estados-Unidos del Norte de América*," which forms part of chapter 1. This article was originally published in the Instituto Franklin-UAH's academic journal, *Camino Real* 10 (2015): 24–36. And I would also like to thank Arte Público Press for generously granting me extensive use of Wallace Woolsey's translation, *Journey to the United States of North America / Viaje a los Estados Unidos del Norte de América*, written by Lorenzo de Zavala and edited by John-Michael Rivera (Houston: Arte Público Press, 2005).

At Purdue University, I have been fortunate to find very supportive and welcoming colleagues who have also contributed to the book's development. Marcia Stephenson, Patty Hart, and Paul Dixon all read portions of my book at different points. They have also been amazing mentors and colleagues. Niall Peach and Ricardo Quintana Vallejo were excellent research assistants, and they also helped me refine my thoughts through their engaging questions and discussions in class. Niall assisted with many of the English translations. All errors are, of course, my own. Members of my writing groups at Purdue— Katie Brownell, Elena Coda, Jennifer Kaufmann-Buhler, Maren Linett, Erin Moodie, Shelley Staples, Laura Zanotti, and Stephanie Zywicki—provided invaluable feedback, support, and friendship throughout my first years. Antonia Syson was also a key member of this group and one of the first faculty members to welcome me to Purdue. She was a generous friend, colleague, and writing partner who read and gave detailed feedback on many chapters of this book. We deeply miss her sharp wit, eye for detail, and boisterous laughter.

I am grateful to Greg Clingham and Pam Dailey at Bucknell University Press for their support of this project and their guidance in preparing the manuscript for publication. I am also greatly indebted to Sam Brawand at Brawand Consulting for her skilled and efficient editing at a crucial moment in the manuscript preparation process.

My deepest thanks go to my entire family for their encouragement and support, which came in so many different forms over the years that it would be impossible for me to list them all here. I would not have completed this book without their love and support, especially that of my partner and husband, Greg.

Notes

Introduction

1 Jovita González and Eve Raleigh (a.k.a. Margaret Eimer), *Caballero: A Historical Novel*, ed. José E. Limón and María E. Cotera (College Station: Texas A&M University Press, 1996) (hereafter cited as *Caballero* by page).

2 I use *Texas Mexican* and *Tejano* interchangeably. *Tejano* (or *Texas Mexican*) as I use it refers to Mexicans and those of Hispanic ancestry living in the territory of Texas, and with cultural and ancestral ties to Texas. It is therefore a regional rather than national term and can be applied to the communities of Hispanic origin living in Texas during Mexican or U.S. rule of the territory (i.e., from 1821 to the present).

3 For more information on Jovita González's life and her work, see chapter 3 of José E. Limón, *Dancing with the Devil: Society and Cultural Poetics in Mexican-American South Texas* (Madison: University of Wisconsin Press, 1994), 60–75.

4 Numerous literary critics have interpreted *Caballero* as a commentary on cross-cultural collaboration and accommodation. See María E. Cotera, *Native Speakers: Ella Deloria, Zora Neale Hurston, Jovita González, and the Poetics of Culture* (Austin: University of Texas Press, 2008); and her "Hombres Necios: A Critical Epilogue," in *Caballero*, 359–350. As a rewriting of history that positions Anglos and Tejanos as complementary participants in a foundational moment in Texan history and culture, see Vincent Pérez, *Remembering the Hacienda: History and Memory in the Mexican American Southwest* (College Station: Texas A&M University Press, 2006).

5 The manuscript, along with other significant documents related to the life and work of Jovita González and her husband, E. E. Mireles, was donated to the Special Collections and Archives Department of the Mary and Jeff Bell Library, Texas A&M University–Corpus Christi in 1992 (see Thomas H. Kreneck, foreword to *Caballero*, ix). For more on the recovery of *Caballero* and the history of the E. E. Mireles and Jovita González de Mireles Papers in the Special Collections and Archives at Texas A&M University–Corpus Christi, see archivist Kreneck's foreword to *Caballero* (ix–x).

6 Letters suggest that from 1938 to 1939, González and Eimer sent the novel to at least three major publishers—Macmillan, Houghton-Mifflin, and Bobbs-Merrill—but it was never selected for publication. Limón, introduction to *Caballero*, xix.

7 In his introduction to *Caballero* (1996), José Limón notes that González received a one-year fellowship from the Rockefeller Foundation in 1934 that relieved her of

her duties as a high school Spanish teacher in order to research and write a book on South Texan history and culture. He concludes that she most likely began the process of writing and researching for *Caballero* (along with another collection of folkloric sketches, *Dew on the Thorn*) in 1934 (xvii). González invited Eimer to coauthor the novel with her in 1937 (xviii–xix).

8 Kreneck, foreword to *Caballero*, ix.

9 For a reading of *Caballero* as a foundational fiction, following Doris Sommer's *Foundational Fictions: The National Romances of Latin America* (1984; Berkeley: University of California Press, 1991), see José E. Limón, "Mexicans, Foundational Fictions, and the United States: *Caballero*, a Late Border Romance," *Modern Language Quarterly* 57, no. 2 (1996): 341–353.

10 At the end of the novel, for example, the narrator also makes sure to point out that Susanita, one of the main characters, gives birth to a blue-eyed baby girl who is "blond and so white and the loveliest thing in the world." *Caballero*, 333.

11 For analyses of the feminist critiques voiced through the female characters in *Caballero*, see Monica Kaup, "The Unsustainable Hacienda: The Rhetoric of Progress in Jovita González and Eve Raleigh's *Caballero*," *Modern Fiction Studies* 51, no. 3 (2005): 561–591; María E. Cotera, "Recovering 'Our' History: *Caballero* and the Gendered Politics of Form," *Aztlán: A Journal of Chicano Studies* 32, no. 2 (2007): 157–171; and John M. González, "Terms of Engagement: Nation or Patriarchy in Jovita González's and Eve Raleigh's *Caballero*," in *Recovering the U.S. Hispanic Literary Heritage*, ed. José F. Aranda and Silvio Torres-Saillant (Houston: Arte Público Press, 2002), 4:264–276.

12 Pablo A. Ramirez, "Resignifying Preservation: A Borderlands Response to American Eugenics in Jovita González and Eve Raleigh's *Caballero*," *Canadian Review of American Studies / Revue canadienne d'études américaines* 39, no. 1 (2009): 22. Ramirez convincingly argues that the 1930s therefore mark a formative moment in U.S. history when "Mexican Americans are being driven out of the nation and officially expelled from the category of whiteness" (22).

13 For example, Nicole M. Guidotti-Hernández argues that González's oeuvre "replicates a hegemonic vision of Spanish caste and U.S.-based race relations in her rendering of the Texas-Mexican national imaginary, one that incisively critiques gender inequality but that colludes with rather than offering a critique of U.S. and Mexican racial ideologies." *Unspeakable Violence: Remapping U.S. and Mexican National Imaginaries* (Durham, N.C.: Duke University Press, 2011), 170.

14 *Caballero*, 54.

15 *Caballero*, 54.

16 Vincent Pérez similarly argues that "interethnic romance thus projects Mexican American inclusion within a liberal and modern New South(west), an imagined bicultural society in which the pre-modern agrarian culture of its Mexican (i.e., southern) minority has not been lost but has ideally served to enrich and transform a modern Anglo American society driven by individualism and commercialism." *Remembering the Hacienda*, 96.

17 Limón, introduction to *Caballero*, xix.

18 Limón, xviii.

19 Limón, xxi–xxii.

20 For more on the historical and cultural context of the Chicano movement in reaction to earlier assimilationist currents in the Mexican American community, see Rodolfo Acuña, *Occupied America: A History of Chicanos*, 4th ed. (New York:

Longman, 2000), 328–385; Randy Ontiveros, *In the Spirit of a New People: The Cultural Politics of a New Movement*, E-book Library (New York: New York University Press, 2013); and Juan Gómez-Quiñones and Irene Vásquez, *Making Aztlán: Ideology and Culture of the Chicana and Chicano Movement, 1966–1977*, E-book Library (Albuquerque: University of New Mexico Press, 2014). For a thorough discussion and problematization of the (supposedly) oppositional poles of assimilation and authenticity, see John Alba Cutler's *Ends of Assimilation: The Formation of Chicano Literature* (Oxford: Oxford University Press, 2015).

21 Numerous critics have examined and critiqued this reified image of Chicano identity and community. Groundbreaking examples include Juan Bruce-Novoa, "Canonical and Non-canonical Texts," in *Retrospace: Collected Essays on Chicano Literature* (Houston: Arte Público Press, 1990), 132–145; and Chabram-Dernersesian, "I Throw Punches for My Race, but I Don't Want to Be a Man: Writing Us—Chica-nos (Girl, Us) / Chicana—into the Movement Script," in *Cultural Studies*, ed. Lawrence Grossberg, Cary Nelson, and Paula A. Treichler (New York: Routledge, 1992), 81–95. See also Dennis López, "Good-Bye Revolution—Hello Cultural Mystique: Quinto Sol Publications and Chicano Literary Nationalism," *MELUS* 35, no. 3 (2010): 183–210, for an analysis of the development of an exclusionary Chicano literary nationalism over time; and Julie Avril Minich, *Accessible Citizenships: Disability, Nation, and the Cultural Politics of Greater Mexico* (Philadelphia: Temple University Press, 2014), for a critique of able-bodied exclusionary forms of Chicano nationalism as well as an analysis of alternatives to this sort of able-bodied cultural nationalism.

22 Cotera, *Native Speakers*, 202.

23 Cotera, 202.

24 See Cotera, 199–224. See also Guidotti-Hernández, *Unspeakable Violence*, 133–170, for a critique of elitist discourses and racism present in González's oeuvre as a whole.

25 Critics have debated the historical accuracy of *Caballero*. Limón, for example, finds the novel's depiction of resolving ethnic conflict between Mexicans and Anglos through marriage as "too much romance" ("Mexicans," 346). But Kaup finds that the "forging of interethnic political alliances through kinship bonds among the new and old social elites in *Caballero* is historically accurate" ("Unsustainable Hacienda," 565). John M. González reaches similar conclusions ("Terms," 4:264–276).

26 Historian David Montejano also supports the historical accuracy of interethnic alliance-making through marriage in the time period immediately following the U.S.-Mexican War. See part 1, "Incorporation, 1836–1900," of his comprehensive history *Anglos and Mexicans in the Making of Texas, 1836–1986* (Austin: University of Texas Press, 1987), 13–99; and his introduction, in which he describes this "peace structure" or "accommodative arrangement" between Anglos and Texas Mexicans through which the "new Anglo elite was generally Mexicanized and frequently intermarried or became *compadres* ('god-relatives') with landowning Mexican families" (8).

27 Raúl Coronado, *A World Not to Come: A History of Latino Writing and Print Culture* (Cambridge, Mass.: Harvard University Press, 2013).

28 I use the term *America* (and *American*) to refer to all the Americas, not just the United States of America. I use the term *U.S. American* to refer to people from the United States. I have also chosen to use the masculine ending for gender-variable terms such as *Hispano*, *Chicano*, and so on for several reasons. See "A Note on Translations, Terminology, and the Limits of Language" for an explanation of

174 • Notes to Pages 7–10

my reasoning behind this choice. For a thorough discussion of the evolution and cooptation of the fraught terms *American* and *Americano*, see Kirsten Silva Gruesz, "America," in *Keywords for American Cultural Studies*, Credo Reference e-book, 2nd ed., ed. Bruce Burgett and Glenn Hendler (New York: New York University Press, 2014), 21–25.

29 Rodrigo Lazo, "Confederates in the Hispanic Attic: The Archive against Itself," in *Unsettled States: Nineteenth-Century American Literary Studies*, ed. Dana Luciano and Ivy G. Wilson (New York: New York University Press, 2014), 35.

30 Lazo, 34.

31 See Martha Menchaca, *Recovering History, Constructing Race: The Indian, Black, and White Roots of Mexican Americans* (Austin: University of Texas Press, 2001); and Laura E. Gómez, *Manifest Destinies: The Making of the Mexican American Race* (New York: New York University Press, 2007), for discussions of how Mexican Americans became racialized through legal discourses within the United States after 1848. See Cervantes-Rodríguez for a discussion of how the Spanish language became a racial marker within the United States. See Walter Mignolo, *Local Histories, Global Designs: Coloniality, Subaltern Knowledge, and Border Thinking* (Princeton: Princeton University Press, 2000); and his *The Idea of Latin America* (Malden, Mass.: Blackwell, 2005) for a broader discussion of the racialization of Spanish and Hispanos within the Americas and Europe.

32 See, for example, Amy Kaplan, *The Anarchy of Empire in the Making of U.S. Culture* (Cambridge, Mass.: Harvard University Press, 2002); Gretchen Murphy, *Hemispheric Imaginings: The Monroe Doctrine and Narratives of U.S. Empire* (Durham, N.C.: Duke University Press, 2005); Amy Kaplan and Donald E. Pease, eds., *Cultures of United States Imperialism* (Durham, N.C.: Duke University Press, 1994); James T. Campbell, Matthew Pratt Guterl, and Robert G. Lee, eds., *Race, Nation, and Empire in American History* (Chapel Hill: University of North Carolina Press, 2007); Alfred W. McCoy and Francisco A. Scarano, eds., *Colonial Crucible: Empire in the Making of the Modern American State* (Madison: University of Wisconsin Press, 2009); and Gilbert M. Joseph, Catherine C. LeGrand, and Ricardo D. Salvatore, eds., *Close Encounters of Empire: Writing the Cultural History of U.S.-Latin American Relations* (Durham, N.C.: Duke University Press, 1998).

33 Lazo, "Confederates in the Hispanic Attic," 33.

34 Although it is not the main critical or theoretical lens I use in this book, disability theory similarly suggests that just as a normate body is "an impossible ideal for most people, so is it an inappropriate idea for nations, which struggle to hide the inequalities of race, gender, ability, and class that mark the body politic." Julie Avril Minich, "Mestizaje as National Prosthesis: Corporeal Metaphors in Héctor Tobar's *The Tattooed Soldier*," *Arizona Journal of Hispanic Cultural Studies* 17 (2013): 213.

35 Minich's concept of "national prosthesis," which she uses to describe "how unifying discourses . . . that bolster the formation of national identity also imply a body politic predicated upon able-bodiedness," has also been particularly helpful in working through these ideas. "Mestizaje," 212–213.

36 When I discuss nations and nationalism(s), I am also referring to cultural nationalism.

37 A truly comprehensive study of Greater Mexico would examine texts and other popular forms of expression in other languages in addition to Spanish and English.

38 For studies of Américo Paredes's life, work, and lasting influence in multiple fields (Chicano studies, border studies, folklore, American studies, etc.), see José E. Limón, *Américo Paredes: Culture and Critique* (Austin: University of Texas Press, 2012); Ramón Saldívar, *The Borderlands of Culture: Américo Paredes and the Transnational Imaginary* (Durham, N.C.: Duke University Press, 2006); and José R. López Morín, *The Legacy of Américo Paredes*, Proquest e-book (College Station: Texas A&M University Press, 2006).

39 Américo Paredes, *A Texas-Mexican Cancionero* (Urbana: University of Illinois Press, 1976), xiv.

40 Mary Louise Pratt, *Imperial Eyes: Travel Writing and Transculturation* (New York: Routledge, 2008), 6.

41 Pratt, 7.

42 For examples of critiques of the shortcomings of borderlands studies that focus solely on the (present-day) U.S. Southwest, the northern side of the U.S.-Mexican border, and texts written in English and/or published in the United States, see Robert McKee Irwin, *Bandits, Captives, Heroines, and Saints: Cultural Icons of Mexico's Northwest Borderlands* (Minneapolis: University of Minnesota Press, 2007), xi-xxvi, and 1–37; and Debra Castillo and María Socorro Tabuenca Córdoba, "Reading the Border, North and South."

43 Gloria Anzaldúa, *Borderlands / La Frontera: The New Mestiza*, 2nd ed. (San Francisco: Aunt Lute, 1999), 84; emphasis in the original. All references to works in the original language will be cited directly following the quotation, followed by the English translation in brackets.

44 Unless otherwise noted, all translations are mine.

45 It should be noted, however, that *Mexican American* was not a term used by U.S. citizens of Mexican descent in the nineteenth-century; nonetheless, it is the only term I find simultaneously both broad and specific enough to successfully encompass U.S. citizens of Mexican descent in a variety of different contexts. For more on the development of the term *Mexican American* and its connection to the assimilation policies of the League of United Latin American Citizens during the 1930s, see John Michael Rivera, *The Emergence of Mexican America: Recovering Stories of Mexican Peoplehood in U.S. Culture* (New York: New York University Press, 2006), 135–164.

46 For a more thorough discussion of the evolution of the terms *Chicano* and *Latino*, see F. Arturo Rosales, *Chicano! The History of the Mexican American Civil Rights Movement* (Houston: Arte Público Press, 1996); Juana María Rodríguez, "Latino / Latina / Latin@," in *Keywords for American Cultural Studies*, Credo Reference e-book, 2nd ed., ed. Bruce Burgett and Glenn Hendler (New York: New York University Press, 2014), 146–148; and Rodrigo Lazo, "Introduction: Historical Latinidades and Archival Encounters," in *The Latino Nineteenth Century*, ed. Rodrigo Lazo and Jesse Alemán (New York: New York University Press, 2016), 1–19.

47 For more historical and cultural contextualization of Yucatán as a periphery of the Mexican nation and a crossroads of culture, see Lorena Careaga Viliesid, *De llaves y cerrojos: Yucatán, Texas y Estados Unidos a mediados del siglo XIX)* [On keys and locks: Yucatán, Texas, and the United States in the mid-nineteenth century] (México D.F.: Instituto Mora, UNAM, 2000); David Kazanjian, *The Colonizing Trick: National Culture and Imperial Citizenship in Early America* (Minneapolis: University of Minnesota Press, 2003), 173–212; Kirsten Silva Gruesz, "The Gulf of

Mexico System and the 'Latinness' of New Orleans," *American Literary History* 18, no. 3 (2006): 468–495; and Restall, "Manuel's Worlds."

48 Gruesz, "Gulf of Mexico System," 470.

49 Anzaldúa, *Borderlands / La Frontera*, 25. Yucatán served—and still serves in many ways—as a liminal economic and political space between the United States, the Caribbean, and the rest of Mexico. See Terry Rugeley, *Rebellion Now and Forever: Mayas, Hispanics, and Caste War Violence in Yucatán, 1800–1880* (Stanford: Stanford University Press, 2009), 13. It was a region in which freed African slaves, indigenous Maya peasants, mestizos, and *criollos* interacted and lived alongside one another (see Rugeley, *Rebellion*, 11–15). In the nineteenth century and during the colonial period, Yucatán also served as a frontier "buffer" zone between New Spain / Mexico and other colonial enterprises, such as British Honduras. For more on freed slaves and their interaction with mestizo and indigenous communities in Yucatán, see Matthew Restall, "Manuel's Worlds: Black Yucatan and the Colonial Caribbean," in *Slaves, Subjects, and Subversives: Blacks in Colonial Latin America*, ed. Jane G. Landers and Barry M. Robinson (Albuquerque: University of New Mexico Press, 2006), 147–174; and Restall, *The Black Middle: Africans, Mayas, and Spaniards in Colonial Yucatan* (Stanford: Stanford University Press, 2009).

50 I am using Pierre Bourdieu's idea of cultural workers (artists and writers, for example) who operate (produce art) in a "field of power." The field of power, he explains, "is the space of relations of force between agents or between institutions having in common the possession of the capital necessary to occupy the dominant positions in different fields (notably economic or cultural)" (*The Rules of Art: Genesis and Structure of the Literary Field*, ed. Werner Hamacher and David E. Wellbery, trans. Susan Emanuel [Stanford: Stanford University Press, 1996], 215). In other words, cultural workers possess and create cultural capital, but always in relation and subordination to those agents or institutions that possess and create economic capital. This is the field of power in which artists and writers must operate and create their art, or cultural capital. It is a site of struggle between these competing producers and possessors of different kinds of capital, and the relative value of these different powers is constantly being played out here.

51 In their introduction to *Imagined Transnationalism*, Kevin Concannon, Francisco A. Lomelí, and Marc Priewe critique this "celebratory" image of the transnational, which they contend many critics conceptualize as "a means of challenging those myths of the nation that seek to marginalize others based upon race, gender, or sexual orientation." In doing so, they argue, "a transnational approach can sometimes be mistakenly believed to be a libratory one, as conceiving of the world in terms of a mixture of flows of capital and individuals, and less in terms of boundaries" (3). Concannon, Lomelí, and Priewe, eds., introduction to *Imagined Transnationalism: U.S. Latino/a Literature, Culture, and Identity* (New York: Palgrave Macmillan, 2009), 1–12.

52 Bryce Traister discusses this tendency to critique the "Americanist field imaginary" on the premise that "nations and nationalisms, national subjects and subjects of/to nationalism, are for all intents and purposes interchangeable, and, more to the point, just altogether bad." "Border Shopping: American Studies and the Anti-nation," in *Globalization on the Line: Culture, Capital, and Citizenship at U.S. Borders*, ed. Claudia Sadowski-Smith (New York: Palgrave Macmillan, 2002), 44.

53 Bryce Traister points out that the idea of the *nation* and *nationalisms* are frequently

and oftentimes erroneously conflated in this sort of analysis. "Risking Nationalism: NAFTA and the Limits of the New American Studies," *Canadian Review of American Studies / Revue canadienne d'études américaines* 27, no. 3 (1997): 202.

54 Traister summarizes, "This is what I find most alarming with the postnational and transnational challenge: that the denial of America perversely camouflages precisely those political formations and cultural effects whose *covert* operations it is the critic's task to uncover." "Risking," 203; emphasis in the original.

55 See the influential theoretical and critical works of Benedict Anderson, *Imagined Communities: Reflections on the Origin and Spread of Nationalism*, new ed. (London: Verso, 2006); Sommer, *Foundational Fictions*; and Ángel Rama, *La ciudad letrada* (Montevideo, Uruguay: Arca, 1998); among others, on the power of literature and print media in the formation of communities.

56 Mark Wasserman provides these eye-opening statistics: "Between 1824 and 1857, Mexico had 16 presidents and 33 provisional chief executives, for a total of 49 national administrations. Guadalupe Victoria, the first elected president, was the only president to finish his term (1824–29). Cabinet secretaries were even more transient. The war ministry changed leaders 53 times, the foreign ministry 57 times, and the justice ministry 61 times. The average tenure for a cabinet officer was only seven months." *Everyday Life and Politics in Nineteenth Century Mexico: Men, Women, and War* (Albuquerque: University of New Mexico Press, 2000), 46. For a discussion of instability in Mexico, see also José Ortiz Monasterio, "La formación de la literatura nacional y la integración del Estado mexicano" [The formation of national literature and the integration of the Mexican State], in *Empresa y cultura en tinta y papel (1800–1860)* [Enterprise and culture in ink and paper (1800–1860)], ed. Miguel Ángel Castro, coor. Laura Beatriz Suárez de la Torre (México D.F.: Instituto Mora, 2001), 419–420; and Donald Fithian Stevens, *Origins of Instability in Early Republican Mexico* (Durham, N.C.: Duke University Press, 1991).

57 Ortiz Monasterio, "Formación," 420. Monasterio writes, "Y mi pregunta es: ¿Cómo fue posible que el país no se desmembrara aún más?" (420) [And my question is: How was it possible that the country was not even further driven apart?]. Wasserman similarly remarks that given "its colonial tradition of political fragmentation and its involvement in foreign wars, the wonder of newly independent Mexico was that it remained a nation at all" (*Everyday Life*, 4).

58 Ortiz Monasterio, "Formación," 420–421.

59 Tomás Pérez Vejo, "La invención de un nación: La imagen de México en la prensa ilustrada de la primera mitad del siglo XIX (1830–1855)" [The invention of a nation: The image of Mexico in the enlightened press of the first of the nineteenth century], in *Empresa y cultura en tinta y papel (1800–1860)*, ed. Miguel Ángel Castro, coor. Laura Beatriz Suárez de la Torre (México D.F.: Instituto Mora, 2001), 396.

60 Pérez Vejo, "Invención de un nación," 396.

61 See, for example, Rodrigo Lazo, "'La Famosa Filadelfia': The Hemispheric American City and Constitutional Debates," in *Hemispheric American Studies*, ed. Caroline Field Levander and Robert S. Levine (New Brunswick, N.J.: Rutgers University Press, 2008), 57–74; and Nancy Vogeley, *The Bookrunner: A History of Inter-American Relations—Print, Politics, and Commerce in the United States and Mexico, 1800–1830* (Philadelphia: American Philosophical Society, 2011).

62 For a more in-depth discussion of the genesis of the Black Legend, its racial underpinnings, and its role in defining Spain and Spaniards as outside of modernity, see Margaret R. Greer, Walter D. Mignolo, and Maureen Quilligan's introduction to

Rereading the Black Legend: The Discourses of Religious and Racial Difference in Renaissance Empires, ed. Greer, Mignolo, and Quilligan (Chicago: University of Chicago Press, 2007), 1–26.

63 The term *off-white* is part of a racial hierarchy within a broader white community in which a person might be considered simultaneously white and racially distinct from other more "pure" whites, generally of northern European descent. For more on the idea of off-whiteness, see Matthew Frye Jacobson, *Whiteness of a Different Color: European Immigrants and the Alchemy of Race* (Cambridge, Mass.: Harvard University Press, 1998); David R. Roediger, *Working toward Whiteness: How America's Immigrants Became White* (New York: Basic, 2005); and Noel Ignatiev, *How the Irish Became White* (New York: Routledge, 1995).

64 See Jeremy Adelman for more on how Spanish Americans in the late eighteenth and early nineteenth century were starting to identify the two emerging "types" of empires: empires of conquest and empires of commerce. *Sovereignty and Revolution in the Iberian Atlantic* (Princeton: Princeton University Press, 2006), 25.

65 For a more thorough problematization of the use of the term *(post)colonial* in a Latin American context, see J. Jorge Klor de Alva, "The Postcolonization of the (Latin) American Experience: A Reconsideration of 'Colonialism,' 'Postcolonialsm,' and 'Mestizaje,'" in *After Colonialism: Imperial Histories and Postcolonial Displacements*, ed. Gyan Prakash (Princeton: Princeton University Press, 1995), 241–275; Ella Shohat, "Notes on the Post-colonial," in *The Pre-occupation of Postcolonial Studies*, ed. Fawzia Afzal-Khan and Kalpana Seshadri-Crooks (Durham, N.C.: Duke University Press, 2000), 126–139; and Ann Laura Stoler, "Rethinking Colonial Categories: European Communities and the Boundaries of Rule," *Comparative Studies in Society and History* 31, no. 1 (1989): 134–161.

66 Agustín Iturbide's attempts to implement a new empire in Mexico in the early years of Mexican independence and the support by many liberal Mexicans of Archduke Maximilian's empire in the 1860s remind us that independence did not necessarily also entail a complete rupture from previous modes of government and social organization for many Mexicanos.

67 Mignolo, *Idea*, 7.

68 See Jesse Alemán, "Chicano Novelistic Discourse: Dialogizing the *Corrido* Critical Paradigm," *MELUS* 23, no. 1 (1998): 49–64; and Manuel M. Martín Rodríguez, *Life in Search of Readers: Reading (in) Chicano/a Literature* (Albuquerque: University of New Mexico Press, 2003), 139–170; and Martín Rodríguez, "'A Net Made of Holes': Toward a Cultural History of Chicano Literature," *Modern Language Quarterly* 62, no. 1 (2001): 1–18.

69 José F. Aranda, *When We Arrive: A New Literary History of Mexican America* (Tucson: University of Arizona Press, 2003), 5.

70 Aranda, 5.

71 Guidotti-Hernández, *Unspeakable Violence*, 6.

72 Guidotti-Hernández, 6.

73 Guidotti-Hernández, 3–4.

74 Kirsten Silva Gruesz, "Tracking the First Latino Novel: *Un matrimonio como hay muchos* (1849) and Transnational Serial Fiction," in *Transnationalism and American Serial Fiction*, ed. Patricia Okker, Proquest e-book (New York: Routledge, 2012), 36.

75 Silva Gruesz, 37.

76 For intellectual elites during this time period, the most significant distinction was between rational and irrational writing, and what was considered "rational"

literature included many genres that are no longer recognized as "literature" today, such as the dialogue, the allegory, and the sermon, which could all be presented in poetry or prose. Jean Franco, "Waiting for a Bourgeoisie: The Formation of the Mexican Intelligentsia in the Age of Independence," in *Critical Passions: Selected Essays*, ed. Mary Louise Pratt and Kathleen Newman (Durham, N.C.: Duke University Press, 1999), 481.

77 Franco, 481.

78 Vogeley substantiates the massive popular interest in texts dealing with economics and politics—but also the growth of popularity in other literary categories, such as science and technology, religion, travel, school texts, entertainment, and journalism—in both the United States and Latin America in the first decades of the nineteenth century (*Bookrunner*, 8). Indeed, Vogeley's study attests to the fact that it was nonfiction texts—*not* poetry, theater, or novels—that were in highest demand in the first decades of the nineteenth century in Mexico (23).

79 For more on early newspapers in Mexico, see Luis Reed Torres and María del Carmen Ruiz Castañeda, *El periodismo en México: 500 años de historia* [Journalism in Mexico: 500 years of history], 2nd ed. (México, D.F.: EDAMEX, 1998); Íñigo Fernández Fernández, "Un recorrido por la historia de la prensa en México: De sus orígenes al año 1857" [A tour through the history of the press in Mexico: From its origins to the year 1857], *Documentación de las Ciencias de la Información* 33 (2010): 69–89; Jorge Ruedas de la Serna, "Periodismo y literatura en los albores del siglo XIX" [Journalism and literature at the dawn of the nineteenth century], in *Empresa y cultura en tinta y papel (1800–1860)*, ed. Miguel Ángel Castro, coor. Laura Beatriz Suárez de la Torre (México D.F.: Instituto Mora, 2001), 591–598; and Blanca García Gutiérrez, "El papel de la prensa conservadora en la política nacional a mediados del siglo XIX" [The role of the conservative press in national politics in the mid-nineteenth century], in *Empresa y cultura en tinta y papel (1800–1860)*, ed. Castro, coor. Suárez de la Torre, 505–526. For more on early Spanish-language print communities in the present-day U.S. Southwest, see A. Gabriel Meléndez, *Spanish-Language Newspapers in New Mexico, 1834–1958* (Tucson: University of Arizona Press, 2005); Nicolás Kanellos, *Hispanic Periodicals in the United States, Origins to 1960: A Brief History and Comprehensive Bibliography* (Houston: Arte Público Press, 2000); and Doris Meyer, *Speaking for Themselves: Neomexicano Cultural Identity and the Spanish-Language Press, 1880–1920* (Albuquerque: University of New Mexico Press, 1996).

80 Historian Enrique Florescano points out the importance of newspapers in the nineteenth century in Mexico, explaining that "las páginas de los diarios se convirtieron en la arena donde se ventiló la discusión en torno al incierto destino de la nación" [the pages of the daily newspapers were turned into the arena where the debate surrounding the uncertain destiny of the nation was played out]. *Historia de las historias de la nación mexicana* [History of the histories of the Mexican nation] (México D.F.: Taurus, 2002), 336.

81 Vogeley, *Bookrunner*, 23.

82 Spanish-language documents and books began to be printed in Philadelphia and New York in the late eighteenth century, the first Spanish-language newspapers in the United States were published in New Orleans in 1808 and 1809, and the first newspapers in the (present-day) Southwest were published in Texas in 1813 (Kanellos, *Hispanic Periodicals*, 4–5). See also, Nicolás Kanellos, *Hispanic Literature of the United States: A Comprehensive Reference* (Westport, Conn.: Greenwood Press, 2003), 1–44.

83 Vogeley convincingly argues that the Spanish-language presence in the United States was probably also erased from U.S. literary history as a way of asserting dominance in the hemisphere over a new rival, Mexico. Vogeley concludes, "As the U.S.-Mexican border fell into dispute, it was expedient to say that the United States was English-speaking and its was the only voice in the hemisphere." *Bookrunner*, 23.

84 Werner Sollors, Nicolás Kanellos, Caroline Field Levander, Rodrigo Lazo, Ralph Bauer, Kirsten Silva Gruesz, and Anna Brickhouse are among some of the most prominent scholars to develop and promote multilingual, comparative, hemispheric, and transnational approaches to and reassessments of the U.S. literary canon.

85 Vogeley, *Bookrunner*, 24.

86 Florescano similarly argues that writing and written works helped make sense of, but also rewrite, the formation of Mexico as a nation. Writing, he contends, served a political function, helping construct and defend territorial integrity and national unity (*Historia de las historias de la nación mexicana*, 362). See Ignacio M. Sánchez Prado, "Canon *interruptus*: La *Antología del Centenario* en la encrucijada de 1910" [Canon *interruptus*: The anthology of the centenary at the crossroads of 1910], *Revista de Crítica Literaria Latinoamericana* 36, no. 71 (2010): 55–74, for a discussion of how the national literary canon has been created and reinvented for political purposes at important crossroads in Mexican history, such as the Mexican Revolution of 1910. See also on this topic Emmanuel Carballo, *Historia de las letras mexicanas en el siglo XIX* [History of Mexican letters in the nineteenth century] (Guadalajara, Jalisco: Universidad de Guadalajara, 1991); and Martínez, *La expresión nacional: Letras mexicanas del siglo XIX* [National expression: Mexican literature in the nineteenth century] (Guadalajara, Jalisco: Universidad de Guadalajara, 1991).

87 According to Naomi Lindstrom, the novel did not have as much prestige as other literary forms, such as heroic poetry, in the early decades of the nineteenth century. It was not until around the mid-nineteenth century that the novel "assumed a more prominent place in Latin American literature and more examples of it came into being." "The Nineteenth-Century Latin American Novel," in *The Cambridge Companion to the Latin American Novel*, ed. Efraín Kristal (Cambridge: Cambridge University Press, 2005), 23.

88 Sommer explains that more "modern novels, sometimes called romances, came at midcentury, after independence had been won (everywhere but Cuba and Puerto Rico), civil wars had raged for a generation, and newspapers had become the medium for serialized European and American fiction." *Foundational Fictions*, 12.

89 In early nineteenth-century Mexico, literature (in a very broad sense) "was the responsibility of small groups of educated persons, mostly self-taught, who considered it in its broadest sense as the foundation of good government" (Franco, "Waiting," 481). This elite intelligentsia saw their literature as a civilizing force that could be used to combat the heterogeneity of popular cultures, "which were viewed as a threat to social order and good government" (482). Pablo Mora supports this conclusion, stating that even fierce liberals and federalists who rejected a centralist state and called for a diminishment of the powers of both the military and the Catholic Church, like their conservative adversaries, recognized the necessity of having what Mora calls "un cuerpo de sabios"—an elite group of wise men or intellectuals—lead the country toward progress, particularly in the face of dangerous popular insurrections of the "unenlightened" masses that threatened the cohesion of the nation.

"Cultura letrada y regneración nacional a partir de 1836," in *Empresa y cultura en tinta y papel (1800–1860)*, ed. Miguel Ángel Castro, coor. Laura Beatriz Suárez de la Torre (México D.F.: Instituto Mora, 2001), 391.

90 See Kirsten Silva Gruesz, "The Once and Future Latino: Notes toward a Literary History *todavía para llegar*," in *Contemporary U.S. Latino/a Literary Criticism*, ed. Lyn Di Iorio and Richard Perez (New York: Palgrave Macmillan, 2007), 115–142, for a more thorough discussion of the perpetual "futurity" of *latinidad*.

91 Gruesz, 121; emphasis in the original.

92 For excellent discussions of the problematic ways in which race is discussed (or elided through "color-blind" coded language) in the present-day United States, see Eduardo Bonilla-Silva, *Racism without Racists: Color-Blind Racism and the Persistence of Racial Inequality in America*, 4th ed. (Lanham, Md.: Rowman & Littlefield, 2014); and Hazel Rose Markus and Paula M. L. Moya's collection of essays, *Doing Race: 21 Essays for the 21st Century* (New York: W. W. Norton, 2010). For a comparison to how race is discussed in Latin America, see Bonilla-Silva, "We Are All Americans! The Latin Americanization of Racial Stratification in the USA," *Race and Society* 5, no. 1 (2002): 3–16. Bonilla-Silva argues that in a tri-racial model, Latin Americans identify more strongly with a national identity than a racial one, deny the existence of racism, and claim that they are "beyond race" and that a similar tri-racial model and discourse of racial color-blindness will eventually dominate in the United States as well. See also Christina Sue's response to his argument, "An Assessment of the Latin Americanization Thesis," *Ethnic and Racial Studies* 32, no. 6 (2009): 1058–1070.

93 For recent discussions in the media of the resurgence of white supremacy and xenophobia, see, for example, Ian Buruma, "The End of the Anglo-American Order," *New York Times Magazine*, November 29, 2016, http://nyti.ms/2gezEtJ (accessed April 12, 2018); in print as "Exit Wounds," December 4, 2016, 39; and Joseph C. Wilson, "The Rise of the Alt-Right: White Supremacy and Anti-Semitism Go Mainstream," *Huffington Post* (blog), November 3, 2016, http://www.huffingtonpost.com/joe-wilson/the-rise-of-the-altright-_b_12778386.html (accessed April 13, 2018).

94 For recent discussions of income inequality in the U.S. American context, see Bill Chappel, "U.S. Kids Far Less Likely to Out-Earn Their Parents, as Inequality Grows," *NPR*, December 9, 2016, http://www.npr.org/sections/thetwo-way/2016/12/09/504989751/u-s-kids-far-less-likely-to-out-earn-their-parents-as-inequality-grows (accessed April 13, 2018); and Teresa Tritch, "The United States of Inequality," *New York Times*, June 21, 2016, http://nyti.ms/28Ni1hU (accessed April 13, 2018). For a discussion of the growth in income inequality on a global scale, see Jason Hickel, "Global Inequality May Be Much Worse Than We Think," *Guardian*, April 8, 2016, https://www.theguardian.com/global-development-professionals-network/2016/apr/08/global-inequality-may-be-much-worse-than-we-think (accessed April 13, 2018).

Chapter 1   Imperial Republics

1 All Spanish quotations of Lorenzo de Zavala, *Viage a los Estados-Unidos del Norte de América, 1500–1926* (Paris: Decourchant, 1834), are from the original 1834 edition, which is accessible in the *Sabin Americana, 1500–1926* digital archive at https://www.nypl.org/collections/articles-databases/sabin-americana (hereafter cited as

Viage by page). I have maintained antiquated spellings, accentuations, and so on as they appear in the original text.

All English translations of *Viage* are from Wallace Woolsey's translation in John-Michael Rivera's Arte Público Press bilingual edition; see Zavala, *Journey to the United States of North America / Viaje a los Estados Unidos del Norte de América*, trans. Wallace Woolsey (Houston: Arte Público Press, 2005) (hereafter cited as *Journey* by page). This is the only English translation available of the text to my knowledge. While not perfect, it conveys the information and ideas that are relevant to my analysis. Exceptional cases where I use my own translation are appropriately noted throughout; I have occasionally made some minor changes to the English translations, which I mark through the use of brackets. All other uncited translations are my own.

2 Mario Sznajder and Luis Roniger, *The Politics of Exile in Latin America* (Cambridge: Cambridge University Press, 2009), 5.

3 Sznajder and Roniger, 5.

4 Sznajder and Roniger, 8.

5 Sznajder and Roniger, 8.

6 D. A. Brading, *The Origins of Mexican Nationalism* (Cambridge: Center for Latin American Studies, University of Cambridge, 1985), 70.

7 Charles A. Hale, *The Transformation of Liberalism in Late Nineteenth-Century Mexico* (Princeton: Princeton University Press, 1989), 4.

8 Hale, 4.

9 Hale, 4.

10 Allen Wells, "Forgotten Chapters of Yucatán's Past: Nineteenth-Century Politics in Historiographical Perspective," *Mexican Studies / Estudios Mexicanos* 12, no. 2 (Summer 1996): 201.

11 Raymond Estep, *Lorenzo de Zavala: Profeta del liberalismo mexicano* [*Lorenzo de Zavala: Prophet of Mexican liberalism*], trans. Carlos A. Echanove Trujillo (México D.F.: Librería de Manuel Porrúa, 1952), 237.

12 For more detailed biographical information on Zavala and his political viewpoints see W. S. Cleaves, "The Political Career of Lorenzo de Zavala" (MA thesis, University of Texas, 1931), 111–120; in Beatriz Urías Horcasitas, *Historia de una negación: La idea de igualdad en el pensamiento político mexicano del siglo XIX* [History of a negation: The idea of equality in Mexican political thought in the nineteenth century] (México D.F.: Instituto de Investigaciones Sociales Universidad Nacional Autónoma de México, 1996); Margaret Swett Henson, "Understanding Lorenzo de Zavala, Signer of the Texas Declaration of Independence," *Southwestern Historical Quarterly* 102, no. 1 (1998): 1–17; and her biography of Zavala, *Lorenzo de Zavala: The Pragmatic Idealist* (Fort Worth: Texas Christian University Press, 1996); and Estep, *Lorenzo de Zavala*.

13 See Stephen J. Mexal, "The Logic of Liberalism: Lorenzo de Zavala's Transcultural Politics," *MELUS* 32, no. 2 (2007): 83–89, for more on Zavala's fall from popularity and his decision to flee Mexico. See chapter 18 in Michael C. Meyer, William L. Sherman, and Susan M. Deeds, *The Course of Mexican History*, 7th ed. (Oxford: Oxford University Press, 2003), 297–307, for more general information on the clash between centralists and federalists in Mexico in the late 1820s through the early 1830s.

14 Henson, "Understanding," 9–10.

15 Henson notes that "Zavala's appointment as minister to the French court was both a

well-deserved honor and a way to isolate the liberal reformer, a fact that Zavala was slow to realize." *Lorenzo de Zavala*, 66–67.

16 Sznajder and Roniger, *Politics of Exile*, 66.

17 Henson, "Understanding," 10.

18 Zavala's travel narrative was published in Mexico only posthumously in Mérida in 1846 under the title *Viaje a los Estados-Unidos del Norte de América*. A print edition of the travel narrative was published in 2005 in a bilingual edition, translated into English by Wallace Woolsey and with a critical introduction by the editor, John-Michael Rivera (see note 1).

19 In *Viage*, Zavala notes that it is on May 25, 1834, when he begins to compose his travel narrative (2–3). By April of that year, Santa Anna had already assumed power in Mexico City and was working toward dismantling congress. Henson notes that "by June, after more letters to Mexico City urging the appointment of a special commissioner to negotiate with the Spanish, Zavala realized that he, as a federalist reformer, was being denied an opportunity to receive credit for any diplomatic success." *Lorenzo de Zavala*, 70.

20 Henson, "Understanding" 10–11. Henson notes that Zavala initially urged Texas's separation from Mexico "not for independence, but to encourage the formation of a north Mexican federation of states favoring the Federalist system" (10).

21 Sznajder and Roniger, *Politics of Exile*, 4.

22 Sznajder and Roniger, 4.

23 Sznajder and Roniger, 58.

24 Estep, *Lorenzo de Zavala*, 237.

25 Estep, 277.

26 Estep also notes that Zavala's later decision to relocate to Texas similarly kept him closely involved in Mexican politics, where he was still viewed as "una seria amenaza para el régimen centralista" [a serious threat to the centralist regime]. *Lorenzo de Zavala*, 284–285.

27 As Henson (*Lorenzo de Zavala*) and Estep show in their biographies of Zavala, even in exile, Zavala's critiques of Mexico and the Mexican government continued to make waves in Mexican politics. His letters (written while in France in August 1834) to Santa Anna and the centralists, for example, caused uproar back in Mexico and foreclosed the possibility of any peaceful relationship between Zavala and Santa Anna, who was enraged by Zavala's critiques of his government (Estep, *Lorenzo de Zavala*, 282). Furthermore, Zavala had important friendships and partnerships with several important international political figures, such as Joel R. Poinsett, a U.S. congressman and the first U.S. minister to Mexico (and later U.S. Secretary of War under Martin Van Buren).

28 John-Michael Rivera, introduction to *Journey*, xvii–xxiii.

29 In *Chicano Nations: The Hemispheric Origins of Mexican American Literature* (New York: New York University Press, 2011), Marissa K. López similarly reads Zavala's depictions of U.S. border zones as "an untamable, truly wild frontier where the logic and rationality of the nation break down, where instead of citizens we find broken people" (40).

30 Historian Eric Foner notes the centrality of morality in abolitionist discourses, explaining that "morality, not economics, was always paramount in their [abolitionists'] minds" (*Free Soil, Free Labor, Free Men: The Ideology of the Republican Party before the Civil War* [Oxford: Oxford University Press, 1995], xxii). See Robin Blackburn, *The American Crucible: Slavery, Emancipation and Human Rights*

(London: Verso, 2011), 150–159, for more on the humanitarian origins of abolitionist movements in Europe and the Americas.

31 Blackburn, *American Crucible*, 295.

32 Blackburn, 283.

33 Blackburn, 305.

34 Zavala explains that North's sentiments reflect "el espíritu general de los inhabitan-
tes de los Estados-Unidos sobre esta clase tan diferente en color, como en cualidades
morales de las otras" (*Viage*, 263) [the general feeling of the people of the United
States concerning this class as different in color as they are in moral qualities from
the others (*Journey*, 142–143)].

35 Blackburn, *American Crucible*, 333.

36 David Kazanjian, *The Colonizing Trick: National Culture and Imperial Citizenship
in Early America* (Minneapolis: University of Minnesota Press, 2003), 91.

37 Kazanjian, 91.

38 Kazanjian, 94.

39 My contention echoes Kazanjian's larger argument: the equality of citizen-subjects
in the United States is dependent on the exclusion of various nonnational subjects; in other words, the "systematic production and maintenance of hierarchically
codified, racial and national forms actually enabled equality to be understood as
formally and abstractly universal" (*Colonizing Trick*, 5). Kazanjian further clarifies
that the "subjection of U.S. citizens as formally and abstractly equal to one another
and to citizens of other nations depended upon the vigorous and substantial subjection of North Americans to racial and national codification" (5). Thus the rise of
egalitarianism and the simultaneous rise of "hierarchically codified, particularist
differences," which are often seen as contradictory forces, are in fact complementary
(2).

40 Beatriz Urías Horcasitas, "Ideas de modernidad en la historia de México: Democracia e igualdad" [Ideas on modernity in the history of Mexico: Democracy and
equality], *Revista Mexicana de Sociología* 53, no. 4 (1991): 45.

41 Urías Horcasitas, 45.

42 Mark Wasserman similarly argues that in the first half of the nineteenth century in Mexico, class mattered more than almost any other division; there were
schisms among elites, but nothing, he contends, outweighed class solidarity
(*Everyday Life and Politics in Nineteenth Century Mexico: Men, Women, and War*
[Albuquerque: University of New Mexico Press, 2000], 51). While the Mexican
Constitution of 1824 permitted and encouraged high levels of participation in the
democratic process, ruling elites actually worked to disenfranchise more of the
lower classes, indigenous, and mixed-race people in the decades to follow (56–58).
Numerous historians and cultural critics have similarly stressed how Mexican
elites, while professing liberal ideals and identifying as liberals and republicans,
feared the rising of the lower classes as well as indigenous and mestizo communities. See, for more examples, Jean Franco, "Waiting for a Bourgeoisie: The
Formation of the Mexican Intelligentsia in the Age of Independence," in *Critical
Passions: Selected Essays*, ed. Mary Louise Pratt and Kathleen Newman (Durham,
N.C.: Duke University Press, 1999), 476–492; Paloa Mora, "Cultura letrada y
regneración nacional a partir de 1836," in *Empresa y cultura en tinta y papel (1800–
1860)*, ed. Miguel Ángel Castro, coor. Laura Beatriz Suárez de la Torre (México
D.F.: Instituto Mora, 2001), 385–393; Mara Loveman, *National Colors: Racial*

Classification and the States in Latin America (Oxford: Oxford University Press, 2014); and Richard Graham, ed., *The Idea of Race in Latin America, 1870–1940* (Austin: University of Texas Press, 1990).

43 Loveman explores the domestic political battles to control states and define nations in Latin America during the nineteenth and twentieth centuries. One of the common concerns explored in these debates revolved around the question of who should be allowed to fully participate in the cultural and political life of the national community. Over the course of the nineteenth century, Loveman shows how these battles took on ethnoracial dimensions. She explains that "changes in the science of human difference over time reverberated in domestic political struggles, influencing how elites drew ethnoracial distinctions within their populations and how they framed the task of dealing with them in pursuit of their nation- and state-building goals." *National Colors*, 23.

44 Zavala expresses this same concern in other works as well. As Urías Horcasitas explains in her insightful analysis of Lorenzo de Zavala's *Ensayo histórico de las revoluciones en México desde 1808 hasta 1830* (Paris: Imprenta de P. Dupont et G. Laguionie, 1831–1832), for Zavala, as for many other of his contemporary liberals, there was a disjuncture between the appearance of democratic institutions and the reality of their implementation ("Ideas," 51). Urías Horcasitas argues that throughout *Ensayo*, Zavala shows how "lo que las doctrinas abstractas habían transformado era el marco jurídico y las instituciones, pero esto no había repercutido sobre la naturaleza misma del orden social" [what abstract doctrines had transformed was the legal framework and the institutions, but this had not had an effect on the nature itself of the social order] (51). In *Ensayo*, Zavala describes Mexico's political system as "instituciones democráticas con elementos monárquicos" [democratic institutions with monarquical elementos], stating that "falta mucho para que las cosas, la esencia del sistema [democrático], la realidad corresponda a los principios que se profesan" [there is still much lacking so that things, the essence of the democratic system, reality may match the principles that are professed] (qtd. in Urías Horcasitas, "Ideas," 51).

45 Urías Horcasitas, 50.

46 Mexal, "Logic of Liberalism," 99.

47 For more on this internalized discourse of inferiority and the reactions to it within Spanish American literary history, see Alejandro Mejías-López's *The Inverted Conquest: The Myth of Modernity and the Transatlantic Onset of Modernism* (Nashville: Vanderbilt University Press, 2009), 44–45. Enrique Florescano similarly points out how late eighteenth- and early nineteenth-century historians, statesmen, and intellectuals distanced themselves from Spain and this supposed inherited degeneracy by working to establish one dominant interpretation of Mexico's past (the conquest and colonization) as the "época negra" of Mexican history (*Historia de las historias de la nación mexicana* [México D.F.: Taurus, 2002], 298). This, Florescano signals, was part of the "difícil proceso que para los americanos significó romper con las ataduras políticas y mentales que los unían con España" (298) [difficult process that it entailed for Americans to break the political and mental ties that connected them to Spain (translation mine)].

48 See Walter Mignolo, *The Idea of Latin America* (Malden, Mass.: Blackwell, 2005), 70–71, for more information on how modernity was viewed by Latin American intellectuals, politicians, and so on and how these discourses of modernity became

linked to the Spanish and Portuguese languages, thus eventually leading to the racialization of these languages.

49 Urías Horcasitas, "Ideas," 52.

50 M. K. López, *Chicano Nations*, 43.

51 Foner explains that belief in the dignity of labor "has been a part of American culture from the very beginning. In large part, it can be traced to the fact that most Americans come from a Protestant background, in which the nobility of labor was an article of faith." *Free Soil*, 12.

52 Foner, 11.

53 See Meyer, Sherman, and Deeds, *Course of Mexican History*, 310–311.

54 Zavala had a conflicted relationship with Catholicism and the Catholic Church (Estep, *Lorenzo de Zavala*, 254–255). Although he remained a devout Catholic throughout his life, he was one of Mexico's most forceful critics of the church as an institution (254). Estep explains that "no precisamente enemigo de la religión, sí lo fué, e irreductible, de los privilegios de la Iglesia y de sus intereses e influencia en la política nacional" (254) [while not exactly an enemy of religion, he was indeed, and unyieldingly, opposed to the privileges of the Church and to its interests and influence in national politics].

55 See Meyer, Sherman, and Deeds, *Course of Mexican History*, 299–300.

56 Urías Horcasitas, *Historia*, 116.

57 Translation mine.

58 Urías Horcasitas, *Historia*, 116.

59 See Dickson D. Bruce Jr., *And They All Sang Hallelujah: Plain-Folk Camp-Meeting Religion, 1800–1845* (Knoxville: University of Tennessee Press, 1974), for a more comprehensive history of the camp meeting in the early nineteenth-century U.S. South.

60 Mark A. Noll, *The Old Religion in a New World: The History of North American Christianity* (Grand Rapids, Mich.: William B. Eerdmans, 2002), 63.

61 See Nathan O. Hatch, *The Democratization of American Christianity* (New Haven: Yale University Press, 1989); and Noll, *Old Religion*, 48–71, for more thorough discussions of democratization as a central discourse in the development of Christianity in the United States.

62 Bruce, *And They All Sang Hallelujah*, 10.

63 Noll, *Old Religion*, 63.

64 Noll, 63.

65 See Hatch, *Democratization*, 9–11, on the reshaping of Christianity in the United States as a democratic process.

66 Zavala notes, "Muy débil barrera es el Niagara y los lagos para evitar que Canadá sea un dia parte de los Estados-Unidos del Norte" (*Viage*, 99) [The Niagara River and the lakes form a very weak barrier to prevent Canada from one day being a part of the United States of the North (*Journey*, 56)].

67 Zavala writes, "Abierta la puerta á la colonizacion [en Texas], como debia ser, bajo un sistema de gobierno libre, era necesario que una generacion nueva apareciese dentro de pocos años poblando parte de la república mejicana, y de consiguiente que esta nueva poblacion fuese enteramente heterogénea" (*Viage*, 141) [Once the way was opened to coloninization [in Texas], as it should have been, under a system of free government, it was necessary that a new generation should appear within a few years and populate a part of the Mexican republic, and consequently that this new population should be entirely heterogeneous (*Journey*, 79)].

68 See, for example, M. K. López, *Chicano Nations*, 48.
69 Loveman, for example, explores how Latin American states, denied membership in the "club" of civilized nations on racial grounds, "fastened on the idea of race—and in particular, of race mixture—to ground their claims of modern nationhood" (*National Colors*, 40). As Loveman shows, Latin American census officials used the census as scientific evidence of the "inevitable 'racial improvement' ('whitening') of their populations" (40). For more on the complexity of discourses of mestizaje and hybridity in Latin America, see, for example, Lourdes Martínez-Echazábal, "Mestizaje and the Discourse of National/Cultural Identity in Latin America, 1845–1959," *Latin American Perspectives* 25, no. 3 (1998): 21–42; and Antonio Cornejo-Polar, "Mestizaje, transculturación, heterogeneidad," *Revista de Crítica Literaria Latinoamericana* 20, no. 40 (1994): 368–371. For a sophisticated discussion of competing discourses and uses of mestizaje in Chicano culture, see Rafael Pérez-Torres, *Mestizaje: Critical Uses of Race in Chicano Culture* (Minneapolis: University of Minnesota Press, 2006).
70 Jeremy Adelman, *Sovereignty and Revolution in the Iberian Atlantic* (Princeton: Princeton University Press, 2006), 25.
71 Juan Gonzalez, *Harvest of Empire: A History of Latinos in America* (New York: Penguin, 2011); and David Montejano, *Anglos and Mexicans in the Making of Texas, 1836–1986* (Austin: University of Texas Press, 1987), are two excellent examples of texts that focus on the late nineteenth and early twentieth centuries as the time period in which the United States' new brand of imperialism took root in Latin America.
72 Gilbert G. González, *Culture of Empire: American Writers, Mexico, and Mexican Immigrants, 1880–1930* (Austin: University of Texas Press, 2004), 5.

Chapter 2   A Proposed Intercultural and (Neo)colonial Coalition

1 Henequen is a fibrous plant related to the agave. Its fibers were used principally to make binder twine, for which there was a major increase in demand in the late nineteenth century with the development of commercial agriculture and shipping. See Allen Wells, *Yucatan's Gilded Age: Haciendas, Henequen, and International Harvester, 1860–1915* (Albuquerque: University of New Mexico Press, 1985), for a history of the growth and eventual collapse of the henequen industry in Yucatán.
2 See Carlos Cámara Gutiérrez, ed., *Cronología histórica y arquitectónica del Paseo de Montejo* [Historical and architectural chronology of the Paseo de Montejo] (Mérida, Yucatán: Ayuntamiento Municipal de Mérida, 2001), 19–21, for an introduction to the economic factors—namely, henequen production—that led to the construction of the Paseo de Montejo; he explains that "gracias a esa bonanza [de henequén] se da un auge de construcciones sumamente elaboradas" (19) [thanks to that [henequen] boom, there was a surge in extremely lavish buildings] (translations for Cámara Gutiérrez are mine). The construction of the Paseo de Montejo was initiated by "un grupo de hacendados, industriales y comerciantes de la época, que consideraron necesario modernizar a la Mérida de las postrimerías del siglo XIX" (19) [a group of landowners, industrialists, and businessmen from the time, who considered it necessary to modernize Mérida from the end of the nineteenth century].
3 See Cámara Gutiérrez, *Cronología histórica*, 61–65, for a description of how the Paseo de Montejo has changed in the twenty-first century.

4 See Cody Barteet, "The Rhetoric of Authority in New Spain: The Casa de Montejo in Mérida, Yucatán," *Canadian Art Review* 35, no. 2 (2010): 5–20, for further analysis of the symbolic and political importance of the architecture of the historic center of Mérida.

5 When I refer to nineteenth-century "Yucatecos" in this chapter, I am referring to criollos and mestizos. Maya Indians, as we will see in Sierra O'Reilly's writing, were considered part of their own communities, different from Yucatecos. In yet another curious evolution of these terms that demonstrates their fluidity, in the present day, *mestizo* in Yucatán frequently refers to someone who is indigenous Maya. Ronald Loewe in fact argues that in Yucatán, *mestizo* is merely a euphemism for the prohibited and offensive *indio* (Loewe, *Maya or Mestizo? Nationalism, Modernity, and Its Discontents* [Toronto: University of Toronto Press, 2011], 62–63). For more on the complexities of naming indigenous communities in Yucatán, see, for example, Loewe, "Making Maya into Mestizo: Identity, Difference, and *Cultura regional Mestiza*," in *Maya or Mestizo?*, 59–78; Wolfgang Gabbert, *Becoming Maya: Ethnicity and Social Inequality in Yucatán since 1500* (Tucson: University of Arizona Press, 2004); and Quetzil E. Castañeda, "'We Are *Not* Indigenous!': An Introduction to the Maya identity of Yucatan," *Journal of Latin American Anthropology* 9, no. 1 (2004): 36–63.

6 See, for example, Bryce Traister, "Border Shopping: American Studies and the Antination," in *Globalization on the Line: Culture, Capital, and Citizenship at U.S. Borders*, ed. Claudia Sadowski-Smith (New York: Palgrave Macmillan, 2002), 31–52; and "Risking Nationalism: NAFTA and the Limits of the New American Studies," *Canadian Review of American Studies / Revue canadienne d'études américaines* 27, no. 3 (1997): 191–204.

7 Following Castañeda, I understand and encourage readers to understand the term *Maya* as an "embattled zone of contestation of belonging, identity, and differentiation" rather than a homogenous and unchanging identity ("We Are *Not* Indigenous!," 41). It is important to recognize the diversity within the Maya communities of Yucatán. In fact, recent research suggests that there is not and has never been any widespread sense of ethnic unity that could be easily identified as Maya (see Gabbert, *Becoming Maya*). Therefore, when I speak about the nineteenth-century Maya, it is with a recognition of the diversity and lack of cohesion of this community but also with an interest in exposing how nineteenth-century elites attempted to define Maya identity in opposition to Yucateco identity, thus both excluding indigenous people from that definition and homogenizing the indigenous community.

8 For a detailed biography of Sierra O'Reilly, see Miguel Ángel Fernández Delgado, *Justo Sierra O'Reilly: Hombre de letras y autor del proyecto del Código Civil* [Justo Sierra O'Reilly: Man of letters and author of the Civil Code project] (México D.F.: Suprema Corte de Justicia de la Nación, 2006). Most of the information I have summarized here about Sierra O'Reilly's life and work comes from Fernández Delgado's text; see 95–120 for details about Sierra O'Reilly's trip to the United States; and 60–69 for more information on his early publications. Justo Sierra Méndez's collection of essays, *Justo Sierra O'Reilly* (Mérida, Yucatán: Consejo Editorial de Yucatán, 1987), also contains a great deal of useful information about Sierra O'Reilly's biography and literary-historical contributions.

9 In a commemorative volume of articles about Sierra O'Reilly's life and contributions, Leopoldo Peniche Vallado comments on Sierra O'Reilly's importance to the Yucatecan canon and the dearth of critical attention he has been given by critics

outside of Yucatán in Mexico: "Pues nada menos que el centenario de la muerte de este mexicano eminente [Justo Sierra O'Reilly] está pasando casi inadvertido para la República entera. Sólo su patria chica, su Yucatán que tanto amó y se desveló por servir, ha recordado y conmemorado la luctuosa fecha. Una obra de la magnitud de la de Sierra sólo ha merecido menciones frías en muchas de las historias literarias que gozan de crédito en las esferas de la cultural nacional" [It is nothing less than the centenary of the death of this eminent Mexican that is passing by nearly unnoticed by the entire republic. Only his home state, his Yucatán that he loved so much and strived to serve, has remembered and commemorated the sorrowful date. A work of the magnitude of that of Sierra has only merited indifferent references in many of the literary histories that are highly respected in the spheres of national culture]. "Sobre Justo Sierra O'Reilly," in *Justo Sierra O'Reilly*, ed. Justo Sierra Méndez (Mérida, Yucatán: Consejo Editorial de Yucatán, 1987), 19; translation mine.

10 For examples of his legends, see Justo Sierra O'Reilly, *El filibustero y otras historias de piratas, caballeros y nobles damas* [The filibusterer and other stories of pirates, gentlemen, and noble women] (1841–1849), ed. Manuel Sol (Xalapa, Mexico: Universidad Veracruzana, 2007). For analysis of Sierra O'Reilly's short stories, legends, and historical novels, see Nina Gerassi-Navarro, *Pirate Novels: Fictions of Nation Building in Spanish America* (Durham, N.C.: Duke University Press, 1999).

11 See Justo Sierra O'Reilly, introduction to *Los tres siglos de la dominación española, o sea historia de esta provincia, desde la conquista hasta la independencia*, by Fr. Diego López Cogolludo, ed. Sierra O'Reilly (Campeche, México: J. M. Peralta, 1842), 1:iii–ix.

12 See, for example, Marte R. Gomez, "Sobre Justo Sierra O'Reilly," *Historia Mexicana* 3, no. 3 (1954): 309–327.

13 All citations of Justo Sierra O'Reilly are from "Noticia sobre la vida pública y escritos del Excmo. Sr. D. Lorenzo de Zavala, antiguo secretario de estado y ministro plenipotenciario de la república en París," in *Viaje a los Estados-Unidos del Norte de América*, by Lorenzo de Zavala, ed. Sierra O'Reilly, *HathiTrust* (Mérida, Yucatán: Castillo y compañía, 1846), 3–57.

14 As noted in chapter 1, Zavala first published his travel narrative *Viage a los Estados-Unidos del Norte de América* [Journey to the United States of North American] (Paris: Decourchant, 1834).

15 Sierra O'Reilly, "Noticia," 55; emphasis in the original.

16 For example, Lorena Careaga Viliesid explains that in the first half of the nineteenth century, "México no era una nación consolidada ni unida ni con identidad propia, sino un conglomerado de regiones, cada una de ellas con su propia problemática social e intereses económicos y políticos particulares" (*De llaves y cerrojos: Yucatán, Texas y Estados Unidos a mediados del siglo XIX* [México D.F.: Instituto Mora, UNAM, 2000], 27–28) [Mexico was not a consolidated nation, nor was it united with its own identity; rather, it was a conglomerate of regions, each of them with its own social problems, economic interests, and unique politics].

17 Careaga Viliesid, *De llaves*, 29. Matthew Restall emphasizes the long history of isolation in Yucatán, explaining that during colonial times, "traveling overland into Yucatan was arduous, even dangerous, rendering the peninsula effectively an island and the port town of Campeche its main gateway." "Manuel's Worlds: Black Yucatan and the Colonial Caribbean," in *Slaves, Subjects, and Subversives: Blacks in Colonial Latin America*, ed. Jane G. Landers and Barry M. Robinson (Albuquerque: University of New Mexico Press, 2006), 149.

18 Careaga Viliesid, *De llaves*, 29.
19 Careaga Viliesid, 29–30.
20 América Paredes, *A Texas-Mexican Cancionero* (Urbana: University of Illinois Press, 1976), xiv.
21 See Matthew Restall, *The Black Middle: Africans, Mayas, and Spaniards in Colonial Yucatan* (Stanford: Stanford University Press, 2009).
22 In "Manuel's Worlds," Restall similarly argues that "Yucatan (especially the city of Mérida and towns of Campeche and Bacalar) was not only a meeting place for Spaniards, Africans, and Mayas, but also a place where three different worlds overlapped—worlds that were social, racial (as defined by Spaniards), and geographical" (164).
23 Careaga Viliesid, *De llaves*, 44–45.
24 Kirsten Silva Gruesz, "The Gulf of Mexico System and the 'Latinness' of New Orleans," *American Literary History* 18, no. 3 (2006): 470. Sierra O'Reilly was not alone in his pondering of other sorts of "border zones" built on collaborative relationships between elite Hispanos and Anglo Americans; nor was this imagining unique to Yucatán or Mexico. Cuba, for example, was long desired by annexationists in the United States, especially Southern slaveholders. For example, Matthew Pratt Guterl, in *American Mediterranean: Southern Slaveholders in the Age of Emancipation* (Cambridge, Mass.: Harvard University Press, 2008), explores how elite slaveholders in both the United States and Cuba (among other spaces in Latin America) saw themselves as part of a larger "slave empire" that transcended national and linguistic borders.
25 As I note in chapter 1, Zavala has long been recognized as an important figure in Mexican history. More recently, he has been recognized as a key figure in early Latino and Chicano history and culture and as evidence of a long and rich Latino presence in the United States. See, for example, Marissa K. López, *Chicano Nations: The Hemispheric Origins of Mexican American Literature* (New York: New York University Press, 2011). There has even been a biography written about Zavala by Kathleen Tracy as part of a series of children's books, Latinos in American History: The Hispanic Influence in the United States. *Lorenzo de Zavala* (Bear, Del.: Mitchell Lane, 2003).
26 Anna Brickhouse, John F. Chuchiak IV, and David Kazanjian discuss Sierra O'Reilly's travel diary and/or his journalistic output, and I will be referring to their research in greater detail later in the chapter. Ludwig Nolte Blanquet wrote his doctoral dissertation, "La imagen de los Estados Unidos de América en la obra del mexicano Justo Sierra O'Reilly" [The image of the United States of America in the work of the Mexican Justo Sierra O'Reilly] (PhD diss., Freie University, Berlin, 2006), on Justo Sierra O'Reilly's travel writings, focusing primarily on Sierra O'Reilly's published narrative, *Impresiones de un viaje a los Estados Unidos de América y al Canadá* (Campeche, Mexico: Gregorio Buenfil, 1849–1851).
27 During the Texas War of Independence, Yucatecos resented Mexico's demand of increased taxes and Yucatecan troops to fight in Mexico's war against Texas, sympathizing more with their fellow profederalist state, Texas, than with central(ist) Mexico. Careaga Viliesid, *De llaves*, 33–34.
28 My brief outline of the Caste War is a simplified rendering of an extremely complicated and long-lasting conflict that historians are still trying to sort out even today. The details of the war are not central to my argument, but I have attempted to touch on the most significant aspects of this brief history. For a more thorough

and nuanced history of the Caste War and its origins, see Nelson A. Reed, *The Caste War of Yucatán* (Stanford: Stanford University Press, 2001); Martha Herminia Villalobos González, *El bosque sitiado: Asaltos armados, concesiones forestales y estrategias de resistencia durante la Guerra de Castas* [The forest under siege: Armed assault, forest concessions and strategies of resistance during the Caste War] (México D.F.: Editorial Miguel Ángel Porrúa, 2006); and Terry Rugeley, *Rebellion Now and Forever: Mayas, Hispanics, and Caste War Violence in Yucatán, 1800–1880* (Stanford: Stanford University Press, 2009).

29 According to John F. Chuchiak IV, in the 1840s, Maya "comprised more than 80 percent of the Yucatán's total population." "Intellectuals, Indians, and the Press: The Politicization of Justo Sierra O'Reilly's Journalism and Views on the Maya while in the United States," in *Strange Pilgrimages: Exile, Travel, and National Identity in Latin America, 1800–1990s*, ed. Ingrid E. Fey and Karen Racine (Wilmington, Del.: Scholarly Resources, 2000), 62.

30 The idea of seeking support, in many different forms, in the United States was not unique to Sierra O'Reilly. In *Our Sister Republics: The United States in an Age of American Revolutions* (New York: Liveright, 2016), Caitlin Fitz explores how Latin American rebels and revolutionaries sought aid, asylum, and physical and financial support from U.S. Americans in the early years of the Spanish American revolutions. Like Sierra O'Reilly, they also used newspapers and their editors to rally public opinion—as well as financial backers—to their cause.

31 Justo Sierra O'Reilly, *Diario de nuestro viaje a los Estados Unidos (La pretendida anexión de Yucatán)*, ed. Héctor Pérez Martínez (México D.F.: Antigua Librería Robredo, de José Porrúa e Hijos, 1938; hereafter referred to in the text as *Diario de nuestro viaje* and in citations as *Diario* by page). All translations are my own.

32 In addition to Zavala's narrative, Sierra O'Reilly also translated and published narratives about travel in Yucatán, including a two-volume translation of John Lloyd Stephens's immensely popular *Incidents of Travel in Yucatán* in Campeche (1848 and 1850).

33 In his prologue to *Diario de nuestro viaje*, Héctor Pérez Martínez notes that in the 1849–1851 published travel narrative, Sierra O'Reilly "no toca de lleno lo íntimo de su misión, que quedó en secreto" (prologue to *Diario*, xlv) [does not fully cover the intimate details of his mission, which remained a secret]. Fernández Delgado describes these volumes as an attempt at forgetting his sad mission to the United States, instead including simply "memorias, anécdotas, relatos históricos y sus impresiones sobre el vecino país del norte" (prologue to *Diario*, xlix) [memories, anecdotes, historical tales and his impressions about the neighbor country to the north (Fernández Delgado, *Justo Sierra O'Reilly*, 143)].

34 Pérez Martínez similarly emphasizes the honesty of Sierra O'Reilly's journal entries, explaining that in his diary, perhaps unlike the later published *Impresiones*, "no se detiene ante la verdad, y ello, a no dudarlo, le añade mayor valía" (*Diario*, xlix) [he does not hesitate before the truth, and that, in not doubting it, makes it more valuable]. *Diario de nuestro viaje*, Pérez Martínez further confirms, "obedece al deseo de presentar a los investigadores, la fuente original de informaciones sobre una etapa de la historia de Yucatán" (*Diario*, xlix) [complies with the desire to present researchers with the original source of information about a period in the history of Yucatán].

35 It is important to note, however, that *Diario de nuestro viaje* is also an edited collection of diary entries. The editor, Pérez Martínez, explains that he decided to eliminate entries or parts of entries from Sierra O'Reilly's diary manuscript in this

edition that had little to do with his mission in the United States—those parts
that dealt more with "el mensaje cotidiano para la esposa ausente, las impresiones y
recuerdos familiares ajenos a las actividades del Comisionado de Yucatán" (*Diario*,
xlix) [the daily messages for the absent wife, the impressions and familial memories
unconnected to the activities of the Commissioner of Yucatán].

36 Philippe Lejeune, *On Diary*, ed. Jeremey D. Popkin and Julie Rak, trans. Katherine
Durnin, Proquest e-book (Honolulu: University of Hawaii Press, 2009), 191.

37 Lejeune, 191.

38 Lejeune, 191.

39 Rachael Langford and Russell West, "Introduction: Diaries and Margins," in
Marginal Voices, Marginal Forms: Diaries in European Literature and History, ed.
Langford and West (Amsterdam: Rodopi, 1999), 8–9.

40 Mexico was greatly divided by regionalist loyalties, and disagreements over the form
of government best suited for Mexico—federalism or centralism—were especially
divisive. In the United States, debates raged about how to incorporate new territories (and their populations), especially racially diverse ones such as Louisiana and
Texas, into the nation.

41 David Kazanjian, *The Brink of Freedom: Improvising Life in the 19th-Century Atlantic World* (Durham, N.C.: Duke University Press, 2016), 137–139. Kazanjian writes
that in "the face of organized Maya resistance to a massive, late eighteenth- and early
nineteenth-century wave of disenfranchisement and dispossession, liberal Creoles
mobilized their periodical culture to represent a multifaceted conflict . . . as a race
war between two utterly distinct and discrete peoples: civilized *blancos* and barbaric
indios" (158).

42 Kazanjian, 157–158.

43 Kazanjian, 158.

44 Chuchiak, "Intellectuals," 64.

45 Chuchiak, 63.

46 Chuchiak, 63.

47 Chuchiak, 62–63.

48 Chuchiak, 64.

49 María DeGuzmán, *Spain's Long Shadow: The Black Legend, Off-Whiteness, and
Anglo-American Empire* (Minneapolis: University of Minnesota Press, 2005), xii.

50 This rhetoric does not, however, completely displace the racial terminology Sierra
O'Reilly repeatedly uses in his description of criollos in the Yucatán as "blancos"
and "la población blanca."

51 Similarly, many people in the United States were against the annexation of Mexican
territories not only because of the diversity of its population but also, as Alejandro
Mejías-López points out, because Mexico had given too many liberties and rights
to its nonwhite population (*The Inverted Conquest: The Myth of Modernity and
the Transatlantic Onset of Modernism* [Nashville: Vanderbilt University Press,
2009], 29). Sierra O'Reilly here echoes the idea prevalent in the United States that
"Spanish America's problem was *too much* democracy," which, in the eyes of Anglo
Americans, entailed a breakdown of established social and racial orders (in *Inverted
Conquest*, 29; emphasis in the original).

52 Gretchen Murphy, *Hemispheric Imaginings: The Monroe Doctrine and Narratives of
U.S. Empire* (Durham, N.C.: Duke University Press, 2005), 5.

53 Lee Joan Skinner, *History Lessons: Refiguring the Nineteenth-Century Historical
Novel in Spanish America* (Newark, Del.: Juan de la Cuesta, 2006), 19.

54 Skinner, 19.
55 The idea to recruit volunteer regiments in the United States or Europe to fight in (or conquer and rule over, as in the famous case of William Walker in Nicaragua) Spanish America was not an unusual occurrence in the nineteenth century; for more examples, see Robert E. May, *Manifest Destiny's Underworld: Filibustering in Antebellum America* (Chapel Hill: University of North Carolina Press, 2002). And in fact, as Careaga Viliesid shows, these proposals to send volunteer regiments to Yucatán were eventually realized, although without the help of Sierra O'Reilly and after the U.S.-Mexican War had already ended. "Filibusteros, mercenarios y voluntarios: Los soldados norteamericanos en la Guerra de Castas de Yucatán, 1848–1850," in *Política y negocios: Ensayos sobre la relación entre México y los Estados Unidos en el siglo XIX*, ed. Ana Rosa Suárez Argüello and Marcela Terrazas Basante (México D.F.: Instituto Mora, UNAM, 1997), 123–200.
56 In a letter to Buchanan on April 3, 1848, Sierra O'Reilly pleads for help from the United States and explains that "México nos mira como enemigos suyos" (*Diario*, 100) [Mexico looks at us as her enemies].
57 Murphy, *Hemispheric Imaginings*, 5.
58 David Kazanjian, *The Colonizing Trick: National Culture and Imperial Citizenship in Early America* (Minneapolis: University of Minnesota Press, 2003), 187.
59 Kazanjian, 175.
60 Chuchiak, "Intellectuals," 61.
61 Chuchiak, 66.
62 Anna Brickhouse, *Transamerican Literary Relations and the Nineteenth-Century Public Sphere* (Cambridge: Cambridge University Press, 2004), 211. See Rugeley, *Rebellion*, 98–99, for more on the sale of Maya "rebels" and prisoners of war as slaves to Cuba.
63 For example, in "Mestizaje, transculturación, heterogeneidad," Antonio Cornejo-Polar argues that "la categoría mestizaje es el más poderoso y extendido recurso conceptual con que América Latina se interpreta a sí misma.... Prevaleció y prevalece una ideología salvífica del mestizo y el mestizaje como síntesis conciliante de las muchas mezclas que constituyen el cuerpo socio-cultural latinoamericano" [mestizaje as a category is the most powerful and widespread conceptual resource by which Latin America understands itself.... There prevailed and still prevails a salvational ideology of the mestizo and mestizaje as a conciliatory synthesis of the many mixtures that constitute the sociocultural Latin American body] (368).
64 Kazanjian, *Colonizing Trick*, 176.
65 For an analysis, see Juan Matú, "Monumento a la Patria, símbolo de mexicanidad del pueblo" [Monument to the Homeland, symbol of the Mexicanness of the Yucate-can community], *Diario de Yucatán*, September 14, 2014, http://yucatan.com.mx/merida/ciudadanos/monumento-a-la-patria-simbolo-de-mexicanidad-del-pueblo-yucateco (accessed September 15, 2016).
66 According to popular mythology, the Mexica left their original homeland, Aztlán (north of what is today Mexico), in search of a promised land. Their gods had directed them to continue to travel until they saw a sign—an eagle devouring a snake while perched on a prickly pear cactus—that they had reached their final destination and the place where they should found the new center of their civilization.
67 Rómulo Rozo Peña, quoted in Matú, "Monumento a la Patria."
68 For an influential history of the Spanish conquest of Yucatán, see Inga Clendinnen,

Ambivalent Conquests: Maya and Spaniard in Yucatán, 1517–1570 (Cambridge: Cambridge University Press, 1987).

69 See, for example, Lee J. Alston, Shannan Mattiace, and Tomas Nonnenmacher, "Coercion, Culture, and Contracts: Labor and Debt on Henequen Haciendas in Yucatán, Mexico, 1870–1915," *Journal of Economic History* 69, no. 1 (2009): 104–137; and Wells, *Yucatan's Gilded Age*, chap. 6. One of the more well-known representations of the injustices of the henequen hacienda is John Kenneth Turner's sensational *Barbarous Mexico* (Chicago: Kerr, 1910), in which he describes in shocking detail the subhuman conditions for workers on henequen plantations.

70 Wells, *Yucatan's Gilded Age*, 2.

71 See Wells, *Yucatán's Gilded Age*, chap. 2, for a thorough history of International Harvester, its relationship with local elites, and its economic incursion into the henequen industry in Yucatán.

72 Wells, 6. In his now classic essay, Robin W. Winks, "On Decolonization and Informal Empire," *American Historical Review* 81, no. 3 (1976): 540–556, offers an engaging discussion of informal empires.

73 For example, numerous studies have shown that for speakers of indigenous languages in Mexico, there are a disproportionate lack of opportunities in education as well as diminished access to quality health care and inadequate representation in legal matters (see Aldo Anzures Tapia, "Evaluations in Mexico: Institutionalizing the Silence of Indigenous Populations," *Working Papers in Educational Linguistics* 20, no. 2 [2015]: 13–33; and "Snapshots of Yucatec Maya Language Practices: Language Policy and Planning Activities in the Yucatán Peninsula," *Working Papers in Educational Linguistics* 32, no. 1 [2017]: 67–90). There are also many ways in which the poor, who are overwhelmingly indigenous Maya in Yucatán, are more informally marginalized and excluded from participation in or access to resources and opportunities. See, for example, Carlos Acuña and Salvador Medina, "Riviera Maya: Sin derecho a la ciudad," [The Riviera Maya: Without rights to the city] *Horizontal*, n.d., http://horizontal.mx/rivieramaya/ (accessed May 17, 2017).

74 See, for example, the essays included in editor Sierra Méndez's collection *Justo Sierra O'Reilly*.

Chapter 3   A Transnational Romance

1 See Rosaura Sánchez and Beatrice Pita, eds., *Conflicts of Interest: The Letters of María Amparo Ruiz de Burton* (Houston: Arte Público Press, 2001), 71–74 (hereafter cited as *Conflicts* by page), for more information on the friendship between Mariano Guadalupe Vallejo and Ruiz de Burton.

2 As noted, all quotations from Ruiz de Burton's personal letters come from Sánchez and Pita's collection of her letters, *Conflicts of Interest: The Letters of María Amparo Ruiz de Burton*. All English translations of Ruiz de Burton's letters in this chapter are my own.

3 There is some uncertainty about the year of Ruiz de Burton's birth. It might have been 1831, 1832, or even 1833. See *Conflicts*, 4–5.

4 As readers will recall from the introduction, I use the term *Mexicano(s)* to refer to the inhabitants of Greater Mexico with ancestral or cultural ties to Mexico, regardless of citizenship status; I employ it as a cultural descriptor and not as a synonym for *Mexican*, which I use to describe the citizens of Mexico. The term *Mexicano(s)* therefore refers to both Mexican Americans and Mexicans. I use the term *Mexican*

American when speaking about a new, more broadly defined identity and community of people with cultural or ancestral ties to Mexico, living in and forming part of the United States after 1848.

5 See the introduction for a more thorough discussion of "Greater Mexico."

6 The idea of a "humbug"—a mask covering up a deeper truth or a "real" self—was a powerful and important concept in the nineteenth-century United States, particularly for white men in the U.S. South. In *Honor and Slavery* (Princeton: Princeton University Press, 1996), Kenneth S. Greenberg explores in depth how "unmasking" someone or something, calling someone out for being a "humbug" or a fake, was one of the greatest challenges to a white man's sense of honor; his ability to maintain appearances—show he was not a humbug—was, Greenberg argues, what also distinguished him from his black slaves.

7 Enrique Florescano explains that the nineteenth century in Mexico "es una época castigada por acontecimientos atroces: erosión de la unidad interna, lucha de facciones, ingobernabilidad, invasiones extranjeras, pérdida de más de la mitad del territorio, guerra civil, trauma político, descalabro moral . . . En el breve lapso de 50 años, de 1821 a 1867, el país imagina ser la nación más poderosa del continente americano para inmediatamente después desplomarse en el deterioro político y la quiebra económica, hasta enfrentar, como siniestra pesadilla, la amenaza de extinción" (*Historia de las historias de la nación mexicana* [México, D.F.: Taurus, 2002], 317) [is an era crippled by atrocious events: the erosion of internal unity, factional fighting, ungovernability, foreign invasions, the loss of more than half of its territory, civil war, political trauma, moral mayhem . . . In the brief span of fifty years, from 1821 to 1867, the country imagines itself to be the most powerful nation on the American continent to then immediately plummet into political disarray and economic bankruptcy, even confronting, like an evil nightmare, the threat of extinction].

8 *Californio* is the regional term that many inhabitants of both Baja and Alta California used for self-identification and is thus a term I will use frequently in this chapter when referring to Ruiz de Burton's regional identity. In fact, many Californios used this term instead of Mexicano, emphasizing the importance of regional rather than national communities. Ruiz de Burton herself uses the term frequently in her letters.

9 In their introduction to *María Amparo Ruiz de Burton: Critical and Pedagogical Perspectives* (Lincoln: University of Nebraska Press, 2004), editors Amelia María de la Luz Montes and Anne Elizabeth Goldman note that Ruiz de Burton's maternal grandfather was a commander of the Mexican northern frontier in Baja California and later was the governor of Baja California; she was also related by blood and marriage to the most prominent (politically, socially) families in Alta California (245). Sánchez and Pita note that while the Ruiz family was not necessarily wealthy, they did enjoy "political recognition and social status" (*Conflicts*, 6). Ruiz de Burton herself claimed that she was related to "all the leading families of Alta California" (9). As Sánchez and Pita explain, Ruiz de Burton was adept at capitalizing on these types of familial and social connections for her own social, political, and even economic gain (6).

10 After the 1848 U.S. acquisition of Mexican territories, "*mestizos* of the Southwest were racially unintelligible in a system designed to support the racial hierarchies of U.S. slavery and whose 'criteria of intelligibility' were, in the 1850 and 1860 censuses, 'white,' 'black,' and 'mulatto.'" Suzanne Bost, "West Meets East: Nineteenth-Century Southern Dialogues on Mixture, Race, Gender, and Nation," *Mississippi Quarterly* 56, no. 4 (2003): 648.

11 For more on the racialization of Mexican Americans after 1848, see my introduction as well as Laura E. Gómez, *Manifest Destinies: The Making of the Mexican American Race* (New York: New York University Press, 2007); Ilona Katzew and Susan Deans-Smith, eds., *Race and Classification: The Case of Mexican America* (Stanford: Stanford University Press, 2009); and Martha Menchaca, *Recovering History, Constructing Race: The Indian, Black and White Roots of Mexican Americans* (Austin: University of Texas Press, 2001).

12 For a classic study of Reconstruction in the United States, see Eric Foner, *Reconstruction: America's Unfinished Revolution, 1863–1877* (New York: Harper and Row, 1988). For a concise historiography of Reconstruction, see the prologue to Foner's *Forever Free: The Story of Emancipation and Reconstruction* (New York: Knopf, 2005).

13 See Naomi Lindstrom, "The Nineteenth-Century Latin American Novel," in *The Cambridge Companion to the Latin American Novel*, ed. Efraín Kristal (Cambridge: Cambridge University Press, 2005), 23.

14 See Doris Sommer, *Foundational Fictions: The National Romances of Latin America* (1984; Berkeley: University of California Press, 1991); and Skinner, *History Lessons: Refiguring the Nineteenth-Century Historical Novel in Spanish America* (Newark, Del.: Juan de la Cuesta, 2006).

15 For more on Mariano Guadalupe Vallejo, a fascinating historical figure in his own right, see Alan Rosenus's biography of Vallejo, *General Vallejo and the Advent of the Americans* (Albuquerque: University of New Mexico Press, 1995).

16 Sánchez and Pita write about Ruiz de Burton's paradoxical status in the United States: "She was an insider, a U.S. citizen and the wife of an army officer, but she was also an outsider, a native Californian woman for whom her 'race,' her Latin culture, and gender meant being positioned on the margins of the centers of power" (*Conflicts*, xiii). Ruiz de Burton's good friend and longtime correspondent Mariano Guadalupe Vallejo also commented upon her position as both insider and outsider, calling her an "alma atravesada" [a pierced soul], thus highlighting her "split and fissured sense of self and place" (Sánchez and Pita, in *Conflicts*, 74).

17 In her June 4, 1858, letter to Matías Moreno, Ruiz de Burton writes about her dedication to her fellow Californios: "California soy y Ud. sabe bien cuán constante es mi cariño e interés hacia mis paisanos en general, no importa en qué suelo se encuentren" (*Conflicts*, 152) [I am a Californiana, and you know well how constant my affection and interest are toward my fellow countrymen (*paisanos*) in general, regardless of the soil on which they find themselves].

18 For more on the popularity of *Uncle Tom's Cabin* in the United States and abroad, see Claire Parfait, *The Publishing History of Uncle Tom's Cabin, 1852–2002*, Proquest e-book (New York: Taylor and Francis, 2007), 90–94.

19 Parfait, 96.

20 In *The Romance of Reunion: Northerners and the South, 1865–1900* (Chapel Hill: University of North Carolina Press, 1993), Nina Silber offers a compelling reading of images and narratives of romantic unions as a dominant figure of reconciliation in the United States following the Civil War.

21 In *Rewriting Womanhood: Feminism, Subjectivity, and the Angel of the House in the Latin American Novel, 1887–1903* (University Park: Pennsylvania State University Press, 2009), Nancy LaGreca explores how Latin American women writers used the novel to break down stereotypes of women as the "angel[s] of the house." Mary Louise Pratt similarly discusses the emergence of Spanish American women writers in the postrevolutionary period, which she argues "marked a historical

aperture for women, an experimental moment in which they could be players in the drama of nation-building." "Women, Literature, and National Brotherhood," *Nineteenth-Century Contexts* 18 (1994): 35.

22 See Jane Tompkins, *Sensational Designs: The Cultural Work of American Fiction, 1790–1860*, Proquest e-book (Oxford: Oxford University Press, 1985), chap. 5, 131–153, for a discussion of the sentimental novel—a genre considered to be written exclusively by and for women in nineteenth-century United States—and its political and cultural power.

23 Nathaniel Hawthorne, quoted in Fred Lewis Pattee, *The Feminine Fifties* (New York: D. Appleton-Century, 1940). Nina Baym, *Woman's Fiction: A Guide to Novels by and about Women in America, 1820–1870* (Ithaca, N.Y.: Cornell University Press, 1978), explores the women novelists who dominated the U.S. reading public for much of the nineteenth century. Because novels by women appealed to a mass, and mostly female, audience, their work was almost never considered as aesthetically or artistically pleasing as that written by men (13–14). Instead, it was frequently used as "evidence of the deplorable feminine taste in literature.... [and] the horrible situation facing any would-be serious writer in America" (14).

24 Sánchez and Pita describe Ruiz de Burton as "an intellectual who was well read in European history and literature, especially in British, Spanish, French, Greek and American literature, and trilingual (Spanish, English, and French), [and] although she never attended a university, MARB [María Amparo Ruiz de Burton] ha[d] access to multiple experiences and discourses that fueled her writing" (*Conflicts*, 550).

25 See Sánchez and Pita, in *Conflicts*, 554–555, for more on her two known plays. See also 560–561 for more on her newspaper articles and 561–562 for more on the legal brief she wrote.

26 In "The Vanishing Mexicana/o: (Dis)Locating the Native in Ruiz de Burton's *Who Would Have Thought It?* and *The Squatter and the Don*," *Aztlán: A Journal of Chicano Studies* 36, no. 2 (2011): 89–120, Tereza M. Szeghi contends that one of the central goals of Ruiz de Burton's novels is to educate her readers about the history, culture, and social systems of Mexicanos (and particularly Californios) in order to make it clear to Anglos that elite Mexicanos are the equals of Anglo Americans in terms of race, culture, and civilization.

27 See Kirsten Silva Gruesz, *Ambassadors of Culture: The Transamerican Origins of Latino Writing* (Princeton: Princeton University Press, 2002), 1–29.

28 I have gleaned most of this biographical information from the chapter introductions in Sánchez and Pita's meticulously researched *Conflicts of Interest*. Each chapter, advancing chronologically through Ruiz de Burton's life, carefully analyzes the many places in which she lived and traveled and how these locales impacted her writing and world view, as evidenced by the primary sources also included in each chapter.

29 Ruiz de Burton's other novel, *The Squatter and the Don* (1885; New York: Modern Library, 2004), focuses on landed Californio families and their fates following the arrival of large numbers of Anglo American squatters to California during the 1870s and 1880s.

30 All citations are from María Amparo Ruiz de Burton, *Who Would Have Thought It?*, ed. Rosaura Sánchez and Beatrice Pita (1872; Houston: Arte Público Press, 1995).

31 As I discuss in the introduction, the idea of the cultural worker comes from Pierre Bourdieu. A cultural worker (an artist or writer, for example) creates and possesses cultural capital. The field of power in which a cultural worker creates her art is a

constant site of struggle between competing producers and possessors of different forms of capital. See Bourdieu, *The Rules of Art: Genesis and Structure of the Literary Field*, trans. Susan Emanuel, ed. Werner Hamacher and David E. Wellberry (Stanford: Stanford University Press, 1996), 214–282.

32 Ruiz de Burton, *Who Would Have Thought It?*, 16.

33 Ruiz de Burton, 28.

34 Sánchez and Pita, introduction to Ruiz de Burton, *Who Would Have Thought It?*, x.

35 Sánchez and Pita, lviii.

36 Rosaura Sánchez posits that Ruiz de Burton, from her unique position "within the belly of the beast," is able to "view events from a critical distance and to disarticulate hegemonic constructions of 'Anglo-Saxon America' by positing the Other America, Latin or Spanish America." "Dismantling the Colossus: Martí and Ruiz de Burton on the Formulation of Anglo América," in *José Martí's "Our America": From National to Hemispheric Cultural Studies*, ed. Jeffrey Belnap and Raúl Fernández (Durham, N.C.: Duke University Press, 1998), 116.

37 José F. Aranda penned one of the first essays on this topic, "Contradictory Impulses: María Amparo Ruiz de Burton, Resistance Theory, and the Politics of Chicano/a Studies," *American Literature* 70, no. 3 (1998): 551–579, that questions the usefulness and appropriateness of using resistance theory or theories of the subaltern to understand a pre-Chicano text like Ruiz de Burton's *Who Would Have Thought It?*

38 For example, in "Dismantling the Colossus," Sánchez sets up a binary antithesis between Anglo America and Latin America. She argues that Ruiz de Burton's dismantling of the U.S. national community in *Who Would Have Thought It?* lays "a foundation for a continental [Latin American] solidarity, a position from which U.S. hegemony can better be repudiated at home as well as globally" (126).

39 This is a general trend in criticism about Ruiz de Burton's other works as well: critics repeatedly label her as a transnational figure or a representative voice of a larger pan-Latino or Latin American community yet focus almost exclusively on her position within an Anglo American and U.S. American context. For example, José David Saldívar, *Border Matters: Remapping American Cultural Studies* (Berkeley: University of California Press, 1997), looks at Ruiz de Burton as a transnational figure, yet nearly all his analysis focuses on Ruiz de Burton's position within an Anglo American context; he sees her as offering readers "a subaltern literature of the U.S.-Mexican borderlands" (168).

40 Jesse Alemán, "Citizenship Rights and Colonial Whites: The Cultural Work of María Amparo Ruiz de Burton's Novels," in *Complicating Constructions: Race, Ethnicity, and Hybridity in American Texts*, ed. David S. Goldstein and Audrey B. Thacker, Proquest e-book (Seattle: University of Washington Press, 2007), 10.

41 Robert McKee Irwin, *Bandits, Captives, Heroines, and Saints: Cultural Icons of Mexico's Northwest Borderlands* (Minneapolis: University of Minnesota Press, 2007), 95.

42 Irwin, 95.

43 For criticism on the captivity narrative in the Americas, see Andrea Tinnemeyer, *Identity Politics of the Captivity Narrative after 1848* (Lincoln: University of Nebraska Press, 2006); June Namias, *White Captives: Gender and Ethnicity on the American Frontier* (Chapel Hill: University of North Carolina Press, 1993); Susana Rotker, *Cautivas: Olvidos y memoria en la Argentina* (Buenos Aires: Ariel, 1999); Christopher Castiglia, *Bound and Determined: Captivity,*

Culture-Crossing, and White Womanhood from Mary Rowlandson to Patty Hearst (Chicago: University of Chicago Press, 1996); and Fernando Operé, *Historias de la frontera: El cautiverio en la América hispánica* (Havana, Cuba: Fondo de la Cultura Económica, 2001). For more on captivity narratives specifically in northern Mexico, see also Irwin, *Bandits*.

44 Szeghi explains that Ruiz de Burton uses the genre of the captivity narrative "in order to conflate Mexicana/os with white elites while assigning the negative stereotypes Anglo Americans typically deployed against both Mexicans and Indians only to the latter" ("Vanishing Mexicana/o," 93). Tinnemeyer similarly contends that by "casting a Mexican heroine into the role traditionally played by white women, Ruiz de Burton not only makes a case for the 'whiteness' of Mexicans but also for their status within the United States as equals, as family" (*Identity Politics*, xx).

45 Ruiz de Burton, *Who Would Have Thought It?*, 36.

46 Ruiz de Burton, 201.

47 Ruiz de Burton, 201.

48 Josef Raab argues, "That Mrs. Norval uses and abuses Lola and that she appropriates Lola's fortune can be taken as an allegorical representation of the relationship between the countries which Lola and Mrs. Norval stand for." "The Imagined Inter-American Community of María Amparo Ruiz de Burton," *Amerikastudien / American Studies* 53, no. 1 (2008): 83.

49 Alemán explains that "the U.S.'s expansion into Mexico displaced Mexican landowners and made them vulnerable to attacks, but indigenous groups attacked landowners such as Doña Theresa in the first place precisely because they dispossessed Native Americans of their land and natural resources" ("Citizenship," 11). Szeghi similarly argues that "When we view Doña Theresa's captors as victims of multiple colonizations and displacements, and Doña Theresa herself as a symbol of the Mexican elite (whose wealth is predicated on the co-optation of Indian land and labor), we can read against the grain of Ruiz de Burton's narrative and identity the Indians' attack on the Almenara hacienda, and their abduction of Doña Theresa, as forms of anticolonial resistance rather than as senseless savagery" ("Vanishing Mexicana/o," 95).

50 Alemán, "Citizenship," 11.

51 Ruiz de Burton, *Who Would Have Thought It?*, 29.

52 Szeghi, "Vanishing Mexicana/o," 101.

53 Ruiz de Burton, *Who Would Have Thought It?*, 36.

54 Ruiz de Burton, 200.

55 Ruiz de Burton, 202.

56 Pablo A. Ramirez, "Conquest's Child: Gold, Contracts, and American Imperialism in María Amparo Ruiz de Burton's *Who Would Have Thought It?*," *Arizona Quarterly: A Journal of American Literature, Culture, and Theory* 70, no. 4 (2014): 151.

57 Walter Mignolo's *The Darker Side of the Renaissance: Literacy, Territoriality, and Colonization* (Ann Arbor: University of Michigan Press, 1995) explores how European forms of literacy, such as the encyclopedia, were key to the colonization and destruction of the New World.

58 Ruiz de Burton, *Who Would Have Thought It?*, 81.

59 Ruiz de Burton, 81.

60 Anne E. Goldman and Beth Fisher both explore in more detail the significance of Lola's second captivity in New England at the hands of Mrs. Norval. Fisher argues

that this second captivity narrative works to establish the barbarity of New England and Protestant discourses of womanhood and domesticity (in contrast with Lola's virtue and purity), contest convent captivity narratives and negative stereotypes of Catholics, and highlight anxieties about the desiring and fashionable bourgeois woman (Fisher, "The Captive Mexicana and the Desiring Bourgeois Woman: Domesticity and Expansionism in Ruiz de Burton's *Who Would Have Thought It?*," *Legacy* 16, no. 1 [1999]: 59–69). For Goldman, see "'Who ever heard of a blue-eyed Mexican?': Satire and Sentimentality in María Amparo Ruiz de Burton's *Who Would Have Thought It?*," in *Recovering the U.S. Hispanic Literary Heritage*, 9 vol., ed. Erlinda Gonzales-Berry and Chuck Tatum (Houston: Arte Público Press, 1996), 2:59–78.

61 José Enrique Rodó, *Ariel*, ed. Belén Castro (1900; Madrid: Cátedra, 2004).

62 Fisher, "Captive Mexicana," 61.

63 See Alemán, "Citizenship," 7–14. John Michael Rivera similarly contends that Lola's dyed skin disrupts normative concepts of whiteness and marks race and racial constructions as central preoccupations of the novel; he argues that what "constitutes the 'white race' and who can claim a white body as a collective people is one of the complicated racial and political questions the novel explores." *The Emergence of Mexican America: Recovering Stories of Mexican Peoplehood in U.S. Culture* (New York: New York University Press, 2006), 94.

64 Matthew Frye Jacobson, *Whiteness of a Different Color: European Immigrants and the Alchemy of Race* (Cambridge, Mass.: Harvard University Press, 1998), 120.

65 Ruiz de Burton, *Who Would Have Thought It?*, 25.

66 Ruiz de Burton, 47.

67 Ruiz de Burton, 25.

68 Ruiz de Burton, 16.

69 See Eric Foner's *Free Soil, Free Labor, Free Men: The Ideology of the Republican Party before the Civil War* (Oxford: Oxford University Press, 1995) for an analysis of the growth of the Republican Party in the United States in the decades building up to the U.S. Civil War and their ideology of "free labor" as an essential component of U.S. identity that belonged particularly to the U.S. North.

70 Noel Ignatiev, *How the Irish Became White* (New York: Routledge, 1995), 77.

71 Ruiz de Burton, *Who Would Have Thought It?*, 28.

72 Irwin, *Bandits*, 101.

73 Ruiz de Burton, *Who Would Have Thought It?*, 20.

74 Ruiz de Burton, 31.

75 Jesse Alemán, "'Thank God, Lolita Is Away from Those Horrid Savages': The Politics of Whiteness in *Who Would Have Thought It?*," in *María Amparo Ruiz de Burton: Critical and Pedagogical Perspectives*, ed. Amelia María de la Luz Montes and Anne Elizabeth Goldman (Lincoln: University of Nebraska Press, 2004), 105.

76 Ruiz de Burton, *Who Would Have Thought It?*, 16.

77 Irwin, *Bandits*, xiv.

78 Ruiz de Burton, *Who Would Have Thought It?*, 192.

79 Ruiz de Burton, 199.

80 Sánchez and Pita note that when Ruiz de Burton moved from Baja California to San Diego, she was "made painfully aware of the *californios'* position as targets of racist and ignorant remarks from an ever-growing and ever more powerful Anglo population" (*Conflicts*, 95).

81 See Aranda, "Contradictory Impulses," 551–579, for a critique of both the usefulness

of resistance theory to understanding Ruiz de Burton's work and the tendency to view Ruiz de Burton's work as "subaltern."

82 Ruiz de Burton, *Who Would Have Thought It?*, 67.

83 Ruiz de Burton, 211.

84 Ruiz de Burton, 241.

85 Alemán, "Citizenship," 15.

86 Ruiz de Burton, *Who Would Have Thought It?*, 201.

87 For a thorough discussion of the nineteenth-century debate over forms of government and representation in Spanish America, see François-Xavier Guerra's essay, "The Spanish-American Tradition of Representation and Its European Roots," *Journal of Latin American Studies* 26, no. 1 (1994): 1–35.

88 Historian Claudio Lomnitz explains that "the intensity of discussions surrounding citizenship in the first five decades after Independence reflected both the complex politics of including or excluding popular classes from the political field and the fact that national unity seemed unattainable by any means other than through unity among citizens and violence against traitors." "Modes of Citizenship in Mexico," *Public Culture* 11, no. 1 (1999): 292.

89 Guerra, "Spanish-American Tradition," 10.

90 Guerra, 10.

91 Ruiz de Burton, *Who Would Have Thought It?*, 197.

92 Ruiz de Burton, 197; emphasis mine.

93 Guerra, "Spanish-American Tradition," 12.

94 Guerra, 10.

95 Ruiz de Burton, *Who Would Have Thought It?*, 197.

96 Ruiz de Burton, 198; emphasis in the original.

97 Ruiz de Burton, 198; emphasis in the original.

98 *Oxford English Dictionary (OED Online)*, Oxford University Press, March 2017, http://www.oed.com/ (accessed July 12, 2017), s.v. "Cackle."

99 Brook Thomas, "Ruiz de Burton, Railrods, Reconstruction," *ELH* 80, no. 3 (2013): 871.

100 Thomas, "Ruiz de Burton," 871.

101 Ruiz de Burton, *Who Would Have Thought It?*, 298.

102 Ruiz de Burton, 18.

103 Gretchen Murphy, "A Europeanized New World: Colonialism and Cosmopolitanism in *Who Would Have Thought It?*," in *María Amparo Ruiz de Burton: Critical and Pedagogical Perspectives*, ed. Amelia María de la Luz Montes and Anne Elizabeth Goldman (Lincoln: University of Nebraska Press, 2004), 135.

104 Murphy, "Europeanized New World," 148.

105 Murphy, 148.

106 Ruiz de Burton, *Who Would Have Thought It?*, 194.

107 In *Transamerican Literary Relations and the Nineteenth-Century Public Sphere* (Cambridge: Cambridge University Press, 2004), Anna Brickhouse explains that Americans (both Latin and Anglo) sought to recuperate histories of the New World conquest as foundational elements in their own national literary histories; they often used historical romances set during the Spanish Conquest as an imaginative recuperation of their national histories (44–45). For more on the ways in which both Anglo Americans and Latin Americans appropriated indigenous as well as Spanish imperial histories as parts of distinctly "American" histories, see Brickhouse, *Transamerican*, 37–83; and Debra A. Castillo, *Redreaming America: Toward*

a Bilingual American Culture (Albany: State University of New York Press, 2005), 1–14.

108 Ruiz de Burton, *Who Would Have Thought It?*, 194.

109 Ruiz de Burton, 194.

110 Ruiz de Burton, 195.

111 Ruiz de Burton, 200.

112 John M. Nieto-Phillips, *The Language of Blood: The Making of Spanish-American Identity in New Mexico, 1880s–1930s* (Albuquerque: University of New Mexico Press, 2004), 146–147. The "White Legend" and nostalgic fantasies about the Spanish colonial past were forerunners for the "Spanish fantasy heritage" described by Carey McWilliams in his influential book *North from Mexico: The Spanish-Speaking People of the United States* (1948; New York: Greenwood Press, 1968).

113 Nieto-Phillips, *Language of Blood*, 147. As María DeGuzmán notes in *Spain's Long Shadow: The Black Legend, Off-Whiteness, and Anglo-American Empire* (Minneapolis: University of Minnesota Press, 2005), these sorts of histories of noble Spanish conquistadores, discoverers, and/or colonizers "served to reinforce the 'white Spaniard' typology of Spain" (76). The White Legend is thus also very much a racial discourse. For more on the ambiguities in nineteenth-century Anglo American discourses of the "white Spaniard," who is a figure of moral blackness and off-whiteness and simultaneously a signifier of Europe and the Old World, see DeGuzmán, *Spain's Long Shadow*, 75–90.

114 See Ramirez, "Conquest's Child," 145–147, for an analysis of Lola's symbolic "adoption" by Dr. Norval.

Chapter 4   Between Two Empires

1 Throughout this chapter, all quotations of Eusebio Chacón's poetry and essays come from *The Writings of Eusebio Chacón*, ed. and trans. A. Gabriel Meléndez and Francisco A. Lomelí (Albuquerque: University of New Mexico Press, 2012); all English translations of Chacón's writings come from that same collection (hereafter cited as *Writings* by page). All quotations from *El hijo de la tempestad* and *Tras la tormenta la calma* come from the original edition: Eusebio Chacón, *El hijo de la tempestad; Tras la tormenta la calma: Dos novelitas originales* (Santa Fé, N.Mex.: El Boletín Popular, 1892) (hereafter cited as *Novelitas* by page).

2 In the last two verses of this stanza, there are some significant differences between the original Spanish and the English translation provided by Meléndez. In the original, there is no comma at the end of the penultimate verse, and he also leaves the word *novel*, used as an adjective to describe "la Méjico," out of the English translation. Therefore, "La Méjico novel," the "novel" or "new" Mexico, could be the direct object of the sentence rather than the interlocutor. Thus another way of translating these last verses is the following: "I was born under those who took from you / new Mexico, my beloved land" (my translation). This is significant because in Meléndez's English translation, there is some ambiguity as to whether "the land that I love" is Mexico or New Mexico—that is, whether "the land that I love" is an adjective clause describing Mexico, or a direct object referring to New Mexico. He also chose to omit the word *novel*, or *new*, whereas in the original, there is less ambiguity: the "beloved land" is a "new" or "novel" Mexico, his New Mexico, which had been taken away from Mexico.

3 I will be using the term *Nuevomexicanos* to refer to New Mexico's Spanish-speaking population. This term was frequently used for self-identification by the Spanish-speaking residents of New Mexico during this time period.

4 Critics have certainly debated the idea that Mexican Americans (or, more broadly, Latinos) might constitute a diasporic community (see, for example, William Safran, "Diasporas in Modern Societies: Myths of Homeland and Return," *Diaspora: A Journal of Transnational Studies* 1, no. 1 [Spring 1991]: 83–99). Nonetheless, studies abound that make use of the concept of diaspora when understanding the experiences of Mexican Americans in the United States. And less rigid understandings of diaspora as "a category of practice, project, claim and stance" would certainly include Mexican Americans as a type of diaspora. Rogers Brubaker, "The 'Diaspora' Diaspora," *Ethnic and Racial Studies* 28, no. 1 (2005): 13.

5 Sarah Deutsch, *No Separate Refuge: Culture, Class and Gender on an Anglo-Hispanic Frontier in the American Southwest, 1880–1940* (Oxford: Oxford University Press, 1987), 19–23.

6 For more on the nineteenth-century New Mexican print history, see Doris Meyer, *Speaking for Themselves: Neomexicano Cultural Identity and the Spanish-Language Press, 1880–1920* (Albuquerque: University of New Mexico Press, 1996); A. Gabriel Meléndez, *Spanish-Language Newspapers in New Mexico, 1834–1958* (Tucson: University of Arizona Press, 2005); and Francisco A. Lomelí, "Eusebio Chacón: An Early Pioneer of the New Mexican Novel," in *Pasó por Aquí: Critical Essays on the New Mexican Literary Tradition, 1542–1988*, ed. Erlinda Gonzales-Berry (Albuquerque: University of New Mexico Press, 1989), 149–166.

7 A. Gabriel Meléndez and Francisco A. Lomelí, introduction to *The Writings of Eusebio Chacón*, ed. and trans. Meléndez and Lomelí (Albuquerque: University of New Mexico Press, 2012), 5.

8 Meléndez, *Spanish-Language Newspapers*, 147.

9 See *Writings*, 10–13, for a more thorough biographical sketch of Chacón's life and family history.

10 Chacón was elected assistant district attorney and later deputy district attorney in Trinidad, Colorado. Meléndez and Lomelí, introduction to *Writings*, 12.

11 Chacón, as a successful lawyer and gifted spokesman in New Mexico, has received some critical attention in historical studies for his speeches, essays, and role as a community leader in Colorado and New Mexico. John M. Nieto-Phillips, in *The Language of Blood: The Making of Spanish American Identity in New Mexico, 1880s–1930s* (Albuquerque: University of New Mexico Press, 2004), discusses Chacón as an important public figure in New Mexico.

12 Francisco A. Lomelí has written several articles and encyclopedic entries about Eusebio Chacón's importance as an early link in the development of the Hispanic literary tradition in the United States and as the first Spanish-language novelist of New Mexico ("Eusebio Chacón," in *Pasó por Aquí*, ed. Gonzales-Berry, 149–166; and "Eusebio Chacón: Eslabón temprano de la novela chicana," *La Palabra: Revista de la Literatura Chicana* 2 [1980]: 47–55). In *Spanish-Language Newspapers in New Mexico, 1834–1958*, Meléndez briefly discusses Chacón's writings—both novelistic and political—in the context of a broader New Mexican literary movement. In this comprehensive and meticulously researched book, he looks at Chacón (and his writings) as part of a generation of New Mexican writers (*periodiqueros*) who aimed to create *una literatura nacional* as a means "to mobilize community resources and engage them in literary codification by which questions of ethnicity, identity, and

group participation might reflect the status of Mexican Americans in the national life of the country" (136). For more on Chacón's contributions to the establishment of a New Mexican literary tradition, see Meléndez's *Spanish-Language Newspapers*, 133–175.

13 For more on the critical reception of Chacón's writings since his rediscovery in the 1970s, see Meléndez and Lomelí, introduction to *Writings*, 13–19.

14 The Gypsy woman implies that the son killed his mother upon his birth and warns about his future evilness, singing to the villagers, "El que á su madre mató / Cuando nació en la tormenta / ¿Qué no hará cuando crecido?" (*El hijo*, in *Novelitas*, 5) [He who killed his mother / When he was born during the storm, / What won't he do when he is grown? (*Writings*, 51)].

15 Benedict Anderson, *Imagined Communities: Reflections on the Origin and Spread of Nationalism*, new ed. (London: Verso, 2006), 6.

16 Meléndez, *Spanish-Language Newspapers*, 134.

17 Meléndez and Lomelí, introduction to *Writings*, 18.

18 Nieto-Phillips, *Language of Blood*, 80.

19 New Mexico was incorporated into the United States as a territory as a result of the U.S.-Mexican War, ending with the Treaty of Guadalupe Hidalgo in 1848. It would not become a state until 1912. For an in-depth history of New Mexico's fight for statehood and the complex politics and cultural dynamics that precluded its entry for so long, see David V. Holtby, *Forty-Seventh Star: New Mexico's Struggle for Statehood* (Norman: University of Oklahoma Press, 2012).

20 Nieto-Phillips, *Language of Blood*, 9.

21 Nieto-Phillips, 8.

22 This speech was a reaction to racist comments against Nuevomexicanos that had been written by Nellie Snyder, a Protestant missionary, in *The Review* of Las Vegas. Chacón's speech was later published in the newspapers *La Voz del Pueblo* and *El Independiente*. For more historical information about Chacón's speech or the details of its publication, see Nieto-Phillips, *Language of Blood*, 13–16, 82.

23 María DeGuzmán, *Spain's Long Shadow: The Black Legend, Off-Whiteness, and Anglo-American Empire* (Minneapolis: University of Minnesota Press, 2005), 73.

24 Ramón Gutiérrez, "Hispanic Identities in the Southwestern United States," in *Race and Classification: The Case of Mexican America*, ed. Ilona Katzew and Susan Deans-Smith (Stanford: Stanford University Press, 2009), 183.

25 R. Gutiérrez, 185.

26 R. Gutiérrez, 186.

27 R. Gutiérrez, 186.

28 DeGuzmán, *Spain's Long Shadow*, 72.

29 DeGuzmán, 5.

30 The *novela ejemplar*, or exemplary novel, is perhaps most associated with Miguel de Cervantes Saavedra, who first published his collection *Novelas ejemplares* [Exemplary Novels] in 1613, see Cervantes Saavedra, *Novelas ejemplares*, ed. Harry Sieber (Madrid: Cátedra, 2004). Each *novela* (short story) is intended to teach a moral lesson to the reader; however, Cervantes Saavedra often teaches his moral lesson by directly engaging with vice and brutality. In his romantic *novelas*, he often engages with questions of liberty and honor, as well as marriage, virtue, morality, and true nobility. All these themes likewise appear in Chacón's novelettes, especially *Tras la tormenta la calma*.

31 See Erlinda Gonzales-Berry for an exploration of how Chacón plays with the

comedia genre and the theme of honor in *Tras la tormenta la calma*. "Erotics and Politics in Nineteenth-Century New Mexico: Eusebio Chacón's *Tras la tormenta la calma*," *Western American Literature* 35, no. 1 (2000): 58–74.

32 See Cutler's article "Eusebio Chacón's America" for an analysis of the connections between Shakespeare's *The Tempest* and Chacón's *El hijo de la tempestad*, as well as a reading of Romantic literature and Romantic Don Juan figures in Chacón's novelettes.

33 Cervantes Saavedra, *Novelas ejemplares*, 52; translation mine.

34 Cervantes Saavedra, 52; translation mine.

35 Meléndez, *Spanish-Language Newspapers*, 59.

36 John Alba Cutler, "Eusebio Chacón's America," *MELUS* 36, no. 1 (Spring 2011): 109–134.

37 This desire to break from Spanish tradition is certainly not unique to Chacón's writings. Throughout Spanish America in the nineteenth century, newly independent Spanish Americans had to reconceptualize Spanish American identity "as founded on a break with Spain and, more specifically, with Spanish history." Lee Joan Skinner, *History Lessons: Refiguring the Nineteenth-Century Historical Novel in Spanish America* (Newark, Del.: Juan de la Cuesta, 2006), 19.

38 Nieto-Phillips, *Language of Blood*, 83.

39 Gonzales-Berry, "Erotics and Politics," 61.

40 DeGuzmán, *Spain's Long Shadow*, 70.

41 DeGuzmán, 134.

42 DeGuzmán, 137.

43 Returning once again to Cervantes Saavedra's *Novelas ejemplares*, the first *novela* in that collection, "La gitanilla," certainly speaks to the long-lasting prominence of a popular discourse even *within* Spain that saw and portrayed the Gypsy as morally black and racially "other." The opening lines of the *novela* state unequivocally, "Parece que los gitanos y gitanas solamente nacieron en el mundo para ser ladrones: nacen de padres ladrones, críanse con ladrones, estudian para ladrones, y, finalmente, salen con ser ladrones corrientes y molientes a todo ruedo, y la gana de hurtar y el hurtar son en ellos como ac[c]identes inseparables, que no se quitan sino con la muerte" (Cervantes Saavedra, *Novelas ejemplares*, 61) ["It seems that gypsies, both male and female, were born into this world to be thieves; they are born of thieving parents, they are brought up with thieves, they study to be thieves, and finally they become fully qualified thieves and the desire to steal and stealing itself are in them essential characteristics, which they lose only in death." Miguel de Cervantes Saavedra, "The Little Gypsy Girl," in *Exemplary Novels*, ed. B. W. Ife, trans. Harriet Price (Warminster, U.K.: Aris and Phillips, 1992), 13].

44 Alejandro Mejías-López, *The Inverted Conquest: The Myth of Modernity and the Transatlantic Onset of Modernism* (Nashville: Vanderbilt University Press, 2009), 44.

45 Mejías-López, 44.

46 For more on the creation and dissemination of popular nineteenth-century scientific and social discourses with regard to superior and inferior racial hierarchies, see Reginald Horsman, *Race and Manifest Destiny: The Origins of American Racial Anglo-Saxonism* (Cambridge, Mass.: Harvard University Press, 1981), 98–138.

47 See Heather Winlow, "Mapping Moral Geographies: W. Z. Ripley's Races of Europe and the United States," *Annals of the Association of American Geographers* 96, no. 1 (2006): 119–141. In this essay, she examines W. Z. Ripley's 1899 influential

text *The Races of Europe*, in which he concluded that the so-called Mediterranean races, such as those in Spain, shared an "Africanoid" origin. His work reflects the growing popularity at the end of the nineteenth century of the idea that Spain shared perhaps more links to Africa than Europe.

48 DeGuzmán, *Spain's Long Shadow*, 75.

49 Mejías-López, *Inverted Conquest*, 46.

50 Mejías-López, 46.

51 Juan Pablo Dabove, *Nightmares of the Lettered City: Banditry and Literature in Latin America, 1816–1929* (Pittsburgh, Pa.: University of Pittsburgh Press, 2007), 6.

52 Dabove, 14.

53 Dabove, 34.

54 Laura E. Gómez, *Manifest Destinies: The Making of the Mexican American Race* (New York: New York University Press, 2007), 44.

55 L. E. Gómez, 44–45.

56 Cutler, "Eusebio," 117.

57 Cutler, 119.

58 Dabove, *Nightmares*, 31.

59 Cutler, "Eusebio," 111.

60 Mejías-López, *Inverted Conquest*, 48.

61 Robert McKee Irwin, *Bandits, Captives, Heroines, and Saints: Cultural Icons of Mexico's Northwest Borderlands* (Minneapolis: University of Minnesota Press, 2007), 95.

62 For more general information on the captivity narrative, see Rebecca Blevins Faery, *Cartographies of Desire: Captivity, Race, and Sex in the Shaping of an American Nation* (Norman: University of Oklahoma Press, 1999); and Susana Rotker, *Cautivas: Olvidos y memoria en la Argentina* (Buenos Aires: Ariel, 1999). Faery focuses on the captivity narrative in the United States, while Rotker examines the captivity narrative in Argentina.

63 Faery, *Cartographies of Desire*, 10.

64 Andrea Tinnemeyer, *Identity Politics of the Captivity Narrative after 1848* (Lincoln: University of Nebraska Press, 2006), xvii, and xvi–xvii.

65 Irwin, *Bandits*, 101.

66 Irwin, 101.

67 Nieto-Phillips, *Language of Blood*, 89.

68 Gonzales-Berry, "Erotics and Politics," 67.

69 Carrie C. Chorba, *Mexico, from Mestizo to Multicultural: National Identity and Recent Representations of the Conquest* (Nashville: Vanderbilt University Press, 2007), 10.

70 Chorba, 10.

71 Joseba Gabilondo, "Genealogía de la 'raza latina': Para una teoría atlántica de las estructuras raciales hispanas," *Revista Iberoamericana* 75, no. 228 (2009): 804–805; translation mine.

72 Gabilondo, 805; translation mine.

73 Gabilondo, 805; translation mine.

74 For more on the racialization of Spanish, the creation of language hierarchies, and language as a racial and ethnic marker in the United States, see Ofelia García, "Racializing the Language Practices of U.S. Latinos: Impact on Their Education," in *How the United States Racializes Latinos: White Hegemony and Its Consequences*, ed. José A. Cobas, Jorge Duany, and Joe. R. Feagin (Boulder: Paradigm, 2009), 101–115;

and Ana Margarita Cervantes-Rodríguez and Amy Lutz, "Coloniality of Power, Immigration, and the English-Spanish Asymmetry in the United States," *Nepantla: Views from South* 4, no. 3 (2003): 523–560.

Conclusion

1 Many legends surround the heroes and their actions in the final hours of fighting at the Alamo. Randy Roberts and James S. Olson explore these legends and how they have changed but also endured over time in *A Line in the Sand: The Alamo in Blood and Memory* (New York: Free Press, 2001).

2 "Texas Travel," *Perryman Report & Texas Letter*, March 2012, 2.

3 Richard R. Flores, "Private Visions, Public Culture: The Making of the Alamo," *Cultural Anthropology* 10, no. 1 (1995): 99.

4 Flores, 99.

5 L. Robert Ables, "The Second Battle for the Alamo," *Southwestern Historical Quarterly* 70, no. 3 (1967): 412.

6 Ables, 403–404.

7 See Holly Beachley Brear, *Inherit the Alamo: Myth and Ritual at an American Shrine* (Austin: University of Texas Press, 1995), 84–90, for a brief history of the formation of the DRT.

8 See Ables, "Second Battle," 383–384; and Flores, "Private Visions, Public Culture," 103.

9 Ables, "Second Battle," 405–407.

10 Flores, "Private Visions, Public Culture," 103.

11 Although the DRT did eventually officially recognize Adina De Zavala's role in the preservation of the Alamo, the group still places greater historical emphasis on Driscoll as the main actor in this drama. Brear, *Inherit the Alamo*, 92–94.

12 Brear, 92–93.

13 Grantland Rice, "Ghosts of the Alamo," quoted in Adina De Zavala, *History and Legends of the Alamo and Other Missions in and around San Antonio*, ed. Richard R. Flores (Houston: Arte Público Press, 1996), 50.

14 Rice, "Ghosts," in De Zavala, *History and Legends*, 50.

15 I use the term *Tejano* to refer to Texans of Mexican descent, thus emphasizing their regional affiliations.

16 Richard R. Flores concludes that overall, "De Zavala weaves a clear and putatively accurate narrative that chronicles the Indian, Spanish, Mexican, Texan and U.S. presence at the Alamo." Introduction to *History and Legends*, xxxiii.

17 Brear, *Inherit the Alamo*, 2.

18 Brear, 1.

19 Brear, 1.

20 Brear, 1.

21 Brear, 3.

Bibliography

Ables, L. Robert. "The Second Battle for the Alamo." *Southwestern Historical Quarterly* 70, no. 3 (1967): 372–413.

Acuña, Carlos, and Salvador Medina. "Riviera Maya: Sin derecho a la ciudad." *Horizontal.* n.d. http://horizontal.mx/rivieramaya/ (accessed May 17, 2017).

Acuña, Rodolfo. *Occupied America: A History of Chicanos.* 4th ed. New York: Longman, 2000.

Adelman, Jeremy. *Sovereignty and Revolution in the Iberian Atlantic.* Princeton: Princeton University Press, 2006.

Alemán, Jesse. "Chicano Novelistic Discourse: Dialogizing the *Corrido* Critical Paradigm." *MELUS* 23, no. 1 (1998): 49–64.

———. "Citizenship Rights and Colonial Whites: The Cultural Work of María Amparo Ruiz de Burton's Novels." In *Complicating Constructions: Race, Ethnicity, and Hybridity in American Texts*, edited by David S. Goldstein and Audrey B. Thacker, 3–30. Proquest e-book. Seattle: University of Washington Press, 2007.

———. "'Thank God, Lolita Is Away from Those Horrid Savages': The Politics of Whiteness in *Who Would Have Thought It?*" In *María Amparo Ruiz de Burton: Critical and Pedagogical Perspectives*, edited by Amelia María de la Luz Montes and Anne Elizabeth Goldman, 95–111. Lincoln: University of Nebraska Press, 2004.

Alston, Lee J., Shannan Mattiace, and Tomas Nonnenmacher. "Coercion, Culture, and Contracts: Labor and Debt on Henequen Haciendas in Yucatán, Mexico, 1870–1915." *Journal of Economic History* 69, no. 1 (2009): 104–137.

Anderson, Benedict. *Imagined Communities: Reflections on the Origin and Spread of Nationalism.* New ed. London: Verso, 2006.

Andrews, Anthony P., Rafael Burgos Villanueva, and Luis Millet Cámara. "The Henequen Ports of Yucatan's Gilded Age." *International Journal of Historical Archaeology* 16, no. 1 (2012): 25–46.

Anzaldúa, Gloria. *Borderlands / La Frontera: The New Mestiza.* 2nd ed. San Francisco: Aunt Lute, 1999.

Anzures Tapia, Aldo. "Evaluations in Mexico: Institutionalizing the Silence of Indigenous Populations." *Working Papers in Educational Linguistics* 20, no. 2 (2015): 13–33.

———. "Snapshots of Yucatec Maya Language Practices: Language Policy and Planning Activities in the Yucatán Peninsula." *Working Papers in Educational Linguistics* 32, no. 1 (2017): 67–90.

Aranda, José F. "Contradictory Impulses: María Amparo Ruiz de Burton, Resistance Theory, and the Politics of Chicano/a Studies." *American Literature* 70, no. 3 (1998): 551–579.

———. *When We Arrive: A New Literary History of Mexican America*. Tucson: University of Arizona Press, 2003.

Avelar, Idelber. "Toward a Genealogy of Latin Americanism." *Dispositio* 22, no. 49 (1997): 121–133.

Barteet, Cody. "The Rhetoric of Authority in New Spain: The Casa de Montejo in Mérida, Yucatán." *Canadian Art Review* 35, no. 2 (2010): 5–20.

Bartosik-Vélez, Elise. *The Legacy of Christopher Columbus in the Americas: New Nations and a Transatlantic Discourse of Empire*. Nashville: Vanderbilt University Press, 2014.

Bauer, Ralph. *The Cultural Geography of Colonial American Literatures: Empire, Travel, Modernity*. Cambridge: Cambridge University Press, 2003.

Baym, Nina. *Woman's Fiction: A Guide to Novels by and about Women in America, 1820–1870*. Ithaca, N.Y.: Cornell University Press, 1978.

Bazant, Jan. "From Independence to the Liberal Republic, 1821–1867." In *Mexico since Independence*, edited by Leslie Bethell, 1–48. Cambridge: Cambridge University Press, 1991.

Bhabha, Homi K. *The Location of Culture*. New York: Routledge, 2004.

Blackburn, Robin. *The American Crucible: Slavery, Emancipation, and Human Rights*. London: Verso, 2011.

Bonilla-Silva, Eduardo. *Racism without Racists: Color-Blind Racism and the Persistence of Racial Inequality in America*. 4th ed. Lanham, Md.: Rowman & Littlefield, 2014.

———. "We Are All Americans! The Latin Americanization of Racial Stratification in the USA." *Race and Society* 5, no. 1 (2002): 3–16.

Bost, Suzanne. "West Meets East: Nineteenth-Century Southern Dialogues on Mixture, Race, Gender, and Nation." *Mississippi Quarterly* 56, no. 4 (2003): 647–656.

Bourdieu, Pierre. *The Rules of Art: Genesis and Structure of the Literary Field*. Edited by Werner Hamacher and David E. Wellbery. Translated by Susan Emanuel. Stanford: Stanford University Press, 1996.

Brading, D. A. "Monuments and Nationalism in Modern Mexico." *Nations and Nationalism* 7, no. 4 (2001): 521–531.

———. *The Origins of Mexican Nationalism*. Cambridge: Center for Latin American Studies, University of Cambridge, 1985.

Brear, Holly Beachley. *Inherit the Alamo: Myth and Ritual at an American Shrine*. Austin: University of Texas Press, 1995.

Brickhouse, Anna. *Transamerican Literary Relations and the Nineteenth-Century Public Sphere*. Cambridge: Cambridge University Press, 2004.

———. *The Unsettlement of America: Translation, Interpretation, and the Story of Don Luis Velasco, 1560–1945*. Oxford: Oxford University Press, 2015.

Brubaker, Rogers. "The 'Diaspora' Diaspora." *Ethnic and Racial Studies* 28, no. 1 (2005): 1–19.

Bruce, Dickson D., Jr. *And They All Sang Hallelujah: Plain-Folk Camp-Meeting Religion, 1800–1845*. Knoxville: University of Tennessee Press, 1974.

Bruce-Novoa, Juan. "Canonical and Non-canonical Texts." In *Retrospace: Collected Essays on Chicano Literature*, 132–145. Houston: Arte Público Press, 1990.

Buruma, Ian. "The End of the Anglo-American Order." *New York Times Magazine*, November 29, 2016. http://nyti.ms/2gezEtJ (accessed April 12, 2018). In print as "Exit Wounds." December 4, 2016, 39.

Cámara Gutiérrez, Carlos, ed. *Cronología histórica y arquitectónica del Paseo de Montejo*. Mérida, Yucatán: Ayuntamiento Municipal de Mérida, 2001.

Campbell, James T., Matthew Pratt Guterl, and Robert G. Lee, eds. *Race, Nation, and Empire in American History*. Chapel Hill: University of North Carolina Press, 2007.

Carballo, Emmanuel. *Historia de las letras mexicanas en el siglo XIX.* Guadalajara, Jalisco: Universidad de Guadalajara, 1991.

Careaga Viliesid, Lorena. *De llaves y cerrojos: Yucatán, Texas y Estados Unidos a mediados del siglo XIX.* México D.F.: Instituto Mora, UNAM, 2000.

———. "Filibusteros, mercenarios y voluntarios: Los soldados norteamericanos en la Guerra de Castas de Yucatán, 1848–1850." In *Política y negocios: Ensayos sobre la relación entre México y los Estados Unidos en el siglo XIX,* edited by Ana Rosa Suárez Argüello and Marcela Terrazas Basante, 123–200. México D.F.: Instituto Mora, UNAM, 1997.

Castañeda, Quetzil E. "'We Are *Not* Indigenous!': An Introduction to the Maya Identity of Yucatan." *Journal of Latin American Anthropology* 9, no. 1 (2004): 36–63.

Castiglia, Christopher. *Bound and Determined: Captivity, Culture-Crossing, and White Womanhood from Mary Rowlandson to Patty Hearst.* Chicago: University of Chicago Press, 1996.

Castillo, Debra A. *Redreaming America: Toward a Bilingual American Culture.* Albany: State University of New York Press, 2005.

Castillo, Debra A., and María Socorro Tabuenca Córdoba. *Border Women: Writing from La Frontera.* Minneapolis: University of Minnesota Press, 2002.

Cervantes-Rodríguez, Ana Margarita, and Amy Lutz. "Coloniality of Power, Immigration, and the English-Spanish Asymmetry in the United States." *Nepantla: Views from South* 4, no. 3 (2003): 523–560.

Cervantes Saavedra, Miguel de. "The Little Gypsy Girl." In *Exemplary Novels,* edited by B. W. Ife, translated by Harriet Price, 7–101. Warminster, U.K.: Aris and Phillips, 1992.

———. *Novelas ejemplares.* Edited by Harry Sieber. Madrid: Cátedra, 2004.

Chabram-Dernersesian, Angie. "I Throw Punches for My Race, but I Don't Want to Be a Man: Writing Us—Chica-nos (Girl, Us) / Chicana—into the Movement Script." In *Cultural Studies,* edited by Lawrence Grossberg, Cary Nelson, and Paula A. Treichler, 81–95. New York: Routledge, 1992.

Chacón, Eusebio. *El hijo de la tempestad; Tras la tormenta la calma: Dos novelitas originales.* Santa Fé, N.Mex.: El Boletín Popular, 1892.

———. *The Writings of Eusebio Chacón.* Edited and translated by A. Gabriel Meléndez and Francisco A. Lomelí. Albuquerque: University of New Mexico Press, 2012.

Chappel, Bill. "U.S. Kids Far Less Likely to Out-Earn Their Parents, as Inequality Grows." *NPR,* December 9, 2016. http://www.npr.org/sections/thetwo-way/2016/12/09/504989751/u-s-kids-far-less-likely-to-out-earn-their-parents-as-inequality-grows (accessed April 13, 2018).

Chatterjee, Partha. *The Nation and Its Fragments: Colonial and Postcolonial Histories.* Princeton: Princeton University Press, 1993.

Chorba, Carrie C. *Mexico, from Mestizo to Multicultural: National Identity and Recent Representations of the Conquest.* Nashville: Vanderbilt University Press, 2007.

Chuchiak, John F., IV. "Intellectuals, Indians, and the Press: The Politicization of Justo Sierra O'Reilly's Journalism and Views on the Maya While in the United States." In *Strange Pilgrimages: Exile, Travel, and National Identity in Latin America, 1800–1990s,* edited by Ingrid E. Fey and Karen Racine, 59–72. Wilmington, Del.: Scholarly Resources, 2000.

Cleaves, W. S. "The Political Career of Lorenzo de Zavala." MA thesis, University of Texas, 1931.

Clendinnen, Inga. *Ambivalent Conquests: Maya and Spaniard in Yucatán, 1517–1570.* Cambridge: Cambridge University Press, 1987.

Concannon, Kevin, Francisco A. Lomelí, and Marc Priewe. Introduction to *Imagined Transnationalism: U.S. Latino/a Literature, Culture, and Identity,* edited by Kevin Concannon, Francisco A. Lomelí, and Mark Priewe, 1–12. New York: Palgrave Macmillan, 2009.

Cornejo-Polar, Antonio. "Mestizaje, transculturación, heterogeneidad." *Revista de Crítica Literaria Latinoamericana* 20, no. 40 (1994): 368–371.

———. "Mestizaje e hibridez: Los riesgos de las metáforas." *Revista de Crítica Literaria Latinoamericana* 24, no. 47 (1998): 7–11.

Coronado, Raúl. *A World Not to Come: A History of Latino Writing and Print Culture*. Cambridge, Mass.: Harvard University Press, 2013.

Cotera, María E. "Hombres Necios: A Critical Epilogue." In *Caballero: A Historical Novel*, by Jovita González and Eve Raleigh, edited by José E. Limón, 339–350. College Station: Texas A&M University Press, 1996.

———. *Native Speakers: Ella Deloria, Zora Neale Hurston, Jovita González, and the Poetics of Culture*. Austin: University of Texas Press, 2008.

———. "Recovering 'Our' History: *Caballero* and the Gendered Politics of Form." *Aztlán: A Journal of Chicano Studies* 32, no. 2 (2007): 157–171.

Cutler, John Alba. *Ends of Assimilation: The Formation of Chicano Literature*. Oxford: Oxford University Press, 2015.

———. "Eusebio Chacón's America." *MELUS* 36, no. 1 (Spring 2011): 109–134.

Dabove, Juan Pablo. *Nightmares of the Lettered City: Banditry and Literature in Latin America, 1816–1929*. Pittsburgh, Pa.: University of Pittsburgh Press, 2007.

De Armond, Louis. "Justo Sierra O'Reilly and Yucatecan-United States Relations, 1847–1848." *Hispanic American Historical Review* 31, no. 3 (August 1951): 420–436.

DeGuzmán, María. *Spain's Long Shadow: The Black Legend, Off-Whiteness, and Anglo-American Empire*. Minneapolis: University of Minnesota Press, 2005.

Deutsch, Sarah. *No Separate Refuge: Culture, Class and Gender on an Anglo-Hispanic Frontier in the American Southwest, 1880–1940*. Oxford: Oxford University Press, 1987.

De Zavala, Adina. *History and Legends of the Alamo and Other Missions in and around San Antonio*. Edited by Richard Flores. Houston: Arte Público Press, 1996.

Drake, Paul W. *Between Tyranny and Anarchy: A History of Democracy in Latin America, 1800–2006*. Stanford: Stanford University Press, 2009.

Estep, Raymond. *Lorenzo de Zavala: Profeta del liberalismo mexicano*. Translated by Carlos A. Echanove Trujillo. México D.F.: Librería de Manuel Porrúa, 1952.

Faery, Rebecca Blevins. *Cartographies of Desire: Captivity, Race, and Sex in the Shaping of an American Nation*. Norman: University of Oklahoma Press, 1999.

Fernández Delgado, Miguel Ángel. *Justo Sierra O'Reilly: Hombre de letras y autor del proyecto del Código Civil*. México D.F.: Suprema Corte de Justicia de la Nación, 2006.

Fernández Fernández, Íñigo. "Un recorrido por la historia de la prensa en México: De sus orígenes al año 1857." *Documentación de las Ciencias de la Información* 33 (2010): 69–89.

Fisher, Beth. "The Captive Mexicana and the Desiring Bourgeois Woman: Domesticity and Expansionism in Ruiz de Burton's *Who Would Have Thought It?*" *Legacy* 16, no. 1 (1999): 59–69.

Fitz, Caitlin. *Our Sister Republics: The United States in an Age of American Revolutions*. New York: Liveright, 2016.

Flores, Richard R. Introduction to *History and Legends of the Alamo and Other Missions in and around San Antonio*, by Adina De Zavala, edited by Richard Flores, v–lviii. Houston: Arte Público Press, 1996.

———. "Private Visions, Public Culture: The Making of the Alamo." *Cultural Anthropology* 10, no. 1 (1995): 99–115.

Florescano, Enrique. *Historia de las historias de la nación mexicana*. México D.F.: Taurus, 2002.

Foner, Eric. *Forever Free: The Story of Emancipation and Reconstruction*. New York: Knopf, 2005.

———. *Free Soil, Free Labor, Free Men: The Ideology of the Republican Party before the Civil War*. Oxford: Oxford University Press, 1995.

———. *Reconstruction: America's Unfinished Revolution, 1863–1877*. New York: Harper and Row, 1988.

Foucault, Michel. *The Archaeology of Knowledge and the Discourse on Language*. Translated by A. M. Sheridan Smith. New York: Vintage, 2010.

Franco, Jean. *Plotting Women: Gender and Representation in Mexico*. New York: Columbia University Press, 1989.

———. "Waiting for a Bourgeoisie: The Formation of the Mexican Intelligentsia in the Age of Independence." In *Critical Passions: Selected Essays*, edited by Mary Louise Pratt and Kathleen Newman, 476–492. Durham, N.C.: Duke University Press, 1999.

Gabbert, Wolfgang. *Becoming Maya: Ethnicity and Social Inequality in Yucatán since 1500*. Tucson: University of Arizona Press, 2004.

Gabilondo, Joseba. "Genealogía de la 'raza latina': Para una teoría atlántica de las estructuras raciales hispanas." *Revista Iberoamericana* 75, no. 228 (2009): 795–818.

García, Ofelia. "Racializing the Languages Practices of U.S. Latinos: Impact on Their Education." In *How the United States Racializes Latinos: White Hegemony and Its Consequences*, edited by José A. Cobas, Jorge Duany, and Joe. R. Feagin, 101–115. Boulder: Paradigm, 2009.

García Gutiérrez, Blanca. "El papel de la prensa conservadora en la política nacional a mediados del siglo XIX." In *Empresa y cultura en tinta y papel (1800–1860)*, edited by Miguel Ángel Castro, coordinated by Laura Beatriz Suárez de la Torre, 505–526. México D.F.: Instituto Mora, 2001.

Gerassi-Navarro, Nina. *Pirate Novels: Fictions of Nation Building in Spanish America*. Durham, N.C.: Duke University Press, 1999.

Giron, Nicole. "La idea de 'cultura nacional' en el siglo XIX: Altamirano y Ramírez." In *En torno a la cultura nacional*, edited by Héctor Aguilar Camín and others, 53–83. México D.F.: Instituto Nacional Indigenista, 1976.

Glenn, Evelyn Nakano. *Unequal Freedom: How Race and Gender Shaped American Citizenship and Labor*. Cambridge, Mass.: Harvard University Press, 2002.

Goldman, Anne E. "'Who ever heard of a blue-eyed Mexican?': Satire and Sentimentality in María Amparo Ruiz de Burton's *Who Would Have Thought It?*" In *Recovering the U.S. Hispanic Literary Heritage*, vol. 2, edited by Erlinda Gonzales-Berry and Chuck Tatum, 59–78. Houston: Arte Público Press, 1996.

Gómez, Laura E. *Manifest Destinies: The Making of the Mexican American Race*. New York: New York University Press, 2007.

Gomez, Marte R. "Sobre Justo Sierra O'Reilly." *Historia Mexicana* 3, no. 3 (1954): 309–327.

Gómez-Quiñones, Juan, and Irene Vásquez. *Making Áztlán: Ideology and Culture of the Chicana and Chicano Movement, 1966–1977*. E-book Library. Albuquerque: University of New Mexico Press, 2014.

Gonzales-Berry, Erlinda. "Erotics and Politics in Nineteenth-Century New Mexico: Eusebio Chacón's *Tras la tormenta la calma*." *Western American Literature* 35, no. 1 (2000): 58–74.

González, Gilbert G. *Culture of Empire: American Writers, Mexico, and Mexican Immigrants, 1880–1930*. Austin: University of Texas Press, 2004.

———. "Mexican Labor Migration, 1876–1924." In *Beyond la Frontera: The History of Mexico-U.S. Migration*, edited by Mark Overmyer-Velázquez, 28–50. Oxford: Oxford University Press, 2011.

González, John M. "Terms of Engagement: Nation or Patriarchy in Jovita González's and Eve Raleigh's *Caballero*." In *Recovering the U.S. Hispanic Literary Heritage*, vol. 4, edited by José F. Aranda and Silvio Torres-Saillant, 264–276. Houston: Arte Público Press, 2002.

González, Jovita, and Eve Raleigh [a.k.a. Margaret Eimer]. *Caballero: A Historical Novel.* Edited by José E. Limón and María E. Cotera. College Station: Texas A&M University Press, 1996.

Gonzalez, Juan. *Harvest of Empire: A History of Latinos in America.* New York: Penguin, 2011.

Graham, Richard, ed. *The Idea of Race in Latin America, 1870–1940.* Austin: University of Texas Press, 1990.

Greenberg, Kenneth S. *Honor and Slavery.* Princeton: Princeton University Press, 1996.

Greer, Margaret R., Walter D. Mignolo, and Maureen Quilligan, eds. *Rereading the Black Legend: The Discourses of Religious and Racial Difference in Renaissance Empires.* Chicago: University of Chicago Press, 2007.

Gruesz, Kirsten Silva. *Ambassadors of Culture: The Transamerican Origins of Latino Writing.* Princeton: Princeton University Press, 2002.

———. "America." In *Keywords for American Cultural Studies.* Credo Reference e-book, 2nd ed., edited by Bruce Burgett and Glenn Hendler, 21–25. New York: New York University Press, 2014.

———. "The Gulf of Mexico System and the 'Latinness' of New Orleans." *American Literary History* 18, no. 3 (2006): 468–495.

———. "The Once and Future Latino: Notes toward a Literary History *todavía para llegar.*" In *Contemporary U.S. Latino/a Literary Criticism,* edited by Lyn Di Iorio and Richard Perez, 115–142. New York: Palgrave Macmillan, 2007.

———. "Tracking the First Latino Novel: *Un matrimonio como hay muchos* (1849) and Transnational Serial Fiction." In *Transnationalism and American Serial Fiction,* edited by Patricia Okker, 36–63. Proquest e-book. New York: Routledge, 2012.

Guerra, François-Xavier. "The Spanish American Tradition of Representation and Its European Roots." *Journal of Latin American Studies* 26, no. 1 (1994): 1–35.

Guidotti-Hernández, Nicole M. *Unspeakable Violence: Remapping U.S. and Mexican National Imaginaries.* Durham, N.C.: Duke University Press, 2011.

Guterl, Matthew Pratt. *American Mediterranean: Southern Slaveholders in the Age of Emancipation.* Cambridge, Mass.: Harvard University Press, 2008.

Gutiérrez, David G. *Walls and Mirrors: Mexican Americans, Mexican Immigrants, and the Politics of Ethnicity.* Berkeley: University of California Press, 1995.

Gutiérrez, Ramón. "Hispanic Identities in the Southwestern United States." In *Race and Classification: The Case of Mexican America,* edited by Ilona Katzew and Susan Deans-Smith, 174–193. Stanford: Stanford University Press, 2009.

Gutiérrez Nájera, Lourdes, M. Bianet Castellanos, and Arturo J. Aldama. "Introduction: Hemispheric *Encuentros* and Re-memberings." In *Comparative Indigeneities of the Américas: Toward a Hemispheric Approach,* edited by M. Bianet Castellanos, Lourdes Gutiérrez Nájera, and Arturo J. Aldama, 1–19. Tucson: University of Arizona Press, 2012.

Hale, Charles A. *The Transformation of Liberalism in Late Nineteenth-Century Mexico.* Princeton: Princeton University Press, 1989.

Hames-García, Michael. "How to Tell a Mestizo from an Enchirito: Colonialism and National Culture in the Borderlands." *Diacritics* 30, no. 4 (2000): 102–122.

———. "Which America Is Ours? Martí's 'Truth' and the Foundations of 'American Literature.'" *Modern Fiction Studies* 49, no. 1 (2003): 19–53.

Hatch, Nathan O. *The Democratization of American Christianity.* New Haven: Yale University Press, 1989.

Henson, Margaret Swett. *Lorenzo de Zavala: The Pragmatic Idealist*. Fort Worth: Texas Christian University Press, 1996.

———. "Understanding Lorenzo de Zavala, Signer of the Texas Declaration of Independence." *Southwestern Historical Quarterly* 102, no. 1 (1998): 1–17.

Hernandez-Jason, Beth. "Squatting in Uncle Tom's Cabin: Intertextual References and Literary Tactics of Nineteenth-Century U.S. Women Writers." In *Recovering the U.S. Hispanic Literary Heritage*, vol. 8, edited by Gabriela Baeza Ventura and Clara Lomas, 37–57. Houston: Arte Público Press, 2011.

Hickel, Jason. "Global Inequality May Be Much Worse Than We Think." *Guardian*, April 8, 2016. https://www.theguardian.com/global-development-professionals-network/2016/apr/08/global-inequality-may-be-much-worse-than-we-think (accessed April 13, 2018).

Holtby, David V. *Forty-Seventh Star: New Mexico's Struggle for Statehood*. Norman: University of Oklahoma Press, 2012.

Horsman, Reginald. *Race and Manifest Destiny: The Origins of American Racial Anglo-Saxonism*. Cambridge, Mass.: Harvard University Press, 1981.

Ignatiev, Noel. *How the Irish Became White*. New York: Routledge, 1995.

Irwin, Robert McKee. *Bandits, Captives, Heroines, and Saints: Cultural Icons of Mexico's Northwest Borderlands*. Minneapolis: University of Minnesota Press, 2007.

———. *Mexican Masculinities*. Minneapolis: University of Minnesota Press, 2003.

Jacobs, Margaret D. "Mixed-Bloods, Mestizas, and Pintos: Race, Gender, and Claims to Whiteness in Helen Hunt Jackson's *Ramona* and María Amparo Ruiz de Burton's *Who Would Have Thought It?*" *Western American Literature* 36, no. 3 (2001): 212–231.

Jacobson, Matthew Frye. *Whiteness of a Different Color: European Immigrants and the Alchemy of Race*. Cambridge, Mass.: Harvard University Press, 1998.

Joseph, Gilbert M., Catherine C. LeGrand, and Ricardo D. Salvatore, eds. *Close Encounters of Empire: Writing the Cultural History of U.S.-Latin American Relations*. Durham, N.C.: Duke University Press, 1998.

Kanellos, Nicolás, ed. *Hispanic Literature of the United States: A Comprehensive Reference*. Westport, Conn.: Greenwood Press, 2003.

———. *Hispanic Periodicals in the United States, Origins to 1960: A Brief History and Comprehensive Bibliography*. Houston: Arte Público Press, 2000.

Kaplan, Amy. *The Anarchy of Empire in the Making of U.S. Culture*. Cambridge, Mass.: Harvard University Press, 2002.

Kaplan, Amy, and Donald E. Pease, eds. *Cultures of United States Imperialism*. Durham, N.C.: Duke University Press, 1994.

Katzew, Ilona, and Susan Deans-Smith, eds. *Race and Classification: The Case of Mexican America*. Stanford: Stanford University Press, 2009.

Kaup, Monika. "The Unsustainable Hacienda: The Rhetoric of Progress in Jovita González and Eve Raleigh's *Caballero*." *Modern Fiction Studies* 51, no. 3 (2005): 561–591.

Kazanjian, David. *The Brink of Freedom: Improvising Life in the 19th-Century Atlantic World*. Durham, N.C.: Duke University Press, 2016.

———. *The Colonizing Trick: National Culture and Imperial Citizenship in Early America*. Minneapolis: University of Minnesota Press, 2003.

Klor de Alva, J. Jorge. "The Postcolonization of the (Latin) American Experience: A Reconsideration of 'Colonialism,' 'Postcolonialsm,' and 'Mestizaje.'" In *After Colonialism: Imperial Histories and Postcolonial Displacements*, edited by Gyan Prakash, 241–275. Princeton: Princeton University Press, 1995.

Kreneck, Thomas H. Foreword to *Caballero: A Historical Novel*, by Jovita González and Eve

Raleigh, edited by José E. Limón and María E. Cotera, ix–x. College Station: Texas A&M University Press, 1996.

LaGreca, Nancy. *Rewriting Womanhood: Feminism, Subjectivity, and the Angel of the House in the Latin American Novel, 1887–1903.* University Park: Pennsylvania State University Press, 2009.

Langford, Rachael, and Russell West. "Introduction: Diaries and Margins." In *Marginal Voices, Marginal Forms: Diaries in European Literature and History,* edited by Rachael Langford and Russell West, 6–21. Amsterdam: Rodopi, 1999.

Lazo, Rodrigo. "Confederates in the Hispanic Attic: The Archive against Itself." In *Unsettled States: Nineteenth-Century American Literary Studies,* edited by Dana Luciano and Ivy G. Wilson, 31–54. New York: New York University Press, 2014.

———. "'La Famosa Filadelfia': The Hemispheric American City and Constitutional Debates." In *Hemispheric American Studies,* edited by Caroline Field Levander and Robert S. Levine, 57–74. New Brunswick, N.J.: Rutgers University Press, 2008.

———. "Introduction: Historical Latinidades and Archival Encounters." In *The Latino Nineteenth Century,* edited by Rodrigo Lazo and Jesse Alemán, 1–19. New York: New York University Press, 2016.

Lejeune, Philippe. *On Diary.* Edited by Jeremey D. Popkin and Julie Rak. Translated by Katherine Durnin. Proquest e-book. Honolulu: University of Hawaii Press, 2009.

Levander, Caroline Field, and Robert S. Levine, eds. *Hemispheric American Studies.* New Brunswick, N.J.: Rutgers University Press, 2008.

Limón, José E. *American Encounters: Greater Mexico, the United States, and the Erotics of Culture.* Boston: Beacon Press, 1998.

———. *Américo Paredes: Culture and Critique.* Austin: University of Texas Press, 2012.

———. "Border Literary Histories, Globalization, and Critical Regionalism." *American Literary History* 20, nos. 1–2 (2008): 160–182.

———. *Dancing with the Devil: Society and Cultural Poetics in Mexican-American South Texas.* Madison: University of Wisconsin Press, 1994.

———. Introduction to *Caballero: A Historical Novel,* by Jovita González and Eve Raleigh, xii–xxii. College Station: Texas A&M University Press, 1996.

———. "Mexicans, Foundational Fictions, and the United States: *Caballero,* a Late Border Romance." *Modern Language Quarterly* 57, no. 2 (1996): 341–353.

Lindstrom, Naomi. "The Nineteenth-Century Latin American Novel." In *The Cambridge Companion to the Latin American Novel,* edited by Efraín Kristal, 23–43. Cambridge: Cambridge University Press, 2005.

Loewe, Ronald. *Maya or Mestizo? Nationalism, Modernity, and Its Discontents.* Toronto: University of Toronto Press, 2011.

Lomelí, Francisco A. "Eusebio Chacón: An Early Pioneer of the New Mexican Novel." In *Pasó por Aquí: Critical Essays on the New Mexican Literary Tradition, 1542–1988,* edited by Erlinda Gonzales-Berry, 149–166. Albuquerque: University of New Mexico Press, 1989.

———. "Eusebio Chacón: Eslabón temprano de la novela chicana." *La Palabra: Revista de la Literatura Chicana* 2 (1980): 47–55.

Lomnitz, Claudio. "Modes of Citizenship in Mexico." *Public Culture* 11, no. 1 (1999): 269–293.

López, Dennis. "Good-Bye Revolution—Hello Cultural Mystique: Quinto Sol Publications and Chicano Literary Nationalism." *MELUS* 35, no. 3 (2010): 183–210.

López, Marissa K. *Chicano Nations: The Hemispheric Origins of Mexican American Literature.* New York: New York University Press, 2011.

López Morín, José R. *The Legacy of Américo Paredes*. Proquest e-book. College Station: Texas A&M University Press, 2006.

Loveman, Mara. *National Colors: Racial Classification and the States in Latin America*. Oxford: Oxford University Press, 2014.

Luis-Brown, David. *Waves of Decolonization: Discourses of Race and Hemispheric Citizenship in Cuba, Mexico, and the United States*. Durham, N.C.: Duke University Press, 2008.

Markus, Hazel Rose, and Paula M. L. Moya, eds. *Doing Race: 21 Essays for the 21st Century*. New York: W. W. Norton, 2010.

Martí, José. "Nuestra America." In *Política de nuestra América*, prologue by Roberto Fernández Retamar, 39–47. Havana, Cuba: Fondo Cultural del ALBA, 2006.

Martin, Leona S. "Nation Building, International Travel, and the Construction of the Nineteenth-Century Pan-Hispanic Women's Network." *Hispania* 87, no. 3 (2004): 439–446.

Martín Rodríguez, Manuel M. *Life in Search of Readers: Reading (in) Chicano/a Literature*. Albuquerque: University of New Mexico Press, 2003.

———. "'A Net Made of Holes': Toward a Cultural History of Chicano Literature." *Modern Language Quarterly* 62, no. 1 (2001): 1–18.

Martínez, José Luisz. *La expresión nacional*. México D.F.: Editorial Oasis, 1984.

Martinez-Echazábal, Lourdes. "Mestizaje and the Discourse of National/Cultural Identity in Latin America, 1845–1959." *Latin American Perspectives* 25, no. 3 (1998): 21–42.

Matú, Juan. "Monumento a la Patria, símbolo de mexicanidad del pueblo." *Diario de Yucatán*. September 14, 2014. http://yucatan.com.mx/merida/ciudadanos/monumento-a-la-patria -simbolo-de-mexicanidad-del-pueblo-yucateco (accessed September 15, 2016).

May, Robert E. *Manifest Destiny's Underworld: Filibustering in Antebellum America*. Chapel Hill: University of North Carolina Press, 2002.

McClennen, Sophia A. "Inter-American Studies or Imperial American Studies?" *Comparative American Studies* 3, no. 4 (2005): 393–413.

McCoy, Alfred W., and Francisco A. Scarano, eds. *Colonial Crucible: Empire in the Making of the Modern American State*. Madison: University of Wisconsin Press, 2009.

McWilliams, Carey. *North from Mexico: The Spanish-Speaking People of the United States* (1948). New York: Greenwood Press, 1968.

Mejías-López, Alejandro. *The Inverted Conquest: The Myth of Modernity and the Transatlantic Onset of Modernism*. Nashville: Vanderbilt University Press, 2009.

Meléndez, A. Gabriel. *Spanish-Language Newspapers in New Mexico, 1834–1958*. Tucson: University of Arizona Press, 2005.

Meléndez, A. Gabriel, and Francisco A. Lomelí. Introduction to *The Writings of Eusebio Chacón*, edited and translated by A. Gabriel Meléndez and Francisco A. Lomelí, 1–24. Albuquerque: University of New Mexico Press, 2012.

Menchaca, Martha. *Recovering History, Constructing Race: The Indian, Black, and White Roots of Mexican Americans*. Austin: University of Texas Press, 2001.

Mexal, Stephen J. "The Logic of Liberalism: Lorenzo de Zavala's Transcultural Politics." *MELUS* 32, no. 2 (2007): 79–106.

Meyer, Doris. *Speaking for Themselves: Neomexicano Cultural Identity and the Spanish-Language Press, 1880–1920*. Albuquerque: University of New Mexico Press, 1996.

Meyer, Michael C., William L. Sherman, and Susan M. Deeds. *The Course of Mexican History*. 7th ed. Oxford: Oxford University Press, 2003.

Mignolo, Walter. *The Darker Side of the Renaissance: Literacy, Territoriality, and Colonization*. Ann Arbor: University of Michigan Press, 1995.

———. *The Idea of Latin America*. Malden, Mass.: Blackwell, 2005.

———. *Local Histories, Global Designs: Coloniality, Subaltern Knowledge, and Border Think-ing*. Princeton: Princeton University Press, 2000.

Minich, Julie Avril. *Accessible Citizenships: Disability, Nation, and the Cultural Politics of Greater Mexico*. Philadelphia: Temple University Press, 2014.

———. "Mestizaje as National Prosthesis: Corporeal Metaphors in Héctor Tobar's *The Tat-tooed Soldier*." *Arizona Journal of Hispanic Cultural Studies* 17 (2013): 211–226.

Monsiváis, Carlos. "La nación de unos cuantos y las esperanzas románticas (Notas sobre la historia del término 'Cultura Nacional' en México)." In *En torno a la cultura nacional*, 161–221. México D.F.: Instituto Nacional Indigenista, 1976.

Montejano, David. *Anglos and Mexicans in the Making of Texas, 1836–1986*. Austin: University of Texas Press, 1987.

Montes, Amelia María de la Luz, and Anne Elizabeth Goldman, eds. *María Amparo Ruiz de Burton: Critical and Pedagogical Perspectives*. Lincoln: University of Nebraska Press, 2004.

Mora, Pablo. "Cultura letrada y regneración nacional a partir de 1836." In *Empresa y cultura en tinta y papel (1800–1860)*, edited by Miguel Ángel Castro, coordinated by Laura Beat-riz Suárez de la Torre, 385–393. México D.F.: Instituto Mora, 2001.

Mora-Torres, Juan. "'Los de casa se van, los de fuera no vienen': The First Mexican Immi-grants, 1848–1900." In *Beyond la Frontera: The History of Mexico-U.S. Migration*, edited by Mark Overmyer-Velázquez, 3–27. Oxford: Oxford University Press, 2011.

Murphy, Gretchen. "A Europeanized New World: Colonialism and Cosmopolitanism in *Who Would Have Thought It?*" In *María Amparo Ruiz de Burton: Critical and Pedagogi-cal Perspectives*, edited by Amelia María de la Montes and Anne Elizabeth Goldman, 135–152. Lincoln: University of Nebraska Press, 2004.

———. *Hemispheric Imaginings: The Monroe Doctrine and Narratives of U.S. Empire*. Dur-ham, N.C.: Duke University Press, 2005.

Namias, June. *White Captives: Gender and Ethnicity on the American Frontier*. Chapel Hill: University of North Carolina Press, 1993.

Nieto-Phillips, John M. *The Language of Blood: The Making of Spanish-American Identity in New Mexico, 1880s–1930s*. Albuquerque: University of New Mexico Press, 2004.

Noll, Mark A. *The Old Religion in a New World: The History of North American Christianity*. Grand Rapids, Mich.: William B. Eerdmans, 2002.

Nolte Blanquet, Ludwig. "La imagen de los Estados Unidos de América en la obra del mexi-cano Justo Sierra O'Reilly." PhD diss., Freie University, Berlin, 2006.

Ontiveros, Randy. *In the Spirit of a New People: The Cultural Politics of a New Movement*. E-book Library. New York: New York University Press, 2013.

Operé, Fernando. *Historias de la frontera: El cautiverio en la América hispánica*. Havana, Cuba: Fondo de la Cultura Económica, 2001.

Ortiz Monasterio, José. "La formación de la literatura nacional y la integración del Estado mexicano." In *Empresa y cultura en tinta y papel (1800–1860)*, edited by Miguel Ángel Castro, coordinated by Laura Beatriz Suárez de la Torre, 419–428. México D.F.: Instituto Mora, 2001.

Overmyer-Velázquez, Mark. "Introduction: Histories and Historiographies of Greater Mexico." In *Beyond la Frontera: The History of Mexico-U.S. Migration*, edited by Mark Overmyer-Velázquez, xix–xlv. Oxford: Oxford University Press, 2011.

Oxford English Dictionary (OED Online). Oxford University Press, March 2017. http://www.oed.com/ (accessed July 12, 2017).

Paredes, Américo. *A Texas-Mexican Cancionero*. Urbana: University of Illinois Press, 1976.

Parfait, Claire. *The Publishing History of Uncle Tom's Cabin, 1852–2002*. Proquest e-book. New York: Taylor and Francis, 2007.

Pattee, Fred Lewis. *The Feminine Fifties*. New York: D. Appleton-Century, 1940.

Peniche Vallado, Leopoldo. "Sobre Justo Sierra O'Reilly." In *Justo Sierra O'Reilly*, edited by Justo Sierra Méndez, 17–19. Mérida, Yucatán: Consejo Editorial de Yucatán, 1987.

Pérez, Vincent. *Remembering the Hacienda: History and Memory in the Mexican American Southwest*. College Station: Texas A&M University Press, 2006.

Pérez-Torres, Rafael. *Mestizaje: Critical Uses of Race in Chicano Culture*. Minneapolis: University of Minnesota Press, 2006.

Pérez Vejo, Tomás. "La invención de una nación: La imagen de México en la prensa ilustrada de la primera mitad del siglo XIX (1830–1855)." In *Empresa y cultura en tinta y papel (1800–1860)*, edited by Miguel Ángel Castro, coordinated by Laura Beatriz Suárez de la Torre, 395–408. México D.F.: Instituto Mora, 2001.

Pratt, Mary Louise. *Imperial Eyes: Travel Writing and Transculturation*. New York: Routledge, 2008.

———. "Las mujeres y el imaginario nacional en el siglo XIX." *Revista de Crítica Literaria Latinoamericana* 19, no. 38 (1993): 51–62.

———. "Women, Literature, and National Brotherhood." *Nineteenth-Century Contexts* 18 (1994): 27–47.

Raab, Josef. "The Imagined Inter-American Community of María Amparo Ruiz de Burton." *Amerikastudien / American Studies* 53, no. 1 (2008): 77–95.

Rama, Ángel. *La ciudad letrada*. Montevideo, Uruguay: Arca, 1998.

Ramirez, Pablo A. "Conquest's Child: Gold, Contracts, and American Imperialism in María Amparo Ruiz de Burton's *Who Would Have Thought It?*" *Arizona Quarterly: A Journal of American Literature, Culture, and Theory* 70, no. 4 (2014): 143–165.

———. "Resignifying Preservation: A Borderlands Response to American Eugenics in Jovita González and Eve Raleigh's *Caballero*." *Canadian Review of American Studies / Revue canadienne d'études américaines* 39, no. 1 (2009): 21–39.

Reed, Nelson A. *The Caste War of Yucatán*. Stanford: Stanford University Press, 2001.

Reed Torres, Luis, and María del Carmen Ruiz Castañeda. *El periodismo en México: 500 años de historia*. 2nd ed. México D.F.: EDAMEX, 1998.

Restall, Matthew. *The Black Middle: Africans, Mayas, and Spaniards in Colonial Yucatan*. Stanford: Stanford University Press, 2009.

———. "Manuel's Worlds: Black Yucatan and the Colonial Caribbean." In *Slaves, Subjects, and Subversives: Blacks in Colonial Latin America*, edited by Jane G. Landers and Barry M. Robinson, 147–174. Albuquerque: University of New Mexico Press, 2006.

Rivera, John Michael. *The Emergence of Mexican America: Recovering Stories of Mexican Peoplehood in U.S. Culture*. New York: New York University Press, 2006.

———. Introduction to *Journey to the United States of North America / Viaje a los Estados Unidos del Norte de América*, by Lorenzo de Zavala, translated by Wallace Woolsey, xii–xxxiii. Houston: Arte Público Press, 2005.

Roberts, Randy, and James S. Olson. *A Line in the Sand: The Alamo in Blood and Memory*. New York: Free Press, 2001.

Rodó, José Enrique. *Ariel* (1900). Edited by Belén Castro. Madrid: Cátedra, 2004.

Rodríguez, Ileana. *Liberalism at Its Limits: Crime and Terror in the Latin American Cultural Text*. Pittsburgh, Pa.: University of Pittsburgh Press, 2009.

Rodríguez, Juana María. "Latino / Latina / Latin@." In *Keywords for American Cultural Studies*. Credo Reference e-book, 2nd ed., edited by Bruce Burgett and Glenn Hendler, 146–148. New York: New York University Press, 2014.

Rodríguez Díaz, María del Rosario. "Mexico's Vision of Manifest Destiny during the 1847 War." *Journal of Popular Culture* 35, no. 2 (2001): 41–50.

Roediger, David R. *Working toward Whiteness: How America's Immigrants Became White: The Strange Journey from Ellis Island to the Suburbs.* New York: Basic, 2005.

Rosales, F. Arturo. *Chicano! The History of the Mexican American Civil Rights Movement.* Houston: Arte Público Press, 1996.

Rosenus, Alan. *General Vallejo and the Advent of the Americans.* Albuquerque: University of New Mexico Press, 1995.

Rotker, Susana. *Cautivas: Olvidos y memoria en la Argentina.* Buenos Aires: Ariel, 1999.

Ruedas de la Serna, Jorge. "Periodismo y literatura en los albores del siglo XIX." In *Empresa y cultura en tinta y papel (1800–1860),* edited by Miguel Ángel Castro, coordinated by Laura Beatriz Suárez de la Torre, 591–598. México D.F.: Instituto Mora, 2001.

Rugeley, Terry. *Rebellion Now and Forever: Mayas, Hispanics, and Caste War Violence in Yucatán, 1800–1880.* Stanford: Stanford University Press, 2009.

Ruiz, Julie. "Captive Identities: The Gendered Conquest of Mexico in *Who Would Have Thought It?*" In *María Amparo Ruiz de Burton: Critical and Pedagogical Perspectives,* edited by Amelia María de la Montes and Anne Elizabeth Goldman, 112–132. Lincoln: University of Nebraska Press, 2004.

Ruiz, Vicki L. "Nuestra América: Latino History as United States History." *Journal of American History* 93, no. 3 (2006): 655–672.

Ruiz de Burton, María Amparo. *The Squatter and the Don* (1885). New York: Modern Library, 2004.

———. *Who Would Have Thought It?* Edited by Rosaura Sánchez and Beatrice Pita. Houston: Arte Público Press, 1995.

Ruiz Guerra, Rubén. "Paso Interoceánico, grupos de interés y opinión pública en Estados Unidos, 1848–1853." In *Política y negocios: Ensayos sobre la relación entre México y los Estados Unidos en el siglo XIX,* edited by Ana Rosa Suárez Argüello and Marcela Terrazas Basante, 249–302. México D.F.: Instituto Mora, UNAM, 1997.

Sabato, Hilda. "On Political Citizenship in Nineteenth-Century Latin America." *American Historical Review* 106, no. 4 (2001): 1290–1315.

Sadowski-Smith, Claudia. *Border Fictions: Globalization, Empire, and Writing at the Boundaries of the United States.* Charlottesville: University of Virginia Press, 2008.

Safran, William. "Diasporas in Modern Societies: Myths of Homeland and Return." *Diaspora: A Journal of Transnational Studies* 1, no. 1 (Spring 1991): 83–99.

Saldívar, José David. *Border Matters: Remapping American Cultural Studies.* Berkeley: University of California Press, 1997.

Saldívar, Ramón. *The Borderlands of Culture: Américo Paredes and the Transnational Imaginary.* Durham, N.C.: Duke University Press, 2006.

Sánchez, Rosaura. "Dismantling the Colossus: Martí and Ruiz de Burton on the Formulation of Anglo América." In *José Martí's "Our America": From National to Hemispheric Cultural Studies,* edited by Jeffrey Belnap and Raúl Fernández, 115–128. Durham, N.C.: Duke University Press, 1998.

Sánchez, Rosaura, and Beatrice Pita, eds. *Conflicts of Interest: The Letters of María Amparo Ruiz de Burton.* Houston: Arte Público Press, 2001.

———. Introduction to *Who Would Have Thought It?,* by María Amparo Ruiz de Burton, edited by Rosaura Sánchez and Beatrice Pita, vii–lxv. Houston: Arte Público Press, 1995.

Sánchez Prado, Ignacio M. "Canon *interruptus*: La *Antología del Centenario* en la encrucijada de 1910." *Revista de Crítica Literaria Latinoamericana* 36, no. 71 (2010): 55–74.

Sarmiento, Domingo Faustino. *Facundo: Civilización y barbarie*. 1845. Edited by Roberto Yahni. Madrid: Cátedra, 1990.

Shohat, Ella. "Notes on the Post-colonial." In *The Pre-occupation of Postcolonial Studies*, edited by Fawzia Afzal-Khan and Kalpana Seshadri-Crooks, 126–139. Durham, N.C.: Duke University Press, 2000.

Sierra Méndez, Justo, ed. *Justo Sierra O'Reilly*. Mérida, Yucatán: Consejo Editorial de Yucatán, 1987.

Sierra O'Reilly, Justo. *Diario de nuestro viaje a los Estados Unidos (La pretendida anexión de Yucatán)*. Edited by Héctor Pérez Martínez. México D.F.: Antigua Librería Robredo, de José Porrúa e Hijos, 1938.

——. *El filibustero y otras historias de piratas, caballeros y nobles damas* (1841–1849). Edited by Manuel Sol. Xalapa, Mexico: Universidad Veracruzana, 2007.

——. *Impresiones de un viaje a los Estados Unidos de América y al Canadá*. Campeche, Mexico: Gregorio Buenfil, 1849–1851.

——. Introduction to *Los tres siglos de la dominación española, o sea historia de esta provincia, desde la conquista hasta la independencia*, vol. 1, by Fr. Diego López Cogolludo, edited by Justo Sierra O'Reilly, iii–ix. Campeche, Mexico: J. M. Peralta, 1842.

——. "Noticia sobre la vida pública y escritos del Excmo. Sr. D. Lorenzo de Zavala, antiguo secretario de estado y ministro plenipotenciario de la república en París." In *Viaje a los Estados-Unidos del Norte de América*, by Lorenzo de Zavala, edited by Justo Sierra O'Reilly, 3–57. *HathiTrust*. Mérida, Yucatán: Castillo y compañía, 1846.

Silber, Nina. *The Romance of Reunion: Northerners and the South, 1865–1900*. Chapel Hill: University of North Carolina Press, 1993.

Skinner, Lee Joan. *History Lessons: Refiguring the Nineteenth-Century Historical Novel in Spanish America*. Newark, Del.: Juan de la Cuesta, 2006.

——. "Martyrs of Miscegenation: Racial and National Identities in Nineteenth-Century Mexico." *Hispanófila* 132 (2001): 25–42.

Smith, Jon, and Deborah Cohn, eds. *Look Away! The U.S. South in New World Studies*. Durham, N.C.: Duke University Press, 2004.

Sollors, Werner, ed. *Multilingual America: Transnationalism, Ethnicity, and the Languages of American Literatures*. New York: New York University Press, 1998.

Sommer, Doris. *Foundational Fictions: The National Romances of Latin America* (1984). Berkeley: University of California Press, 1991.

Stevens, Donald Fithian. *Origins of Instability in Early Republican Mexico*. Durham, N.C.: Duke University Press, 1991.

Stoler, Ann Laura. "Rethinking Colonial Categories: European Communities and the Boundaries of Rule." *Comparative Studies in Society and History* 31, no. 1 (1989): 134–161.

Sue, Christina. "An Assessment of the Latin Americanization Thesis." *Ethnic and Racial Studies* 32, no. 6 (2009): 1058–1070.

Szeghi, Tereza M. "The Vanishing Mexicana/o: (Dis)Locating the Native in Ruiz de Burton's *Who Would Have Thought It?* and *The Squatter and the Don*." *Aztlán: A Journal of Chicano Studies* 36, no. 2 (2011): 89–120.

Sznajder, Mario, and Luis Roniger. *The Politics of Exile in Latin America*. Cambridge: Cambridge University Press, 2009.

"Texas Travel." *Perryman Report & Texas Letter*, March 2012, 1–5.

Thomas, Brook. "Ruiz de Burton, Railrods, Reconstruction." *ELH* 80, no. 3 (2013): 871–895.

Tinnemeyer, Andrea. *Identity Politics of the Captivity Narrative after 1848*. Lincoln: University of Nebraska Press, 2006.

Tompkins, Jane. *Sensational Designs: The Cultural Work of American Fiction, 1790–1860.* Proquest e-book. Oxford: Oxford University Press, 1985.

Tracy, Kathleen. *Lorenzo de Zavala.* Bear, Del.: Mitchell Lane, 2003.

Traister, Bryce. "Border Shopping: American Studies and the Anti-nation." In *Globalization on the Line: Culture, Capital, and Citizenship at U.S. Borders,* edited by Claudia Sadowski-Smith, 31–52. New York: Palgrave Macmillan, 2002.

———. "Risking Nationalism: NAFTA and the Limits of the New American Studies." *Canadian Review of American Studies / Revue canadienne d'études américaines* 27, no. 3 (1997): 191–204.

Tritch, Teresa. "The United States of Inequality." *New York Times,* June 21, 2016. http://nyti .ms/28Ni1hU (accessed April 13, 2018).

Turner, John Kenneth. *Barbarous Mexico.* Chicago: Kerr, 1910.

Urías Horcasitas, Beatriz. *Historia de una negación: La idea de igualdad en el pensamiento político mexicano del siglo XIX.* México D.F.: Instituto de Investigaciones Sociales Universidad Nacional Autónoma de México, 1996.

———. "Ideas de modernidad en la historia de México: Democracia e igualdad." *Revista Mexicana de Sociología* 53, no. 4 (1991): 45–55.

Villalobos González, Martha Herminia. *El bosque sitiado: Asaltos armados, concesiones forestales y estrategias de resistencia durante la Guerra de Castas.* México D.F.: Editorial Miguel Ángel Porrúa, 2006.

Vogeley, Nancy. *The Bookrunner: A History of Inter-American Relations—Print, Politics, and Commerce in the United States and Mexico, 1800–1830.* Philadelphia: American Philosophical Society, 2011.

Wasserman, Mark. *Everyday Life and Politics in Nineteenth Century Mexico: Men, Women, and War.* Albuquerque: University of New Mexico Press, 2000.

Wells, Allen. "Forgotten Chapters of Yucatán's Past: Nineteenth-Century Politics in Historiographical Perspective." *Mexican Studies / Estudios Mexicanos* 12, no. 2 (Summer 1996): 195–229.

———. *Yucatán's Gilded Age: Haciendas, Henequen, and International Harvester, 1860–1915.* Albuquerque: University of New Mexico Press, 1985.

White, Hayden. "The Value of Narrativity in the Representation of Reality." *Critical Inquiry* 7, no. 1 (Autumn 1980): 5–27.

Wilson, Joseph C. "The Rise of the Alt-Right: White Supremacy and Anti-Semitism Go Mainstream." *Huffington Post* (blog), November 3, 2016. http://www.huffingtonpost .com/joe-wilson/the-rise-of-the-altright-_b_12778386.html (accessed April 13, 2018).

Winks, Robin W. "On Decolonization and Informal Empire." *American Historical Review* 81, no. 3 (1976): 540–556.

Winlow, Heather. "Mapping Moral Geographies: W. Z. Ripley's Races of Europe and the United States." *Annals of the Association of American Geographers* 96, no. 1 (2006): 119–141.

Zaragoza, Cosme M. "Del XIX al XX: La novela aztlanense en español." PhD diss., University of Arizona, 1984.

Zavala, Lorenzo de. *Ensayo histórico de las revoluciones en México desde 1808 hasta 1830.* Paris: Imprenta de P. Dupont et G. Laguionie, 1831–1832.

———. *Journey to the United States of North America / Viaje a los Estados Unidos del Norte de América.* Translated by Wallace Woolsey. Houston: Arte Público Press, 2005.

———. *Viage a los Estados-Unidos del Norte de América.* Paris: Decourchant, 1834. *Sabin Americana,* Gale, Cengage Learning, https://www.nypl.org/collections/articles-databases/sabin-americana.

Index

abolitionism: 36–37; as economic issue, 37; fears surrounding, 38–40; as moral issue, 36, 183–184n30; racism and, 110–111, 114

African Americans (United States): free blacks, 37–41, 44; marginalization of, 98, 111–112, 114

Afro-Latinos, 137, 145, 176n49

Alamo: battle of, 159–163; folk heroes of, 159, 162, 207n1; second battle of, 160–164; as symbolic space of public memory, 159–160, 162–165

"A la Patria," (Chacón), 127–129, 157, 202n2

Alemán, Jesse, 16–17, 113

America(n), hemispheric definition of, x, 173–174n28

Anderson, Benedict, 135, 177n55

Anzaldúa, Gloria, 10–11

Aranda, José F., 16–17

archive, Latino, 2, 7–8

Ariel (Rodó), 109

autobiography, 75. *See also* literature: nonfiction

Aztecs: founding mythology, 92–93, 193n66; in nineteenth-century literature, 122–123, 201–202n107

banditry, 140; as site for critiquing the nation, 145–148

barbarism: blackness and, 14–16, 22–23, 98; indigenous communities as figures of, 87, 89, 105–106, 108–109, 148–150; in Mexico, 52–53, 57–59, 78, 87–88, 159; slavery as a form of, 30, 36, 44–45, 59; U.S. government as figure of, 131, 146–149; U.S. materialism as form of, 108–109, 123, 149.

See also Black Legend; blackness; civilization: versus barbarism; empire, Spanish

blackface, 110, 114

Black Legend, 15, 50, 79–80, 123, 138, 139, 142, 177–178n62. *See also* barbarism; blackness; empire, Spanish; Spanishness; White Legend

blackness: anxieties about, 99, 110, 130, 138, 141–145, 150–151; barbarism and, 14–16, 22–23, 98; as degeneracy, 30, 42–44; Spaniards and, 42–44, 138–139, 142–145. *See also* barbarism; Black Legend

borderlands: Caribbean as, 11, 71–72, 190n24; definitions of, 10–11, 175n42; Gulf of Mexico as, 11–12, 71–72, 175–176n47; Latino-Anglo border system, 11, 72; racial hierarchies in Northern Mexican, 105, 112–113, 150, 156; Yucatán as, 11, 23, 70–72, 175–176n47, 176n49, 190n24. *See also* contact zone; Greater Mexico

Bourdieu, Pierre, 176n50, 197–198n31

Caballero: A Historical Novel (González and Eimer), 1–7; authorship and publication history, 1–2, 5–7, 171n5, 171n6, 171–172n7; collaboration in, 3–7, 171n4; as failed Chicano text, 5–6; Texas history in, 4, 6, 173n25, 173n26; as transnational novel, 2–4

Californios, definition of, 195n8

camp meeting (United States), 51–53. *See also* Christianity, U.S. American

canon, literary. *See* literature: national canons and

Tejanos: definition of, 171n2, 207n15; whiteness of elites, 7
Texas Mexican. *See* Tejanos
transnationalism: critiques of, 12, 176n51;
theorization of, 67
travel narrative, 14, 20, 75. *See also* literature:
nonfiction

U.S. American, x
U.S.-Mexican War: as pivotal moment for
Mexican Americans, 2–4, 19, 23–24,
97–98, 99, 100, 104, 129, 136, 204n19;
Yucatán's relationship with Mexico dur-
ing, 69, 73–74, 90–91

Vallejo, Mariano Guadalupe, 96–97,
99–100, 118–119, 186n16, 194n1, 196n15
*Viage a los Estados Unidos del Norte de
América* (Zavala), 28–65, 164–165;
community formation in, 59, 63–65;
comparisons between Mexico and the
United States in, 29–30, 36, 44, 45, 46,
48, 51–53, 59, 63–64; liberalism in, 30–32,
37–38, 40–44, 49, 51–53, 61–62; New
England, depictions of, 46–50, 53–54;
New Orleans, depictions of, 34–36;
publication of, 32, 69–71; as U.S. Latino
text, 58, 72
Vogeley, Nancy, 20–21, 179n78, 180n83

wage labor. *See* labor: slave versus wage
White Legend, 123, 202n112, 202n113. *See
also* Black Legend; empire, Spanish;
Spanishness
Who Would Have Thought It? (Ruiz de
Burton), 23, 98–126; blackface in, 102,
110, 114; captivity narratives in, 105–109,
199n44, 199–200n60; collaboration
in, 98, 121, 124–126; community formation in, 104–108, 110, 114, 116, 121–126;
critiques of U.S. empire and culture in,
103–104, 108–109, 111, 114–116, 120–121,
125; elitism in, 104, 106, 113–116,
121–126; European cultural authority

in, 122–125; as foundational fiction, 116,
121–124; French Intervention in Mexico,
depiction of, 98, 116–118, 121; as Latin
American novel, 98, 103; as transnational
novel, 102, 114, 121–126; U.S. Civil War,
depiction of, 115–116, 120–121; as U.S.
Latino novel, 103, 124; whiteness in,
110–116, 122–126

Yucatán: attempted annexation to United
States, 69, 73–74, 90; as borderlands,
11, 23, 70, 71–72, 175–176n47, 176n49,
190n24; civilization of, 80–82, 84–85,
87; connections with Caribbean and
Texas, 70, 71–72, 190n27; conquest of,
93, 193–194n68; differences from central
Mexico, 71, 87–88, 189n17, 190n27; federalism in, 73; neocolonialism in, 85–89, 91,
93, 95; secession from Mexico, 73, 90, 92;
as sibling country to United States, 81–85,
88; treatment of Maya Indians in, 77, 90,
93–94, 194n69, 194n73. *See also* Maya
Indians (Yucatán); Mérida, Yucatán;
Yucatecos
Yucatecos: commonalities with Anglos, 76,
87, 190n27; definition of, 68, 188n5; as
off-white, 80–81; whiteness of elite, 68,
76–77, 78–80, 86–87, 90, 192n50. *See also*
Mérida, Yucatán; Yucatán

Zavala, Lorenzo de, 21–22, 28–65, 164;
compared to Adina De Zavala, 164–165;
*Ensayo histórico de las revoluciones de
México*, 33, 185n44; experiences in exile,
29–33, 58–59, 183n27; liberal philosophy
of, 31, 51; life and career of, 31–33; role in
Texas Revolution, 31–32, 65, 69, 70; as
U.S. Latino figure, 31, 65, 190n25; *Viage a
los Estados Unidos del Norte de América*,
28–65, 164–165; *Viaje a los Estados Unidos
del Norte de América* (edited by Sierra
O'Reilly), 69–71; views on Catholic
Church and Catholicism, 49, 51–53,
186n54

About the Author

CARA ANNE KINNALLY is an assistant professor of Spanish in the School of Languages and Cultures at Purdue University. Her research focuses on U.S. Latino/a and Mexican literary and cultural production, border studies, race, colonialism, and community formation. She has published articles on related topics in several journals, including *Chasqui*, *Arizona Journal of Hispanic Cultural Studies*, and *Camino Real: Estudios de las hispanidades norteamericanas*.